9/9/71

Books by

KARL E. MEYER

THE
PLEASURES
OF
ARCHAEOLOGY

THE
PLEASURES
OF
ARCHAEOLOGY

A Visa to Yesterday

KARL E. MEYER

ATHENEUM   *NEW YORK*

1971

The author wishes to thank the publishers of the following copyright works for permission to print quotations: E. M. Butler, *The Tyranny of Greece over Germany* (Cambridge University Press, 1935); Cyril Connolly, *Ideas and Places* (Harper and Row, 1953); *Antigone*, translated by Dudley Fitts and Robert Fitzgerald, from Dudley Fitts, ed., *Greek Plays in Modern Translation* (Dial Press, 1947); Graham Greene, *Another Mexico* (British title: *The Lawless Roads*) (Viking Press, 1939); Aldous Huxley, *Beyond the Mexique Bay* (Harper and Brothers, 1934); Nikos Kazantzakis, *Journey to the Morea* (Simon and Schuster, 1965); Arthur Koestler, *Arrow in the Blue* (The Macmillan Company, 1952); Miguel León-Portilla, *Broken Spears* (Beacon Press, 1962); André Malraux, *Anti-memoirs*, copyright © 1967 by André Malraux, translation by Terence Kilmartin copyright © 1968 by Hamish Hamilton, London, and Holt, Rinehart and Winston, New York; Gilbert Murray, "The Value of Greece and the Future of the World," from R. W. Livingstone, ed., *The Legacy of Greece* (Clarendon Press, Oxford, 1921); Lesley Byrd Simpson, *Many Mexicos* (University of California Press, 1952); T. H. White, *The Once and Future King* (G. P. Putnam's Sons, 1958).

Argument

I shall treat alike the small and great cities of men: for most that were great in ancient times are now small; and some have been great in my day that were small. HERODOTUS, Histories, *I, v*

Curiosity led me, pure, disinterested curiosity, the human thrust in time.
FREYA STARK, Ionia: A Quest

I believe in the spade. It has fed the tribes of mankind. It has furnished them water, coal, iron and gold. And now it is giving them truth—historic truth— the mines of which have never been opened till our time.
OLIVER WENDELL HOLMES, London Academy, XXV, 422

Every archaeologist knows in his heart why he digs. He digs, in pity and humility, that the dead may live again, that what is past may not be forever lost, that something may be salvaged from the wreck of ages.
GEOFFREY BIBBY, Testimony of the Spade

Look to the rock whence ye are hewn. ISAIAH II: I

For my Mother

Author's Preface

THIS BOOK, I FEAR, may exasperate any reader with an inordinately tidy mind. It fits no precise category, it is at times discursively subjective, it follows only the most vagrant of patterns—each chapter, generally speaking, begins with an essay about the past of the country described, then discusses how the spade has recovered history, and concludes with a brief guided tour of the major sites in the area. This is a scavenger's scrapbook, written by a layman who has rummaged inquisitively in the crowded attic of the human past.

My rummaging began with a chance visit in 1959 to the Inca city of Machu Picchu; ever since, I have spent my holidays exploring the world unearthed by archaeology. The experience has been in turns illuminating, mystifying, inspiriting, depressing, but never dull. I have written this book for anyone who would like to follow the same itinerary, either on a jetliner or from an armchair. No special knowledge of archaeology is assumed.

Though not aggressively asserted, there is a point of view. My forays have quickened my belief that yesterday prefigures today, just as in an ancient mound the shape of a city is conditioned by the walls buried beneath it. The conventional figure of Father Time, I was interested to discover, derives from Saturn, or Cronus, the god who devoured his children. The image is apt; the one revolution that unfailingly swallows its offspring is the revolution of the clock.

As I complete this book, I am acutely aware of my audacity as a political journalist in even attempting to write it. I am guilty, I know, of trespassing with reckless certitude through four hundred centuries and four continents, finding parables in pots and allegories in kitchen-middens, making rash pronouncements about evidence whose conflicting testimony causes scholars to pause.

If I were to rise in defense, my plea would be a simple one: I have waited vainly for someone else to write a book such as this, a book without scholarly pretension that seeks to celebrate the *pleasures* of archaeology; a book that is reflective without being solemn; a book that is at best an *hors d'œuvre* intended to sharpen the appetite for more substantial fare. Let me finally confess that this volume, completed between deadlines over a five-year period, was composed to please myself as much as any reader.

In these pages I have been generously assisted by scholars whose unfailing kindness has been one of the pleasures I have discovered in archaeology. Among those to whom I am indebted for counsel and criticism are Dr. Clifford Evans and Dr. Betty J. Meggers of the Smithsonian Institution; Professor Michael D. Coe of Yale University; Jacquetta Hawkes; Professor Glyn Daniel of Cambridge University; Professor Paul MacKendrick of the University of Wisconsin; Professor Ahmed Fakhry of Cairo University; Professor Walter Brian Emery of London University; Professor Yigal Yadin of Hebrew University; Professor R. J. C. Atkinson of Wales University (Cardiff); Professor Homer A. Thompson of the American School of Classical Studies in Athens; Dr. Carlo M. Lerici of the Lerici Foundation, Milan; Sir Mortimer Wheeler; the late Harper Kelley of the Musée de l'Homme; the late Dr. Eusebio Dávalos Hurtado of the Mexican Institute of Anthropology and History; and Dr. Miguel León-Portilla of the Inter-American Indian Institute.

Additionally, certain friends have given me the benefit of textual criticism, and I wish to record my debt to them; they include Amos and Beth Elon; Alfred Friendly; David Pryce-Jones; Loic Bouvard; Christopher Booker; Peter Osnos; Robert Kaiser; Steven Armstrong; Joan Bingham; Reginald Bosanquet; Pat Kavanagh; and Theodore M. Draper. Tony Clark of Atheneum has provided cogent advice. To Audrey Frew I owe the excellence of the maps, and to Susan E. Meyer invaluable assistance in selection of illustrations. The manuscript was typed with speed and intelligence by Mrs. Jane Russell and Miss Florence Norton. I also owe thanks to *Esquire* for permission to reprint the first chapter, which appeared in slightly different form in its pages. My wife, Sarah, has been integrally involved in every phase of this seemingly interminable project. Last of all, I must express special gratitude to Simon Michael Bessie of Atheneum, whose patient encouragement gave me the fortitude to continue.

The author himself, superfluous to add, bears full responsibility for any errors in writing about tracts of time and space that are, as the writer fully realizes, dismayingly vast.

Karl E. Meyer
London, March 1970

Contents

Illustrations

MAPS

Chapter One

THE TIME MACHINE

I

PAST IMPROBABLE

ONE OF THE PLEASURES of archaeology is the added savor it gives to the newspapers. The daily political news that I am professionally obliged to follow tends to be predictable and repetitious; this is seldom true of reports about important archaeological finds. Ancient news, paradoxically, is often fresher and more improbable than what passes for instant novelty. The news may concern a Neolithic village whose discovery in Yugoslavia shows, contrary to expectations, that there was an ancient art-producing culture on the Danube; or it could be about a Byzantine shipwreck from which skin divers are extricating Greek bronzes; or perhaps about the unearthing in Ecuador of a few sherds whose shape suggests that Asiatic seamen reached the New World fifteen centuries before Columbus. What all of these items have in common is their uncontrived quality; the soil and sea conceal news that cannot easily be managed. Whatever its other deficiencies, the human past retains a capacity for surprise.

This element of surprise lends an attractive peril to the calling of the archaeologist. In few other fields does the practitioner risk being made to look the fool because a schoolboy happens to chase a stray dog into a cave (as at Lascaux) or because an Arab shepherd is led to a cache of documents by an ambulatory goat (as on the cliffs above the Dead Sea). The archaeologist must pit his judgment not only against the rigor of his colleagues, but also against the whim of chance. This is a hazard other scholars do not so commonly face; the zoologist or economist need not read the paper with a wary eye for an item about a bilingual Etruscan inscription whose fortuitous discovery may menace the published opinions of a lifetime. For the archaeologist, the world is seeded with possibly unwelcome surprises, buried like unexploded bombs from forgotten wars. One might therefore expect that archaeologists would be cautious, even timid, about extending their necks. Happily, this is not generally so. Archaeologists tend to be contentious. They take unwise risks; they exult in argument; some are positively atrabilious in debate. For the bystander, that is another pleasure of archaeology.

Stonehenge Its great trilithons outlined against the Salisbury Plain. (COURTESY MINISTRY OF PUBLIC BUILDINGS AND WORKS)

Consider a controversy, which had an unexpected outcome, that concerns one of my favorite monuments, Stonehenge. "Every age has the Stonehenge it deserves—or desires," Jacquetta Hawkes has percipiently remarked. During the Middle Ages the presence of the grim stones on the Salisbury Plain invited the obvious explanation: they were transported magically from a mountain in Ireland by the wand of Merlin. This pleasant theory did not convince Inigo Jones, who in the seventeenth century surveyed the monument for James II. He concluded that Stonehenge was too "elegant in Order" and too "stately in aspect" to ascribe to early Britons, who were a "savage and barbarous people, knowing no use at all of clothes." Who, then, built Stonehenge? As befits an architect of the classical school, Jones surmised that it was erected under the Romans, who had "reduced the naturall inhabitants of this

Stonehenge Restored Inigo Jones's classical reconstruction (center) accords with his theory that the Romans built the sanctuary. Above and below it are illustrations from Thomas Stukeley's *Stonehenge: A Temple Restored to the Druids* (1740).

Island into a Society of Civill life." The succeeding age was more susceptible to romance, and it preferred the theory vigorously advanced in 1740 by the antiquarian Dr. William Stukeley in his book *Stonehenge: A Temple Restored to the British Druids*. No modern scholar gives any credence to the Druid theory, but it nevertheless has exerted a peculiar popular fascination in Britain, possibly because the Druids, a Celtic cult, furiously resisted Continental Roman ways and were mystically enamored of flowers and trees.

It remained for the present age to entertain seriously a still more sensational theory about Stonehenge—that it was designed by nonliterate space scientists. The most determined advocate of this hypothesis is an American astronomer, Professor Gerald Hawkins, who in 1961 happened to visit Stonehenge and was deeply stirred to see the sun rise over the Heel Stone on Midsummer dawn. Could it be, he wondered as he looked around, that Stonehenge was in fact a celestial observatory designed by a master scientist, a proto-Newton? Dr. Hawkins made some measurements and tested his idea by feeding data into a digital computer to determine whether the stones were aligned to solar and lunar movements. The results seemed to be affirmative, and the Professor announced them first in scientific publications and then in an hour-long American television program. Dr. Hawkins maintained that he had decoded Stonehenge: it was an open-air computer that enabled a nonliterate people to predict lunar eclipses and the equinoxes.

British archaeologists were unpersuaded. The builders of Stonehenge, as one of them put it, were howling barbarians, incapable of such calculations. There was, for example, the problem of the Aubrey Holes. There are fifty-six of these peculiar chalk-filled pits that form a large enclosing circle around the monument. Hawkins contends that the holes were used as "counters" for noting a lunar-eclipse cycle that comes at intervals of 19, 19, and 18 (or 56) years. Recently I visited Stonehenge on Midsummer's Day to write a story about the controversy for my newspaper. I called up Professor R. J. C. Atkinson, a forthright anti-Hawkinsonian and the most recent excavator of Stonehenge. "What about those Aubrey Holes?" exclaimed Atkinson. "If you want to count fifty-six years, that's a damn fool way to do it—to dig fifty-six chalk pits."

Another scientist, as it chanced, was also unhappy about those holes. Professor Fred Hoyle, the eminent Cambridge University astronomer, went Hawkins one better. According to Hoyle, the monument could be used to predict *both* lunar and solar eclipses—and without resort to the holes. His elegantly reasoned and somewhat vertiginous argument ended with a dazzling speculative leap. The proto-Newtons of Stonehenge were confronted by three wonders in the firmament: the sun, the moon, and x, the unseen force that could cancel the others out. Was x the origin of the Invisible God of the Hebrews? And were s, m, and x the basis of the Christian trinity? "It would indeed be ironic," Professor Hoyle wrote in *Antiquity*, a leading British journal of archaeology, "if the roots of much of our present-day culture were determined by the lunar node."

The interested public received these revelations about Stonehenge with delight. The computer magazine, *IBM News*, was predictably entranced: "Those crazy old Druids may have known what they were doing after all." Alas, the acclaim was premature. On occasion, in archaeology, outsiders prove brilliantly right; on other occasions their ideas are brilliantly unprovable. The doubters who subjected the theories of Hawkins and Hoyle to a close analysis were able to argue that the alignment data was arbitrarily chosen to prove a case. Barring further surprises, one must accept the considered judgment of Jacquetta Hawkes, the British archaeologist, who appraised all of the arguments. Her survey, "God in the Machine," appeared in the September 1967 issue of *Antiquity*, and she concluded:

> I see no argument strong or consistent enough to change our previous belief that Stonehenge was intended primarily as a sanctuary, that the intention behind the great horseshoes and circles of stone was architectural and not mechanical, that what went on there was mainly ritualistic and not intellectual. I believe that the orientation was intended to express a religious symbolism just as the orientation of Christian churches expressed a symbolism. I feel that we should show that this is indeed the scientific age by refusing to give way to our own wishful thinking.

However, the story does not end here, because throughout the Stonehenge controversy another line of argument was being developed by another outsider, and he has undermined the citadel which Hawkins and Hoyle failed to seize frontally. The third man is Alexander Thom, Emeritus Professor of Engineering Science at Oxford, who in the 1950s began studying the multitude of megalithic sites found in the British Isles—stones arranged in flattened circles, in egg-shaped rings, ellipses, compound circles, and alignments. Professor Thom worked quietly, and concerned himself with three questions. Was a standard unit of measurement used in building the monuments? Are they oriented to solar and lunar movements? Do they presuppose calendrical knowledge? Thom's calculations suggested that in each case the answer was yes. The monuments were built using a standard "megalithic fathom" of 5.44 feet. Many are aligned to extreme risings and settings of the sun and moon at the solstices. Moreover, the builders had evidently evolved a "megalithic calendar" divided into sixteen periods of twenty-three or twenty-four days. All of this happened, if Thom is correct, some four thousand years ago, before the Babylonians devised the first known calendar.

But was the Professor right? In 1967 he published *Megalithic Sites in*

Britain, and I confess to an impatient curiosity when I began reading the review of it in *Antiquity* (March 1968) by Professor R. J. C. Atkinson, who had scourged Hawkins for his heresies. The review began: "It seldom happens that a single book, by an author who makes no claim to being an archaeologist, compels archaeologists themselves to re-examine their assumptions about a whole section of the past. This one does." Atkinson found no flaw in the argument that a standard unit of measurement was used in building the stone rings "however much it may be at variance with our present view of the societies and the technology of the period concerned." He judged the case for lunar and solar alignments as very strong, adding that "in many instances the accuracy of alignment greatly exceeds that recently alleged for similar alignments at Stonehenge." Finally, he felt that the case for the megalithic calendar was credible, though not backed by the same weight of evidence as the other arguments. Atkinson, who selects his words with a caliper, ended on this note:

> There is no doubt that many readers . . . will find this a disturbing book, because its conclusions conflict with the accepted model of the past. We have tended hitherto to equate the unrefined ruggedness of megalithic construction with a way of life which, intellectually as well as materially, was "nastie, brutish and short." These are not epithets, however, which we can justly apply to a people who possessed the kind of skills implied by the evidence which the author of this book presents.

Coming upon a paragraph like that, I submit, is another of the pleasures of archaeology. Without the gimmickry of digital computers or television publicity, Professor Thom has wrested from the darkness a bright patch of the past. We can now say with some confidence that, however brutish the early Britons may have been, they had their eye on the stars and their hands on a yardstick.

An odd figure is a distinguished predecessor of Professor Thom as a surveyor of megalithic remains: John Aubrey (1626–1697), whom Edmund Wilson has described as "an English country gentleman of lively intellectual interests but rather infirm character." A contemporary unkindly called Aubrey "magotie-headed." He never finished any of his important ventures; even the *Brief Lives*, by which he is best known, remained a muddle of notes at his death. But he was a charter member of the Royal Society, a distinguished antiquary, and the original discoverer of the fifty-six holes which still bear his name and which have vexed all attempts to explain their purpose.

Aubrey was born near Stonehenge in a Wiltshire village. He spent his childhood in "an Eremeticall solitude," and frequently wandered alone

Stonehenge from the Air   The Aubrey Holes are visible in the arc surrounding the sanctuary. (PHOTO AEROFILMS LTD.)

among the many ancient ruins in the area. He said of himself, "I was inclined by my Genius, from my Childhood, to the Love of Antiquities, and my Fate dropt me in a Country most suitable for such Enquiries." In 1648 he rediscovered Avebury, a megalithic circle near Stonehenge with a diameter so large that an entire village fits within it. He also undertook a survey of Stonehenge, and his approach showed a creditable scientific temper. He prepared a careful plan and found the puzzling holes (which were to remain unnoticed by anyone else—astonishingly—until 1929). He rightly concluded that Stonehenge was older than Roman or Saxon times, but guessed that the monument was a temple of "the most eminent Order, viz. Druids," thus originating the theory that Dr. Stukeley later seized upon and popularized.

I was impressed by Aubrey's own assessment of his work: "This Inquiry, I must confess, is a gropeing in the Dark: but although I have not brought it into a clear light, yet I can affirm that I have brought it from an utter darkness to a thin mist, and have gone further in this Essay than any one before me. . . ." No modern archaeologist can claim more, for Stonehenge remains a supreme emblem of a proximate craft. The accepted model of the past is made out of clay, not concrete. Though the archaeologist studies materials that are as indestructibly solid as the immense trilithons of Stonehenge, his conclusions are malleable. One can rejoice in this limitation. The palate can become stale, the crossword can be solved, the detective story has an end, but in archaeology it is always possible to pick up the morning newspaper and learn that the intellectual edifice of a half-century has been reduced to rubble by the discovery of a mere potsherd.

II

THE THERAPEUTIC PAST

> *Without the past, the pursued future has no meaning.*
>
> LOREN EISELEY, The Firmament of Time

A LONGER VARIATION of the same thought has been expressed by Francesco Guicciardini: "Past things shed light on future ones; the world was always of a kind; what is and what will be was at some other time; the same things come back but under different names and colors; not everybody recognizes them, but only he who is wise considers them diligently." Or, as a terse inscription on the National Archives building in Washington, D.C., has it (after Shakespeare): "What's Past Is Prologue."

The sentiment enriches every dictionary of quotations, and yet I wish to take partial exception to it. Sometimes the world that archaeology discloses is of a kind radically different from anything that has succeeded it—sometimes the prologue is followed by an utterly unrelated poem, or even by blank pages. While it is true that at one level the spade confirms that the human condition is notoriously unvarying, at another level it confronts us with civilizations that show a bewildering diversity, in which evolutionary tendencies are at times carried to eccentric extremes, as with the reptiles and birds that Darwin observed on the Galápagos Islands. The sameness of the past may be a reassurance; its originality is a therapy.

This originality is amply illustrated by the Maya of Middle America. In dense rain forests hostile to any urban life, the Maya built lofty ceremonial centers that flourished for centuries. They devised a script, still largely undeciphered, which appears to be the only true form of writing developed by the Indians of the New World. They painted murals whose formalized realism anticipated modern Mexican art. They fashioned sculpture endowed with the baroque luxuriance of the jungle foliage that later engulfed it. They invented a numerical system superior to Roman notation, and calculated a calendar year of a precision unequaled in Europe until the nineteenth century. And then, for still undetermined reasons, the classic Maya abandoned their ceremonial cities in around the ninth century A.D. and migrated northward, allowing the jungle to swallow up their achievement.

One might say that if the Maya civilization had never existed, it surely could not have been invented by non-Maya. Its singularity is the quality that most excites and puzzles the travelers who see such extensive ruins as Tikal, Palenque, or Copán. When he visited Central America in the 1930s, Aldous Huxley was impressed by the obsession with time among the Maya rulers, who parceled out the calendar into a pyramid of units, as if they were determined to defeat time by measuring it. As early as the third or fourth century B.C. the Maya priests had devised a system of numeration involving the concept of the zero, and it was used to compute the following progression:

20 *kins*	– 1 *uinal* or 20 days
18 *uinals*	– 1 *tun* or 360 days
20 *tuns*	– 1 *katun* or 7,200 days
20 *katuns*	– 1 *baktun* or 144,000 days
20 *baktuns*	– 1 *pictun* or 2,880,000 days
20 *pictuns*	– 1 *calabtun* or 57,600,000 days
20 *calabtuns*	– 1 *kinchiltun* or 1,152,000,000 days
20 *kinchiltuns*	– 1 *alautun* or 23,040,000,000 days

The observance of these cycles, which formed interlocking calendars, controlled every ceremonial aspect of Maya life. Temples were periodically rebuilt to celebrate the lapse of time. In *Beyond the Mexique Bay* Huxley reflects:

> What causes a people, or at any rate the thinking part of a people, to become as acutely time-conscious as the priestly mathematicians of the Maya Old Empire? Not geography, not economics, not a high average of general intelligence. Rather a series of personal accidents. A man is born to whom, for whatever reason, time is an obsession. It also happens that he possesses the kind of abilities which enable him to solve the problem—the problem of the intellectual mastery and transformation of time—in comprehensible quantitative terms. Furthermore, as luck will have it, he is in a position to influence his fellows, to find colleagues, to make disciples. A tradition is formed, a technique and an intellectual discipline perfected; it becomes "natural" for succeeding thinkers to turn their attention to time and the process of spatializing it in terms of mathematics.

To the extent that Huxley is right, the cultural forms that distinguish a civilization can be seen as the lengthened shadow of a single man (as was said of Jefferson and the University of Virginia). Environment dictates the limits, but the random appearance of human genius shapes the details of civilizations as different as the authoritarian Utopia of the Incas, the genocidal theocracy of the Aztecs, or the Athens of Pericles.

In this lies one of the salutary appeals of archaeology: its evidence testifies to the variety and originality of the species, and on occasion it can even recover from oblivion the actual identity of the earliest innovator. The first known architect, for example, was Imhotep of Egypt, and we not only know his name but may yet find his tomb. Few centuries have outdone our own in furnishing arguments for the misanthrope; no discipline of study, conversely, has done as much as archaeology to redress the balance. The spade enables us to look with fresh respect at our ancestors, however dimly we may regard our contemporaries.

Nowhere, perhaps, is the past more therapeutic than in the Dordogne of France, where humanity learned to paint. On his way to Greece in the late 1930s Henry Miller passed through the Dordogne, and though he is not congenitally an optimist, the author of *The Air-Conditioned Nightmare* was able to write: "It gives me hope for the future of the race, for the future of the earth itself." In 1940 the magnificent painted cave of Lascaux was discovered, and after the war Cyril Connolly went to see the find, writing about it in words that could as well apply to the regenerative past itself:

> The recently discovered paintings have a scope and freshness that make one proud to belong to a species which so many thousand years ago was able to create this pictorial magic. Lascaux is the Parthenon of prehistory; the valley of the Vézère is the foundation of humanism, a landscape where the work of man is like a mineral flower on the tunnelled rock, as exciting and beautiful as the stalagmites and stalactites of Lacav and Padirac are monotonous and unfriendly. To all who have not quite given up hope for mankind this is holy ground.

There is a second respect in which archaeology allows us to make a more flattering estimate of ourselves, though I mention it with some necessary qualifications—the very process by which the past is recovered. One must recognize the severe limits of what the spade can do. There is an intrinsic distortion in a technique that finds its richest material in the graves and garbage heaps of extinct cultures. It is possible, as Sir Mortimer Wheeler has remarked, to dig up the tub and altogether miss Diogenes. The problem was stated with depressing accuracy by John Donne: "The ashes of an Oak in the Chimney are no epitaph of that oak, to tell me how high or large that was. . . . The dust of great persons' graves is speechless too; it says nothing, it distinguishes nothing."

Yet the dust is not always wholly inarticulate. In 1784, in the State of Virginia, Thomas Jefferson excavated an Indian mound. The third American President was deeply interested in ethnology, and he wanted to find out which of several theories about the mound was correct. Jefferson made a perpendicular cut through the barrow and was able to distinguish four strata of bones, with a layer of earth above each. He also noticed that the bones had not been obviously mutilated by weapons, and he therefore dismissed two traditions about the mound; that it was a sepulcher for fallen warriors or a mortuary in which bodies were buried upright. Appearances showed that the Indians had deposited collections of bones on a common surface, covered them with rocks and earth, and then repeated the process. "The following are the particular circumstances which give it this aspect," Jefferson reported. "1. The number of bones. 2. Their confused position. 3. Their being in different strata. 4. The strata in one part have no correspondence with those in another. 5. The difference in time of inhumation. 6. The existence of infant bones among them."

Jefferson is thus an uncelebrated pioneer in using a technique that has yielded far more astonishing results. Just as the zoologist can reconstruct an entire skeleton from a jawbone or even a tooth, so the archaeologist can at least partly reconstruct a vanished civilization from a spindle whorl, a few beads, and a handful of grave dust. In the case of the Sumerians the existence of an entirely unknown yet formative civilization was conjectured on the basis of linguistic clues found on a scattering of tablets. The conjecture was generously confirmed; museums are now filled with Sumerian art and Samuel Noah Kramer has been able to write a brilliant popular book, *History Begins at Sumer*, in which he describes twenty-seven historical "firsts," including the first known case of juvenile delinquency, the first bicameral congress, and the first case of literary plagiarism.

This achievement was anticipated by John Aubrey in words that constitute a testament to the craft he helped to establish:

> These Remaines are *tanquam Tabulata Naufragy* [like fragments of a shipwreck] that after the Revolution of so many Yeares and Governments have escaped the Teeth of Time and (which is more dangerous) the Hands of mistaken Zeale. So that the retrieving of these Things from Oblivion in some sort resembles the Art of the Conjuror, who makes those walke and appeare that have layen in their graves many hundreds of yeares: and to represent to the eie, the places, Customs and Fashions that were of old Times.

I believe that archaeology ennobles reason, both in the record of mortal ingenuity that it discloses, and in the manner it makes the dead walk again. This is one of the pleasures of archaeology, and from time to time, in this disordered epoch, it is a comfort too.

III

THE PAST AS PARABLE

*Such is the power of the stupendous past
over the astonished mind of man.*
ROSE MACAULAY, Pleasure of Ruins

THAT THERE HAS BEEN a quickening of popular interest in archaeology hardly
needs to be demonstrated. In 1951 C. W. Ceram published *Gods, Graves and
Scholars*, and the book quickly became an international best-seller in twenty-
five languages. Its title has been flattered with shameless imitation, and in the
larger bookstores entire sections and alcoves are devoted to the multiplying
volumes about the past. When I told an academic friend that I was writing a
book on archaeology, he commended my good sense. "A growth field," he
volunteered amiably, "it's an evergreen."

Why? An answer was attempted recently by M. I. Finley, the Cambridge University classicist, in a review of a fresh batch of archaeological
books. The interest derives, he felt, from "a subconscious yearning to recap-
ture the distant past which is filled with wonders and myth, the ambiguous
thrill of grave-robbing, the excitement of a treasure hunt, and, for the large
number of amateurs who 'go on digs,' the satisfaction of engaging in an
outdoor activity that is also cultural."

All that Mr. Finley says is indubitably true, but it is not sufficient. The
thrills of archaeology may be ambiguous, but they are not always related to
grave-robbing. His explanation fails, for example, to account for the widespread interest in such purely ratiocinative feats as the decipherment of Linear
B by Michael Ventris. The recondite problems posed by this Cretan script
have fascinated thousands of nonspecialists, including the journalist Joseph
Alsop, who has written a book about their implications for Bronze Age
Greece.

Can it be, rather, that time has replaced space as our terrestrial frontier?
The blank spots on the map have been filled in, the pith-helmeted explorer is
no longer a conventional idol, and the very strangeness of remote lands has
been domesticated by the camera. The blank spots are now felt to be on the
map of history, and popular interest has been seemingly transferred from the
explorer of places to the explorer of the past. Quite arguably, the same
impulse that creates an audience for archaeology also augments the audience

for science fiction: the past and future are our new Dark Continents.

In any event, no culture since the Maya has surpassed ours in its fixation with time. The clock in all its forms is an artifact that we will plentifully bequeath to future archaeologists. The passing of hours and years is anxiously noted on the television screen, in the pages of *Time*, and on the dressing-room mirror. No doubt a lessening belief in the immortal soul helps to explain our near-worship of the implacable clock. But since Hiroshima we are also more despairingly conscious of the mortality of civilizations. The ground no longer feels so solid beneath us; we live on a quicksand. Small wonder that we plumb its depths, looking for comfort, for lessons, for oracular warnings, much as the Greeks turned to Delphi and the whispering oak of Dodona. Sometimes we find a parable.

Ruins are a form of parable that even the least imaginative can understand. Confronted by a ruin, our eyes turn inward and our thoughts dwell on the cheerless laws of history, making an instant Toynbee of the humblest tourist. At the more exalted end of the scale, there is the example of Gibbon, who wrote of his visit to Rome in 1764: "I must not forget the day, the hour, the most interesting of my literary life. It was on the fifteenth of October, in the gloom of the evening, as I sat musing on the Capitol, while the bare-footed friars were chanting their litanies in the temple of Jupiter, that the idea of writing the decline and fall of the City first started in my mind."

Almost as long as there have been ruins to meditate upon, reflective onlookers have endowed the stones with an unvaryingly commonplace sermon. Egyptian priests inscribed their musings on the pyramids, the Greeks pondered the vast Lion Gate at Mycenae, and in the Roman era Lucretius was moved to ask rhetorically:

> Again, perceivest not
> How stones are also conquered by Time?—
> Not how the lofty towers ruin down,
> And boulders crumble?—Not how the shrines of gods
> And idols crack outward?—Nor how indeed
> The Holy Influence hath yet no power
> To postpone the Terminals of Fate?
> [*Translation by William Ellery Leonard*]

In all such melancholy one detects a slight flavor of satisfaction, a touch of what might be called the *Schadenfreude* of the survivor. Henry James was candid enough to admit the emotion, though he apologized for it: "To delight in the aspects of sentient ruin might appear a heartless pastime, and the pleasure, I confess, shows a note of perversity." But the perversity is so prevalent that Rose Macaulay was able to draw upon hundreds of travel journals to compose her *Pleasure of Ruins,* the definitive threnody on the theme.

Mere contact with ruins has a contagious fascination, even among the most improbable excavators. Recently the inmates of Gartree Prison in England were asked if they would like to help unearth a Roman fort on a hill near Coventry. Brian Hobley, Coventry's Keeper of Archaeology, explained the importance of the dig, and at first the prisoners responded cautiously. But as time went on, more volunteers were forthcoming than could be used on the site. "When they got to work on the site," the Manchester *Guardian* reported in 1967, "and their efforts produced pottery and building foundations in what till last year had been an ordinary field, their enthusiasm grew till they would sometimes work through their lunch and tea breaks, and even carry on in the rain rather than sit in the hut." As months went by, less and less professional supervision was necessary; disciplinary problems were virtually nonexistent. The inmates excavated an area of 14,000 square feet, and Mr. Hobley was able to report that the work force was incomparably the best he had ever had, producing results that in quantity and quality could not have been achieved by other means.

Businessmen no less than jailbirds have succumbed to infection, beginning spectacularly with Heinrich Schliemann, who retired, bored and rich, from the indigo trade and rediscovered Troy. Other instances are less familiar. In 1953 a Guayaquil businessman possessing an almost alarming ebullience burst into the archaeological department of the Smithsonian Institution in Washington, D.C. His name was Emilio Estrada and he told Dr. Clifford Evans that he wanted to learn excavation techniques and dig up Ecuador. Evans was encouraging if wary, and the next year he and his wife, Betty, stopped in Guayaquil and began teaching Señor Estrada. He learned with alacrity. He took time off from his automobile-and-appliance firm and worked with the Evanses at unexplored coastal sites. A series of digs unexpectedly yielded the first convincing evidence that Asiatic sea voyagers had reached the coast of South America at least a thousand years before the Vikings found North America. The evidence was ultimately published by the Smithsonian in a handsome volume dedicated to Estrada, who had died in his forties in 1964.*

There is the case of Carlo M. Lerici, an Italian who in the breadth and energy of his interests personifies Milan. Dr. Lerici retired in 1955 from his full-time duties as head of Fondazione Lerici, an eminently successful engineering firm engaged in geophysical exploration. Lerici was thinking mainly of improving his golf; by chance he visited the admirable Etruscan collection in the Villa Giulia in Rome. Why couldn't the technology of geophysical

---

* I record the story with some pride and sadness. It was my good luck to write the first newspaper account of Estrada's finds (Washington *Post,* December 4, 1960) and my less welcome task to write his obituary.

Carlo M. Lerici The retired engineer who rediscovered over a thousand Etruscan tombs. (COURTESY LERICI FOUNDATION)

Peering into the Past Lerici devised this periscopic probe for penetrating Etruscan tombs. (COURTESY LERICI FOUNDATION)

Tomb at Tarquinia A periscopic view of the Tomba dei Fiorellirini. Each panel is a separate photograph taken through Lerici's invention. (COURTESY LERICI FOUNDATION)

exploration be adapted to archaeology? He put the question to his colleagues, and together they developed some ingenious electronic "spades," such as a potentiometer for detecting tomb-sized cavities in the earth, and a periscopic drill that could scan and photograph unopened tombs. Within a decade Lerici's prospectors had located a thousand Etruscan graves at Cerveteri and fifty painted tombs at Tarquinia; they also found the probable site of Sybaris, the ancient Greek colony in southern Italy whose inhabitants supplied the word *sybarite* to the language.

In Iraklion, Crete, a museum catalogue helped make a patron of archaeology out of Leon Pomerance of New York, who is more normally concerned with the paper business. During a holiday in 1960 Mr. Pomerance was examining, catalogue in hand, the rich Minoan collection in the Iraklion Museum. The catalogue was written by Dr. Nikolaos Platon, then director of the Museum, and it mentioned that some major Minoan sites were still

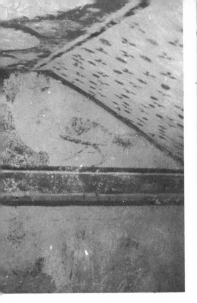

unexcavated. The American met Dr. Platon, and this dialogue ensued:

"Do you mean to tell us that after all these years of digging and bringing to light the palaces of Knossos, Phaestos, and Mallia, you know of others that just lie there?"

"That's right, Mr. Pomerance—I think I know of at least one."

"Then why in heaven's name don't you dig it up?"

"Money, Mr. Pomerance, money. The Greek government sets aside a sizable budget for archaeological work. But the funds go only so far. . . ."

Mr. Pomerance was ensnared on the spot. He offered to underwrite an excavation on condition that he and his wife could come along and watch. His proposal was duly approved by Athens, and in 1962 the Pomerances were on hand as the first spade sank into the melon patch that covered a Minoan palace at Kato Zakro on the extreme eastern tip of Crete. In successive seasons the finds included more than two thousand pottery vessels in a variety of styles, and twelve tablets inscribed in the still-undeciphered Linear A script, all lying amid the tumbled masonry of a palace that may be the "chalk-white Lycastos" which Homer names as one of the seven important cities of Crete.

An Unknown Mural Until photographed, this art in the Tomba dei Giocolieri in Tarquinia had been unseen for nearly two thousand years. (COURTESY LERICI FOUNDATION)

Prison Archaeologists Near Coventry This Coventry encampment was unearthed by prisoners. Left, a prison guard stands above a fully restored Roman wall. (COURTESY HEBERT ART GALLERY AND MUSEUM, COVENTRY. PHOTO B. HOBLEY)

Felons, businessmen, monarchs (Gustav of Sweden and Prince Charles of England), journalists, adventurers (T. E. Lawrence and Malraux), generals (Napoleon, Allenby, Yadin, and Dayan), skin divers, prelates, literary critics (Edmund Wilson), circus strong men (Belzoni), astronomers, and, for all I know, pop singers—such is the vagrant gathering who have nothing whatever in common except the earth beneath them into which they have had occasion to inquire. Yet, curiously, though the company is richly diverse, the story of archaeology often exhibits a startling kind of teleology; its parables have a point, almost as if there were a divinity that shapes our beginnings.

To paraphrase Miss Hawkes's remark about Stonehenge, every nation seems to get the past it deserves. In the Holy Land, where the Word is incontestably more important than masonry, the most important single find has been the Dead Sea Scrolls. In Egypt, where the appetite for prestige prompted the Pharaohs to build indestructible pyramids, a similar impulse led European treasure hunters to ransack the Nile Valley for obelisks and statuary to be taken home as symbols of imperial status. One can say a good deal, as I intend to, about the relationship of the Greek past to the German present, and find an almost macabre parable in the career of Heinrich Schliemann, who brought both the gold of Troy and the swastika to Germany, where both were to perish in the fall of Berlin.

Mexico presents a special case. It is virtually impossible to discuss the Mexican present intelligibly without referring to the Indian past, and to the shock of the Conquest. There is no statue of Cortés in Mexico City—he has not been forgiven for what he did—but there is in the capital the most overwhelming of all archaeological museums. When the new museum was opened in 1964, an odd thing happened. Its designers felt that the garden should be adorned by a monolithic statue of the rain god Tlaloc which is twenty feet high. So big is the idol that its ancient sculptors had been unable to raise him to a vertical position, and he was still lying, like a divine Oblomov, in the bed of his quarry, staring at the sky. Tlaloc was located in a small village outside Mexico City, and the inhabitants indignantly resisted the proposal to transplant their rain god. The government offered to build a new well for the village, but this was not enough; a new school was required as a bonus. Ultimately Tlaloc was sawed from his bed, hoisted onto a special truck with hundreds of rubber tires, and ceremoniously carried to Mexico City. As Victor Alba writes in *The Mexicans:* "Thousands of people were there to see him—standing in a torrential rain. It rained very hard that night, even though it was not the rainy season. People joked about the coincidence, but later, as Tlaloc was being set in place in the museum garden, rain poured down each time he was moved, and the Mexicans began to feel an astonishment not far

"My God, the Campbells! As if we don't see enough of them in Riverdale!"

from superstitious awe, a response they only partly concealed by jokes."

We may look back at the recent past in anger, but as we look back further and further and further still, our emotion, like the Mexicans', gives way to awe. Arthur Koestler, whose books constitute a kind of archaeological report on the ruins of the present, recalled a relevant experience. As a young journalist in the 1920s, Koestler lived for three months in Cairo, where he spent much of his time loitering among the mummies in the Egyptian Museum. He asserts, in *Arrow in the Blue*, that his first faltering steps away from a rigidly scientific to a humanistic view of man were by way of the mummy of Ramses II. In looking at the Pharaoh's face, which seemed as if a damp brush had just passed over his flaxen hair, Koestler felt "a dizzy feeling, as if I were bending over a murky well into which somebody had dropped a stone long ago. To my science-trained mind it seemed atrocious that however deep it travelled in the past, the stone would never reach bottom . . . the well of history opened into a more intimate, humane dimension."

The image is apt. Archaeology in effect has opened wells into the quicksand, providing a glimpse of a past that is, as T. H. Huxley once said of nature, "nowhere inaccessible and everywhere unfathomable." As we hunch over the perforated soil, peering through the semi-darkness, striving to glimpse the pinpoint of water that flickers distantly—as we do this, the chances are that if we succeed, we ultimately see a reflection, reassuring and unnerving, of ourselves.

Tlaloc on Wheels   The Aztec rain god provoked a deluge when he was uprooted and moved. (COURTESY BLACK STAR)

IV

THE PAST AS A VOYAGE

Fly back a thousand years in five hours!
CANADIAN PACIFIC ADVERTISEMENT FOR A
FLIGHT TO MACHU PICCHU, Time, *December 18, 1964*

AMONG THE ACCURATE PROPHECIES of H. G. Wells is one for which he is not generally given credit—the Time Machine. As with so many of Wells's ideas, the laboratories got it slightly wrong, mixing up his conception and misreading his instructions. Our Time Machine goes only one way: backward. The vehicle in the Wellsian novel (written in 1895) looked something like a horseless carriage and was made of an interesting mixture of nickel, ivory, and rock crystal. Our Machine is made of steel, feeds on kerosene, and has the inelegant shape of an overlong swallow with egg-shaped tumors in its wings. Still, the jet plane adequately meets the need of the discerning Time Traveler.

There are few archaeological sites of the first importance that cannot be reached overnight by a jet airliner. Sometimes the tempo is dizzyingly abrupt. The traveler can, as I did in 1964, take off from Washington at 8:00 a.m. and land in Mexico City before noon. If you rent a car at the airport, you can head immediately to a four-lane *autopista* that cuts through the mountains enclosing the Valley of Mexico. In an hour you are in Cholula, a city overshadowed by a pyramid of incredible bulk—its base is twice the length of that of the Great Pyramid in Gizeh. Cholula remembers the visits of two fair-faced visitors: the benign god Quetzalcóatl, who brought the arts of civilization, and Hernán Cortés, who massacred some six thousand of the inhabitants. The friars who accompanied Cortés were shocked by the pyramid; its altars were caked with blood of thousands of human victims. A church arose at the summit to celebrate the gentle Jesus, in whose name massacres could be forgiven. From the top you have a memorable view of hundreds of smaller churches, each with a tiled dome glinting in noonday sun. If you press on from Cholula, in a few hours you can be in Tlaxcala, where Cortés enlisted his first Indian allies and where the first Christian church in the continental New World was consecrated. The timbered roof of the Church of San Francisco is made of old cedar beams hewn from the same forest that provided the lumber for the brigantines that Cortés used in his siege of Mexico City. The pulpit is inscribed: *"Aquí tubo principio al Santo Evangelio en este nuevo mundo"* (Here the Holy Evangel had its beginning in the New World.) A few miles from the church you find villages where Spanish is seldom spoken, and where the events of 1519 have an immanence of something that happened yesterday. Yet your own day began with a cup of coffee in a mobile lounge at Dulles International Airport, Washington, D.C.

It is a measure of our jaded sensibilities that we take the experience for granted. Once a voyage to the past was itself an aging experience; on occasion it could be fatal. Yet the great trophies for the explorer, such places as Petra and Masada, Machu Picchu and Abu Simbel, have ceased to be rare prizes: they are now baggage stickers. Just as grave-robbing has acquired the dignity of a science, so ruin-inspecting has acquired the prosperity of a growth industry. The results are disquieting.

They are disquieting because our Time Machine has a built-in self-destruct. The jet airliner disfigures what it reaches, and the first generation of travelers to arrange an itinerary in terms of time as well as space may be the last. In trampling through the ruins, we efface what we have come to enjoy. The late Dr. Amedeo Maiuri, the great excavator of Pompeii, once said he had lived to see the city destroyed a second time. Moreover, the time gap is inexorably closing to meet the wishes of tourists who will venture anywhere so long as everything remains the same; Conrad Hilton, Thomas Cook, and American Express can not be blamed for trying profitably to oblige.

Romantic Stonehenge Every age gets the Stonehenge it wishes. This is a seventeenth-century version.

Yet the Machine exists, and in one respect its users today have an advantage over the Wellsian Time Traveler. He was a solitary voyager who could never be sure into what century he was venturing or what he would see. We can be more selective, and not only in terms of the past we wish to explore. We can also pick our companions and guides, choosing them from among the pioneers of archaeology, the Victorian travel writers, and such assorted authors as Aldous and Julian Huxley, D. H. and T. E. Lawrence, various Sitwells, Graham Greene, Lawrence Durrell—and Goethe, Stendahl, and Pepys. It is possible to see any given site through five sets of eyes: those of the classical writers like Herodotus and Pausanias, of the first modern rediscoverer, of the excavator, of the literary onlooker, and of the common traveler. To these can be legitimately added a sixth: the perception of the novelist. The historical fiction of authors like Robert Graves and Mary Renault offers a kind of archaeology of the imagination, conjuring dust into flesh and filling old amphoras with an enlivening wine.

Thus we can experience the past as a voyage without even leaving the house. We can follow Emerson and Carlyle on their visit to Stonehenge in 1848. Emerson was deeply affected. From the distance the stones "looked like a group of brown dwarfs in the wide expanse," and within the hewn circle he noticed buttercups, nettles, wild thyme, daisies, meadow-sweet, goldenrod, thistles, and the carpeting grass. Carlyle lit a cigar in the shelter of a stone; they listened to the larks and Carlyle remarked, somewhat portentously, "The larks which were hatched last year, and the wind which was hatched many thousand years ago." Emerson wrote: "We walked in and out, and took again and again a fresh look at the uncanny stones. The old sphinx put our petty differences of nationality out of sight. To these conscious stones we two pilgrims were alike known and near. We could equally well revere their old British meaning." Even Carlyle, for the moment, was "subdued and gentle."

The past, in a sentence, makes the present more bearable; archaeology makes it more sensible; and the jet airliner makes it more available. We can say with Byron:

> What are our woes and sufferance? Come and see
> The cypress, hear the owl, and plod your way
> O'er steps of broken thrones and temples, ye
> Whose agonies are evils of a day!
> A world is at our feet as fragile as our clay. . . .

Now let us venture into the Ice Age.

Chapter Two

INTO THE ICE AGE

FRANCE

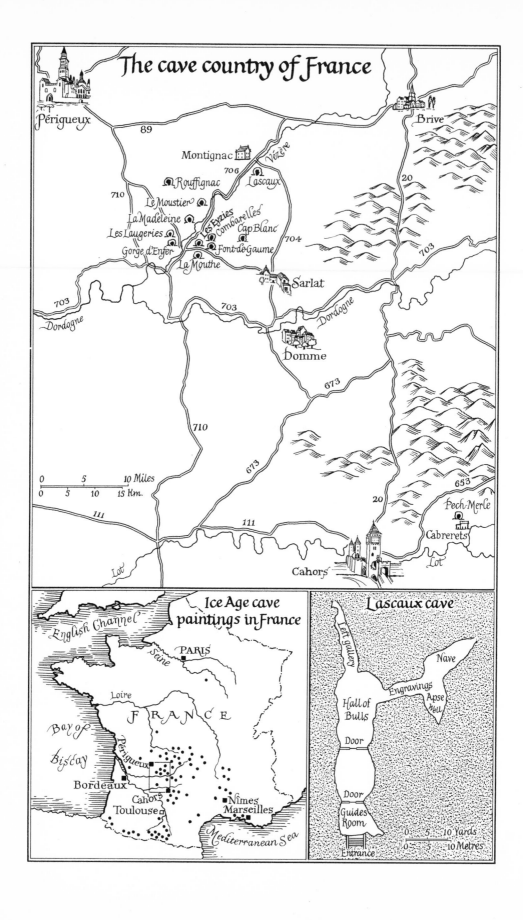

The cave country of France

Périgueux

89

Brive

Montignac
706

Vézère

Rouffignac
710
Lascaux
Le Moustier
La Madeleine
Les Eyzies
Combarelles
Cap Blanc
Les Laugeries
704
Gorge d'Enfer
Font-de-Gaume
La Mouthe
703
Sarlat

703
Dordogne
703
Dordogne

Domme

673

710

673

653

Pech-Merle

20

Cabrerets

0   5   10 Miles
0   5   10   15 Km.

111
111
Lot
Cahors
Lot

Ice Age cave paintings in France

English Channel
Seine
PARIS
Loire
F R A N C E
Bay of Biscay
Périgueux
Bordeaux
Cahors
Toulouse
Nîmes
Marseilles
Mediterranean Sea

Lascaux cave

Left gallery
Nave
Engravings
Hall of Bulls
Apse
Well
Door
Door
Guides Room
0   5   10 Yards
0   5   10 Metres
Entrance

I

THE APE IN THE MIRROR

No man doth exalt Nature to the height it would beare. JOHN DONNE

THE STUDY OF PREHISTORY has the dread fascination of a mirror. We peer into it for a glimpse of our immemorial self, the image of what we have been, and of what we might become. As a species, we are strangely disposed to see the worst—the sagging chin and the manic stare —attributing our ugliness to a primal strain. I think it a measure of our pessimism that we so furiously resist all evidence to the contrary in the glass of prehistory. The creature who can find angels in heaven sees an ape in the mirror.

Take, for example, our picture of Neanderthal man. Who has not looked with a queasy eye at the painting in the natural-history museum that purports to show the Neanderthaler, a club gripped in his burly fist, gazing stupidly at the horizon? He is the repulsive poor relation of *Homo sapiens*, the slinking uncle locked guiltily away in the cellar. This traditional conception impelled Sir Harry Johnston to remark several generations ago: "The dim racial memory of such gorilla-like monsters, with cunning brains, shambling gait, hairy bodies, strong teeth, and possibly cannibalistic tendencies, may be the germ of the ogre in folklore. . . ."

In a brilliant tour de force the novelist William Golding seized on this insight, reversed it, and fashioned a Paleolithic fable in which the coming of modern man is seen through the frightened eyes of the Neanderthalers. To Golding's timid ape-like men, the aggressive, spear-wielding Cro-Magnon hunter was a terrifying newcomer—a creature with a bone-pale face, stick-thin limbs, and an alarming upright posture. "They walked upright and should be dead," runs a passage in *The Inheritors*. "It was as

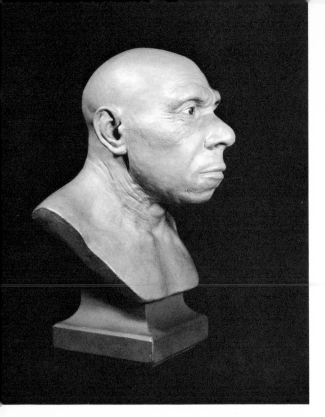

Our Neanderthal Ancestor? The restorations above are deemed acceptable if unflattering versions of the "old man" found at La Chapelle-aux-Saints. The third restoration, based on a skull from Le Moustier, is now regarded as a caricature. (COURTESY AMERICAN MUSEUM OF NATURAL HISTORY)

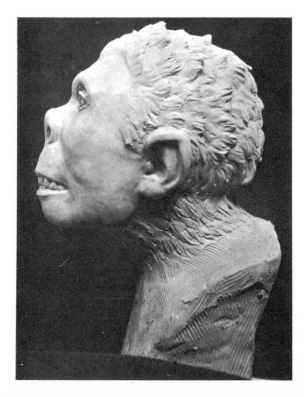

though something Lok could not see were supporting them, holding up their heads, thrusting them slowly and irresistibly forward. Lok knew if he were as thin as they, he would be dead already." Lok's ogres were our murdering ancestors.

Yet both Sir Harry's remark and the novel it inspired spring from a picture that is fundamentally erroneous. The Neanderthal man, I was surprised to learn, did not have a simian gait, his feet were not gorilla-like, and his face did not resemble that of Lon Chaney playing a horrific monster. The conventional caricature derives largely from a universally influential— and highly incompetent—study of a single skeleton found near the French village of La Chapelle-aux-Saints in 1906. The original investigators failed to notice that the skeleton was that of a comparatively old man suffering from arthritis. These qualifying facts emerged in a re-examination of the bones made in 1957 by William Straus of Johns Hopkins University and Alec Cave of St. Bartholomew's Hospital in London. Their reappraisal showed that the posture of Neanderthal man did not differ significantly from our own; in their words: "If he could be reincarnated and placed in a New York subway—providing that he were bathed, shaved and dressed in modern clothing—it is doubtful that he would attract any more attention than some of its other denizens."

The ogre vanishes, his place taken by a subway straphanger: something less than a beauty but nevertheless within the range of human variation. This belated autopsy is only one of many recent discoveries all tending to rehabilitate our most immediate relation, whose bones were first found in the Neander Valley of Germany in 1856. It is now established that Neanderthalers roamed widely through the Old World, and skeletons found in the Middle East and northern Africa show a resemblance closer to modern man than the classic European specimens with their heavier jaws and thicker limbs. Some anthropologists now question whether the Neanderthal man deserves to be listed at all as a separate species.

At the same time, Neanderthal achievements have come to seem less contemptible; he was a skilled hunter, capable of slaying the fearsome eight-foot bear, his tools were impressively various, he could build fires, probably spoke a language, and diligently buried his dead, suggesting the rudiments of a religion. He lived from around 110,000 to 35,000 years ago—a longer run, it may be fairly remarked, than his successors have yet managed. Yet, despite all this, the Neanderthal man continues to have a deplorable image, and museums persist unabashed in displaying slanderous portraits of our unoffending uncle. One is forced to conclude that we *want* the Neanderthaler to be a simian freak, that it somehow gratifies our masochism.

The redemption of Neanderthal man owes much to the meticulous labors of François Bordes, director of the Laboratory of Prehistory at the

University of Bordeaux, who has patiently sifted through the equivalent of an 85,000-year diary of Paleolithic life. The diary was in the form of layered deposits in a cave site known as Combe Grenal, some fourteen miles from the village of Les Eyzies, deep in the Dordogne region of France. No fewer than fifty-five occupation levels were defined in an epochal campaign from 1953 to 1964, and 19,000 Neanderthal tools were found, most of them fitting into four types of "kits." The kits, or associated collections of implements, appear to belong to four traditions, or tribes, since comparable tool groupings were found in 1962 in a cave site near the Sea of Galilee in Israel.

Professor Bordes is an exemplar of a proud French tradition. Growing up near Les Eyzies, he was collecting and digging for flint implements as a teen-ager; during the war he was a Resistance fighter, earning a place on the Nazi death list for his skill at sabotage. His accomplishments include the ability to re-create in minutes the flint tools of the Neanderthal in every known variety—and in his spare time he has written three science-fiction novels. Cautious though he is about generalizations, Bordes is alive to the aesthetic limitations of the people he has done so much to rehabilitate. "They made beautiful things stupidly," he says. "For the first week you are impressed with the tools, but after that you see scrapers and more scrapers and still more scrapers until you are sick of them!" *

As it happens, Bordes is in charge of all excavations in the Dordogne region, and here, more than anywhere else on the globe, one finds an exhilarating corrective to the image of the ape in the mirror.

How can I describe the Dordogne? One must sternly resist travel-brochure clichés or poetic hyperbole (though I like my friend Alan Brien's description of it as "the golf-course of the gods"). Yet to say that it is one of the most generally satisfying places anywhere—satisfying in the friendliness of its people, in its crenelated scenery, in its prehistoric art, and in its amenities, notably the food—is to state a simple truth.

Physically, it is carved by streams into a curious chalky cheesescape of tilted amber hills, chestnut forests, gorges, and canyons. From poplar-lined rivers one sees a medley of truffle farms, cottages tucked in overhanging cliffs, and a castle on an improbable peak. It is rich, above all, in natural and human curiosities of the Ice Age, which are squirreled away in the countless caves that riddle its limestone crust.

The Dordogne has the feel of a place chiseled by glaciers, and its inhabitants have learned to move through the millennia the way the rest of us move through space. In Les Eyzies, rightly called "the capital of prehistory," the average schoolchild knows more about ancient man than most adults

---

* For a fuller account of Bordes's work and of other recent Neanderthal studies, see John E. Pfeiffer's first-rate *The Emergence of Man* (New York: Harper & Row, 1969), which I have gratefully consulted.

elsewhere. For years the local schoolmaster was Denis Peyrony, who was Bordes's predecessor as an official overseer of excavations. "Do you know," Peyrony was apt to remark to visitors, as he did to the German prehistorian Herbert Kühn, "sometimes it seems to me that I'm actually living in the Ice Age, that I'm actually conversing with men of those days. I feel as if they're no strangers, as though I know them. Here, in this rock-shelter, there lives a nice friendly couple, but over there there's a bad pair indeed, always quarreling and fighting, while here there's song and laughter. I seem to be quite close to them. I can almost touch them."

The illusion is understandable, for the past is to the Dordogne what the Alp is to Switzerland: an integral part of the environment. Whole tracts of time take their name from homely features of local topography in Les Eyzies. The era known as Mousterian is named after the cave of Le Moustier, and Magdalenian derives from the cliff site of La Madeleine. Even hotels are affected. One of the best is the Cro-Magnon Hotel, which marks the site where in 1868 road workers found the first known skeleton of Cro-Magnon man (the precise find-spot is now a car-park).

The Dordogne has its country silences and its unique magic. In 1944 the caves of the region were used by the *maquis* as hiding places for air-dropped arms supplies. André Malraux recalls an inspection trip to a cave which he noticed was painted; he and his comrades passed silently through its corridors, wary of the German patrols that might be overhead. With their electric torches throwing a pale halo of light, the Resistance fighters came upon parachutes spread on the ground with machine guns, like odd insects, mounted on them. Overhead, clearly visible, were huge horned animals. The novelist and author of *The Voices of Silence* did not recognize the cave, but was impressed by its sacred calm and its somber beasts, like heraldic emblems. He writes in his *Antimemoirs:*

> We went down by a knotted rope into a fairly shallow pit, on the wall of which was an elementary human form with a bird's head. A pile of bazookas fell over with a weird clang which faded into the shadows, and the silence returned more desolate and more menacing than before. . . . "Are you interested in the paintings?" asked the guide. "Some kids found them when they went in to rescue a puppy in September, 1940. It's very old. Some scientists came, but then, in 1940, you can imagine!"
>
> It was Lascaux.

There is an allegorical quality about the painted caves of the Dordogne —the apposite circumstance that the greatest of ancient ateliers should be found in the country so inordinately proud of its art. Equally curious, France has been the battleground of the debate over Paleolithic art, a dispute that wonderfully accords with the temper of people who, from Montaigne to Camus, have been obsessively concerned with the nature of man. For the Dordogne marks a Rubicon of the species, the place where a hairless biped set himself apart from nature by leaving a lasting testament to his own vision of the world.

"These are not the work of children," the pioneer prehistorian Gabriel de Mortillet excitedly said on first seeing in 1878 a Paleolithic carving found in France. "This is the childhood of art." Few realized how precocious that childhood would prove to be, and one of the remarkable stories of the past century has been the reluctance of our species to accept the evidence of its own genius. The ape in the mirror, it sometimes seems, will believe in anything but himself.

II

THE UNDERGROUND WAR

> *Man can believe the impossible, but never the improbable.* OSCAR WILDE (1892)

IN THE BEGINNING there was certainty. In 1650 James Ussher, Archbishop of Armagh, offered Scriptural proof that the Creation took place in 4004 B.C. The computation was further refined by Dr. John Lightfoot, Master of St. Catherine's and Vice-Chancellor of Cambridge University, who timed it precisely: "Heaven and earth, center and circumference, were created all together in the same instant and clouds full of water. . . . This took place and man was created by the Trinity on October 23, 4004 B.C., at nine o'clock in the morning." Or, as Professor Glyn Daniel, also of Cambridge, has slyly added, at about the beginning of the academic term.

Still, doubts developed. One skeptic was William Buckland, an Oxford geologist and later Dean of Westminster, who wrote in 1836 of the "greatest difficulty in reconciling the early and extended periods which have been assigned to the extinct races of animals with our received chronology." But though Dean Buckland recognized the conflict, he would not recognize the evidence. In 1823 a Paleolithic skeleton was found in a Welsh cave; the pious Dean dated the bones as Romano-Christian.

A bolder investigator was the Frenchman Jacques Boucher de Perthes, who in 1832 became convinced that the flints he had found around Abbeville were manmade. He placed his collection before higher authority, and was dismissed with a condescending smile. "They employed against me," he complained, "a weapon more potent than objections, than criticism, than satire or even persecution—the weapon of disdain. They did not discuss my facts, they did not take the trouble to deny them. They disregarded them."

Across the Channel a self-taught Cornishman, William Pengelly, was investigating caves in the West Country. His first discovery of prehistoric implements were dismissed as modern intrusions. But in 1858 five eminent British geologists were witnesses as Pengelly dug through a sheet of stalagmite covering the floor of a cave above Brixham Harbor. Embedded below were the bones of mammoths, woolly rhinoceros, cave bear, cave lion, hyena, and reindeer. Among these bones were flints unquestionably shaped by man. In 1859 the Royal Society joined in fully accepting the researches of Pengelly and De Perthes.

European scholars were also beginning to accept the idea of the three ages of prehistory—stone, bronze, and iron. This conception originated in a guidebook prepared in 1836 by Christian Thomsen for the collection of the Danish National Museum. Then, in 1851 Daniel Wilson, a British antiquary, won a modest lexical immortality by using the word "prehistory" for the first time.

The soil was thus prepared for the disturbing appearance in 1859 of Darwin's *Origin of Species*, a work which led scandalized believers to insist that man had been brutalized. The view was elegantly expressed by Disraeli in a speech at Oxford in 1864: "The question is this: Is man an ape or an angel? My lord, I am on the side of the angels. I repudiate with indignation and abhorrence the contrary view which is, I believe, contrary to the conscience of mankind."

But, paradoxically, scientists themselves were afflicted with the opposite credulity—so convinced were they that prehistoric man was only an improved version of the ape that they ridiculed the clearest evidence that he could paint like an angel.

The first finds were made in caves. In 1860 Edouard Lartet, a lawyer by training and geologist by avocation, dug carefully into a cave shelter in the foothills of the Pyrénées. Near Aurignac he found the Stone Age burial of a culture now known as Aurignacian. Still more sensational objects turned up near Massat, where in a blackened cave hearth an antler with the picture of a bear scratched on it was found. Lartet instantly linked this with another engraved bone he had found farther north; this was the first evidence that Stone Age (or, in present usage, Paleolithic) man could draw.

Lartet's publication of the find was predictably ignored. Nonetheless, he pursued his researches, turning to the village of Les Eyzies in 1863. Here his collaborator was an Englishman, the banker and ethnologist Henry Christy. At a rock shelter on the Vézère River the pair found flints identical with those Lartet had discovered at Aurignac. In the sites of La Madeleine and Le

Moustier more implements were found, defining two new Paleolithic cultures —and at the former site the excavators came upon the first known engraved picture of the indubitably extinct mammoth.

It happened that an English visitor was present, Hugh Falconer, a friend of Darwin's and a leading paleontologist, and he did what came naturally— he wrote a letter to *The Times*. Here was evidence, he announced in March 1864, that could not be disparaged by "cursory observers and light reasoners" which proved that Paleolithic man had been able to create works that were "marvels both of artistic design and execution."

Yet, notwithstanding this disclosure, scholars dismissed out of hand the first discovery of a painted cave. A visitor to the Paris Exposition of 1878 was impressed by a display of prehistoric implements, and decided to see if he could find any on his own estate in the Basque country of Spain. Don Marcelino Santiago Tomás Sanz de Santuola then explored a cave in Altamira found by a hunter a few years before. His five-year-old daughter Maria was with him, and she was apparently the first to see the marvelous polychrome bison painted on the ceiling. The astounded father carefully copied the picture, and in 1880 published a sober report of the find. It was greeted with scorn; when he died, eight years later, he was virtually alone in insisting that the Altamira paintings were not forged.

Six years later he was vindicated when the archaeologist Emile Rivière explored the cave of La Mouthe, located in the hills near Les Eyzies. Here the entrance was sealed by prehistoric deposits, and within, incised on the wall, were deer, bison, and ibex. Still, it took eight more years for the doubters to concede. In 1901 three young prehistorians—Henri Breuil, Louis Capitan, and Denis Peyrony—entered the sanctuary of Les Comba-relles. With the light of a single candle they saw a menagerie engraved on the walls, and a week later at the nearby cave of Font-de-Gaume more pictures were found, some of them convincingly covered by ancient concretions.

On August 12, 1902—a landmark date in prehistory—an expedition of skeptical scholars inspected La Mouthe, and on that day, in Breuil's words, the "scientific world officially recognized the wall art in the caves of the Reindeer Age."

One of the visiting scholars was Emile Carthailac, Professor at Toulouse University and *doyen* of French prehistorians. Once among the most elo-quent of scoffers, he generously recanted in a paper entitled "*Mea Culpa d'un sceptique*," admitting that he had never visited Altamira but had dismissed the paintings as fakes on the basis of published illustrations. "Here was something absolutely new, strange in every possible way," he confessed. "I took counsel. An influence which had often had happier results quickly made me skeptical. *Take care!*, someone wrote to me, *They want to play tricks with French prehistorians! Don't trust priest-ridden Spaniards!* And I didn't trust them."

Abbé Henri Breuil Conferring with the Abbé is the late Harper Kelley, one of the few Americans to serve on the staff of the Musée de l'Homme.

In a becoming flourish, Carthailac visited Altamira and apologized to Maria, the full-grown daughter of the Spanish don. Accompanying the professor, oddly enough, was a priest, the Abbé Breuil, then twenty-six, who was to become Carthailac's most distinguished disciple. Henri Breuil (1877–1961) was born in Normandy and trained as a priest, but received what was to be a lifetime dispensation from parish duties when he became absorbed by prehistory. He was a self-taught artist with an artist's face: seamed and witty, usually bisected by a drooping Gauloise. Breuil once estimated that he had spent nearly two years crouched in caves, patiently sketching Paleolithic art, his cassock splotched with white candle wax, his back and eyes fatigued with effort. He studied every important cave of Europe, searched the Sahara for still more, and explored the decorated rocks of the Horn of Africa, producing, at regular intervals, fat and wonderful folio volumes packed with sketches. In the process, he added hundreds of centuries to the history of art, and wrested some sort of order out of primeval chaos.

His career had its theological irony. For a century, science and religion had been antagonists in the furor over evolution. Indeed, in 1895 a French Dominican, Father Leroy, was called to Rome and ordered to recant a book he had published defending evolutionary theory. "As a docile son of the Church," the penitent Father asserted, "resolved to live and die in the Faith, and obedient in this case to authority, I hereby declare that I disavow, retract and denounce all that I have said, written and published in favor of [the Darwinian] theory." The same disposition to credit Darwin also proved a source of lifelong trouble to one of Breuil's closest friends, the Jesuit Teilhard de Chardin.

But in the underground war over Paleolithic art the antagonists switched sides; it was a rationalist scientist who suspected a priestly trick when Altamira was discovered, and it was a priest who played the largest role in proving that science had too little belief in man. Breuil himself was untroubled by the metaphysical implications of his work. He was content to remark, "Science and religion are different problems: science observes, ascertains, it does not explain."

The paradox would have delighted Pascal, who dismissed man as "judge of all things and imbecile maggot; depository of truth, and sewer of uncertainty and error, the glory and rubbish of the universe!" For the quarrel over cave art was anticipated in one of Pascal's admonitions: "It is dangerous to let man see how closely he resembles the beasts unless at the same time we show how great he is."

Nor have the caves exhausted their capacity to startle. Only recently a new theory has been advanced about the nature of cave art which, if accepted, will dethrone again the conventional wisdom about early man. Once more it is a Frenchman who is unsettling prehistory—André Leroi-Gourhan, Professor of Ethnology at the Sorbonne and director of the University's Center for Prehistoric and Protohistoric Studies.

In examining the decorated caves of France and Spain, Leroi-Gourhan wondered whether the positioning of the painted animals was wholly arbitrary in the hundred-odd sites that have been discovered. To obtain an answer, he studied the topography of sixty caves in which two thousand animals were visible. After submitting the data to a computer, he was able to offer three remarkable judgments:

> 1. If one defines the "central position" either as the middle of a painted panel or the prominent chamber within the cave, it is in this position that more than 85 percent of all pictures of bison, wild oxen and horses are found.
> 2. The next most prominent animals—deer, ibex, and mammoth—appear in positions other than the central one.
> 3. Three other species—rhinoceros, lion and bear—are found only in the deepest part of the cave.

The implications of this hypothesis are so provocative that Leroi-Gourhan's conclusions have been worriedly challenged by other scholars, particularly the way in which his three conclusions depend on his definition of cave topography. For if he is right, we must believe not only that cave artists worked under cruelly difficult conditions but also that they created, over a wide terrain, an ordered Ark whose conventions persisted for hundreds of centuries.

In a further bold assertion Leroi-Gourhan maintains that the bewildering cave symbols—the rows of dots, barbed lines, hatched rectangles, and macaronic scrawls—can be read as a kind of sexual shorthand. He asserts that there are five groups of female symbols and four of male, and that the symbols are associated with definite species. He argues that man's first epoch of art culminated in a classic period lasting from around 13,000 B.C. to perhaps as late as 8,000 B.C. "Indeed," he goes on, "the uniformity of the classic period suggests not only the existence of contacts between various regional populations but also the existence of a firmly based cosmopolitan artistic tradition." *

In other words, there was a kind of Paleolithic School of Paris whose aesthetic norms were respected over thousands of generations. To put this in perspective, one must bear in mind the broad chronology which is generally accepted by scholars. The creatures that were to become man appeared more than a million years ago, and a half-million years later beings that were recognizably human emerged as the Lower Paleolithic or Early Stone Age began. About 100,000 years ago homonoids like the Neanderthal man began burying their dead, fashioning hand axes and perhaps contriving crude ornaments. But the first unambiguous examples of art have been found thus far only in association with the first *Homo sapiens*, the Cro-Magnon man, who emerged during the fourth and last Ice Age, some 40,000 years ago.

In Breuil's view, the earliest art followed successive cycles, beginning with the Aurignacian-Périgordian and culminating with the Solutrean-Magdalenian, the final cycle ending 10,000 years ago as the Ice Age receded from Europe and the era that prehistorians call "recent" began. Leroi-Gourhan would revise Breuil's cycles, though he accepts the general timetable I have summarized above. His style-cycles are four: two primitive styles, spanning from 30,000 to 17,000 B.C.; an archaic style, from 17,000 to 12,000 B.C.; and a classical style lasting nearly five millennia.

But the dates have a numbing quality, particularly for a species that now thinks of a decade as eternity. Our reflections about timetables dissolve like crystals in a solution when we actually confront the cave drawings themselves.

* For a summary of Leroi-Gourhan's views, see his article "The Evolution of Paleolithic Art," *Scientific American*, Vol. 218, 2 (February 1968), and his magnificent book, *The Art of Prehistoric Man* (London: Thames & Hudson, 1968). For a critical appraisal, consult Peter J. Ucko and Andrée Rosenfeld, *Paleolithic Cave Art* (London: World University Library, 1967).

III

GODS, CAVES, AND SCRAWLERS

Caves are the privileged homes of the documents of prehistory.

PIERRE TEILHARD DE CHARDIN,
The Appearance of Man

BEFORE VISITING the Dordogne in 1962, I saw the late Harper Kelley, one of the few Americans ever to serve on the staff of Musée de l'Homme in Paris. We talked in his cluttered office about a cave controversy that had developed over the authenticity of the art at Rouffignac. He offered an affable warning: "Be careful about forming hard opinions on everything you see. The caves are filled with land-mines, and prehistorians are a volatile breed." I have his warning in mind.

But the caves are as much an emotional as an intellectual experience, and no theory is necessary to savor the sensation of seeing animals executed with supreme grace spring from the blackness. In my own journey to the Valley of Caves, I was unwittingly lucky—I saw Lascaux only a year before it was closed indefinitely to the public that was destroying it.

Lascaux was discovered on September 12, 1940, when France was still divided following the fall of Paris. Five youngsters, two of them refugees from Occupied France, were out rabbit-hunting when their dog Robot tumbled into a hole. The boys climbed into the opening and first saw the splendors of Lascaux by match-light. They hurried to their schoolmaster in the village of Montignac and exuberantly reported their discovery. Ten days later Abbé Breuil, who was in a nearby town, was summoned to inspect the cave, and the find was announced in October. Three of the boys were among the guides at the cave before it was closed.

First opened to the public in 1944, Lascaux was drawing 122,000 visitors by 1962, making it the fourth most popular tourist attraction in France. Elaborate hatches were built to seal the cave, and a machine installed to purify the air. But the machine caused drafts, upsetting the equilibrium that had preserved the paintings. It became evident by 1963 that something was wrong, and a diagnosis showed that a green micro-organism of seaweed structure—called *maladie verte*—was spreading over the paintings. Additionally, flakes of white calcite—called *maladie blanche*—had infected the limestone walls. In August 1969 a detailed report was published by the team of

The Dordogne Valley　A typical chiseled cheesecape at La Roque Sageac. (COUR-
TESY FRENCH GOVERNMENT TOURIST OFFICE)

biologists who had examined the infected walls. The chief blame for the cave's condition was attributed to the shoes of visitors, which carried soil and slime into the cave. The organic debris mingled with sweat, breath, and bacteria to produce a species of green algae, *Palmellococcus*, which leprously disfigured the paintings. Broad-spectrum antibiotic sprays were used to fumigate the cave, and a dilute solution of formaldehyde was applied to kill the algae and bleach the dead cells left on the wall.

The treatment has saved the paintings, but imperiled Lascaux as a tourist attraction—to the distress of everybody, especially the inhabitants of Montignac. As of this writing (1970), nobody can say whether the cave will be opened again to any except a qualified elite of scholarly specialists. (Prince Charles, while an archaeology student at Cambridge, was one of those given special permission to see Lascaux, and from time to time delighted tourists in the area are told that a handful among them may enter the cave.) One proposal under study is to make an exact replica of the cave and locate it nearby—an unsatisfactory solution but possibly the best.

Contemplating the fate of Lascaux, the London *Times* found it no shock to those who believe that culture and art are "the first victims of the revolt of the masses," adding: "What better symbol than the survival of the handiwork of Upper Paleolithic Man through fifteen thousand undisturbed years, so that it might eventually be silently obliterated by the steady footfall and hushed breathing of his remote descendants!" In fairness to the masses who have trooped through Lascaux (myself among them), it could be rejoined that not long ago the devotees of culture and art were themselves the chief predators in the looting of Italy, Greece, and Egypt of antiquities—and that even today, in one of the unpublicized scandals of the Western world, leading museums are the knowing customers of those who pillage and smuggle art from places like Turkey and Mexico (Malraux, too, once engaged in the smuggling of Khmer sculpture from Cambodia). Vandalism does not lend itself easily to class analysis.

Lascaux is compact, but there are on its walls no less than a hundred horses, thirty bovids, at least twenty deer, ten ibexes, seven bison, six or seven felines, and one each of bear, musk-ox reindeer, and rhinoceros. My first feeling on entering was that it is, above all, a strikingly cheerful place; the animals are rendered with affection, yet without Disney-like glucose. Whatever prompted the portrayal of these animals, it was not fear or hate. There is a great cow in one gallery that has a nursery-rhyme quality, as if she had leaped over an underground moon. A frieze of deer in another gallery, where they are shown fording a river, noses tipped up, is drawn with infinite tenderness. As one cranes one's head to stare at the ceiling, the animals seem playful and cinematic—the procession appear actually to move, as in a slow-motion film, and this is an experience no reproduction can ever convey. Painted on a white base, as if an aerosol bomb of sunlight had doused the walls, the Lascaux Ark floats in a lake of light. By lamp flame the creatures must have appeared alive enough to pinch.

There is only a single depiction of a human, a drawing which was not shown to visitors even when the cave was opened; it is located in the Shaft or Well of the Dead Man, a pit at the far end of the Chamber of Engravings. A strangely beaked man is depicted near the base of the shaft, which is about sixteen feet deep. He is sketched in black, with a matchbox body and stick-like limbs; he seems to be falling before a bison whose rump is crossed with a spear. The man's penis is erect, and below him is a queer staff with a bird on its top. What does this cryptic vignette mean? Is the scene related to the nearby picture of a rhinoceros, drawn by another artist? Is it, as Leroi-Gourhan argues, clearly a mythological or allegorical work, or did it refer to a specific incident? And why was it located in the bottom of a shaft?

At Lascaux, as in other caves, there is no agreed answer to exasperating questions, and on the most rudimentary of problems—for example, the motive for using caves as illustrated sanctuaries—there is a depressing cacophony among experts. The caves may have been meeting rooms, they could also have been religious shrines; the art may have been intended as a form of sympathetic magic connected with hunting, or, again, it may have been related to initiation ceremonies in the caves. Or (if Leroi-Gourhan is right) it may be filled with a symbolic language linked to fertility cults. At Lascaux even the simpler matter of dates is a vexed question. Charcoal associated with lamps found in the cave have yielded a carbon date of from 14,500 to 12,500 B.C., but it is not certain that the lamps were contemporaneous with the paintings. Breuil believed the paintings belonged to the Aurignacian-Périgordian cycle and were completed from 35,000 to 25,000 B.C. Leroi-Gourhan, along with most other scholars, feels this is impossibly early; he puts the paintings in his Style III and IV category, or 15,000 to 10,000 B.C.

In the end, the incandescence of Lascaux is augmented by the darkness encompassing it. When I was there, the fact of the paintings made bickering seem irrelevant. I had the feeling of being in a primal wellspring of the human spirit, a place which should be to our world what Delphi was to the Greeks. The oracle's exhortation was "Know thyself"; that of Lascaux should be "Know thy species."

According to Montaigne, who lived near the Dordogne, man sees himself nailed and fastened to the most stagnant part of the universe, at the farthest distance from the vault of Heaven, living among the vilest of animals, "and yet in his imagination he places himself above the circle of the moon, and brings Heaven under his feet." How delighted Montaigne would have been

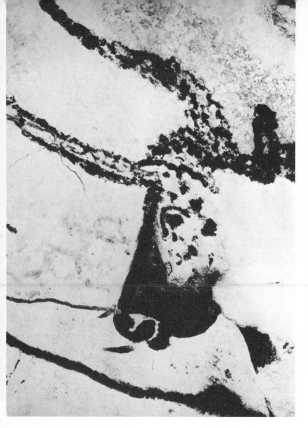

Lascaux: The Great Bull What appears to be an arrow can be seen near the beast's muzzle.

Lascaux: The Painted Shaft At the bottom of this pit, twenty feet deep, archaeologists found the painting of the dead man and the bison. (COURTESY ESTATE OF ABBÉ BREUIL)

to learn that Cro-Magnon man had taken him at his word! *

If Lascaux is closed, the Dordogne provides a consolation to venturers into the Ice Age. Lascaux is the cathedral in a Valley of Caves; there are also abbeys and parish churches, not to speak of the village of Les Eyzies, with its cave shelters like Laugerie Bas, where the old schoolmaster Peyrony eavesdropped on Paleolithic family quarrels, and its fine local museum. (Near the museum there is a statue of the Neanderthal man, in his traditional simian form, gaping blankly at the landscape his ancestors knew. He is a local mascot.)

* Apropos of Montaigne's lunar allusion, on the day when the first men on the moon were returning to earth, an English visitor, Denis Thomas of Chislehurst, Kent, was fortunate enough to visit Lascaux. His reflective letter to the London *Times* seems eminently quotable: "At such a freakish moment the art of men living more than 20,000 years ago, and comprehensible to a space-age mind only at the most superficial level, seemed a crushing rebuke to the present day. I should have thought that any militant modern artist would look on these works with jealous despair. They are impeccably non-aristocratic. They have nothing to do with High Culture, or with any recognizable convention. Even the artists' techniques are enviably non-academic: colors ground from natural minerals, applied by a blowpipe or flattened stick. We could revert to the same methods; but we would still lack our ancestors' innocent spirituality. To have saved the Lascaux paintings is every bit as important as landing on the moon."

Les Eyzies The village and the River Vézère, and the cliffs which overshadow them. (COURTESY PHOTOTEQUE FRANÇAIS)

There are two caves of the first order of importance in the environs of Les Eyzies. At Les Combarelles a voluble guide usually takes one around, flashing his beam and waiting for exclamations of surprise as he identifies some of the interwoven engravings (no cave has more of them) that crowd 116 panels in one gallery and 79 panels in another. The cave is a labyrinth of hairpin turns, and in its penetralia hundreds of drawings are tangled together, requiring sharp eyes and the chattering guide to unsnarl them, but worth the effort. Breuil was one of three original discoverers in 1901; he wrote a friend afterward: "And how we slaved yesterday! I traced eighteen of the beasts— some of them are magnificent . . . all in all, I spent ten hours in the cave. I am half-dead, I am aching all over, but I am very well pleased. Extraordinary, eh?"

Les Combarelles A lion (left) faces mammoth and equines in this tracing by Breuil. (COURTESY ESTATE OF ABBÉ BREUIL)

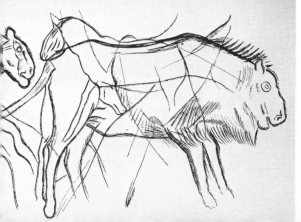

Three Bison from Font-de-Gaume The bulls shown in Breuil's luminous depiction have faded and are ghostly shadows of what he originally copied. (COURTESY ESTATE OF ABBÉ BREUIL)

Font-de-Gaume, not far away, is reached by a more dramatic approach; one scrambles up a footpath that winds around the hill until the entrance at the summit reveals itself. The sanctuary is dimly lit by electricity, and the winding walls contain at least 198 painted and engraved creatures. Its glory is the gallery of the polychrome bison and reindeer, the reds and browns sadly faded but conveying a haunting splendor nonetheless. The cave is also decorated with an abundance of tectiform signs—tent- or roof-shaped symbols sometimes interpreted as being traps. Leroi-Gourhan sees these as female quadrangular symbols. The decorated portion of the cave begins, incidentally, after one passes a narrowing of the walls called "The Rubicon."

What is perhaps the greatest single treasure of Les Eyzies is found at Cap Blanc, the name of the farm that shelters the finest Paleolithic sculptures I know about. The farm is an easy drive from the village, and a sign in front reads: KLAXONNEZ ET ATTENDEZ DIX MINUTES. If after ten minutes the guide does not materialize, toot the horn again and proceed by foot to find the laconic, wooden-shod farmer, smelling agreeably of garlic, who takes one down to a locked shed. Within are three splendid horses hewn from rock in a style that a Periclean master would not scorn. Breuil, who studied the horses shortly after their discovery in 1910, offers the best appreciation. He indignantly rejected the suggestion that the carvings were simply swellings of the rock adapted to the lazy artist's purpose. "No!" the Abbé snorted. "The Magdalenian artist attacked a huge plane surface overhanging at one end, vertical at the other. With his flint tools he cut away the rock for widths of four to twenty inches, and he scraped the silhouette in relief, modeling the projection of the back and muscles, and marking the attaching of limbs and sinews; and he finished off this massive work with the most delicately incised lines." One must marvel at the way in which the sculptor exploited the natural surfaces of the stone while accenting the details of the fetlocks as a visual complement to the broad mass of the body—and did all this in an unsheltered site for no obvious purpose whatever. I like to think it was the sheer pleasure of the feat: art for the artist's sake.

Somewhat farther beyond Les Eyzies is Rouffignac, a cave notorious for the intemperate row it provoked. The reason for the emotion can be simply stated—Rouffignac is one of the best-known caves in the entire region, and yet, if the art within it is authentic, not one of hundreds of modern explorers ever noticed that it was crawling with drawings. This either suggests that the spelunkers were unobservant, which could be true, or that the art was added to the cave by skillful plagiarists of the Cro-Magnon style, which also could be true. Either likelihood is bound to make somebody mad.

The discovery of its art occurred on June 26, 1956, when two prehistorians, Louis-René Nougier and Romain Robert, were invited by the owner of the cave to look around. The two went expecting nothing; they found, to their astonishment, a huge herd of painted game—more than 300 mammoth (the largest collection of any known cave) and smaller herds of horses, bison, and rhinoceros. Abbé Breuil was promptly invited, and he accepted the work as authentic. When this judgment was protested, a delegation of leading specialists solemnly inspected the cave, and most agreed with Breuil. Only a minority insisted the paintings were fake.

A curious twist in *l'affaire Rouffignac* is that one of the cave's most conspicuous paintings, the frieze of rhinoceros, was actually published as an illustration in a book, *Le Périgord Souterrain*, which appeared in 1953—three years before the putative discovery. Why had the author, a young speleologist named Bernard Pierret, made no mention of the rhinoceros clearly shown in his own book? The irate Pierret asserts that he knew they were modern fakes; Nougier and Robert retort that he didn't realize what he saw, and was too embarrassed to confess it.

Glyn Daniel, the distinguished Cambridge prehistorian (and tutor to Prince Charles), was a member of the delegation which visited Rouffignac. He reserved judgment then, and remains skeptical today; his reasoning is set forth in his excellent guide to the Valley of Caves, *The Hungry Archaeologist*, in which he points out that in the forty years between the discovery of

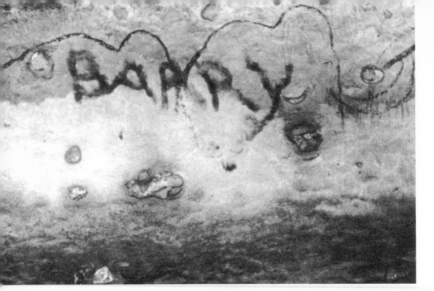

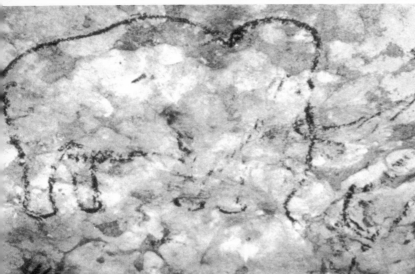

Beasts of Rouffignac The disputed drawings, which most experts accept as authentic, include two mammoths (ABOVE) beneath the eighteenth-century name "Barry"; CENTER, a mammoth under the great ceiling; and BELOW, another in a style derided by some as *à la Babar l'éléphant*

Font-de-Gaume and Combarelles in 1901 and of Lascaux in 1940, nothing was reported at Rouffignac although archaeologists were presumably swarming through all known caves in the region. He cites the statement of a local speleologist, William Martin, a French schoolmaster despite his name, who categorically asserts that he visited Rouffignac in 1948 and saw no paintings or engravings. Moreover, says Daniel (who writes detective stories as well as learned volumes of prehistory), the Cambridge University Speleological Society went caving in Les Eyzies in 1939, and one of its members reports he is "fairly certain" that no art was seen at Rouffignac though the explorers were conscious of the possibility of finding paintings. In the end, Daniel is circumspectly doubtful: "Forgeries can and do happen, great men can and do make mistakes, and equally, people can and do visit sites and not notice what is there!"

For his part, André Leroi-Gourhan, who is emphatically no automatic disciple of Breuil's, shares the Abbé's view about Rouffignac, declaring: "It takes long experience with caves to know that it is quite possible to pass certain details a hundred times without actually seeing them until much later, when they stare you in the face. The quarrel is now a thing of the past." He lists the controversial site as a "typical deep-cave sanctuary."

In any event, the cave manifestly (in the Michelin phrase) *mérite un détour*, if it does not *vaut le voyage*. It is a vast abscess, opening up into chambers of auditorium dimensions, and the owner has built a small electric train to run through it (either the farmer or his wife provides a lively running commentary—and on the way out the couple proffers plates and jugs made of Rouffignac clay and engraved with mammoth heads). Forged or not, the paintings of Rouffignac are distinguished by a sinewy line that catches the curve of a mammoth tusk or the menace of a rhinoceros snout. I was impressed by them, and by the plenitude of names scrawled and carved right across the broad backs of enormous animals; one rhinoceros is formally named "Dubois," after a cave explorer from Brive who years ago gouged his name over a work of art he apparently never saw. Either way, as a fraud or a genuine find, Rouffignac is a monument to human myopia.

In the other direction from Les Eyzies lies the cave of Pech-Merle, near the village of Cabrerets, a full-day trip through luminous country. This cave also was the cause of a scandal. It was rented some years ago by the village mayor, who proceeded to commercialize it, installing a bar, dance floor, and jukebox, improvements that provoked a marked *frisson* among appalled prehistorians. One disapproving visitor in 1952 was the late André Breton, once a grand panjandrum of Dada. As he was being shown around, Breton reached out impulsively to touch a mammoth with his thumb. When the color stuck to his hand, he turned to the mayor and interrupted cheekily, "Forgery, *monsieur*," prompting His Honor—a blacksmith by trade—to heave the artist bodily out of the cave and to lodge a million-franc damage suit against

The Horses of Pech-Merle The profiled man gives an idea of the scale of the creatures so mysteriously surrounded by puffy dots and outlined hands. (PHOTO CARL NOSJAR OF OSLO)

Breton. The trial a year later was *opéra-bouffe*. Malraux, Camus, and Mauriac were among the eminent who protested that Breton was being shamefully persecuted for a misdemeanor. The Ministry of Fine Arts took the offense more seriously, but asked for a token fine of only a single franc. In the event, the court put a value of 20,000 francs on the damaged mammoth trunk, and this was acceptable to the mayor, whose cave by now was packed with curious patrons. (It should be noted that wet paint is not a test of fraudulence in cave art since dampness can keep the original paint wet.)

Pech-Merle is an interminably large cave, with art scattered through a mile and a quarter of serpentine passages. Deep in its entrails is a chamber called the Ossuary, where a trove of cave-bear bones was found, and where countless cryptic lines are traced on the clay face of the wall, meandering ribbons inscribed either with a finger or a pointed tool; in some places there are red dots spread on the wall. It is like being in a surrealist bandbox, perplexing in every way. In the main decorated chamber one finds the famous panel of the spotted horses. A polka-dot horse romps on a hill, his hindquarters intersecting the back of another horse; both equines are hooded in black, like executioners. Mysterious puffs outline one horse's head, and over both animals are stenciled human hands which grope from the wall, as if touching palms with the dark air. It is a spectral apparition. One feels that, perhaps mercifully, here are enigmas that will forever elude the data cards fed into Professor Leroi-Gourhan's computer machines.

IV

FINAL HELPING

Who can help loving the land that has taught us six hundred and eighty-five ways to dress eggs? THOMAS MOORE (1812)

I HAVE MENTIONED earlier that one of the pleasures of the Dordogne is gastronomic, but the matter cannot be simply left there in a book that celebrates hedonism, however specialized. In the strict usage, the cuisine is known as *périgourdine*, after Périgord, the precise name of the district in which the Valley of Caves falls. Suitably enough, in its gastronomy as well as its archaeology, the region derives its distinctive flavor from something underground: the truffle. This peculiar mushroom is a regional specialty, and a Périgord pig with particular gifts has been bred as a truffle-hunter. To harvest wild truffles (writes Waverley Root in his authoritative *Food of France*), "no more efficient way of gathering them has been found than to let the pigs root them up, after which a short, sharp altercation with the pig is necessary to secure possession of the truffle."

Once excavated, the truffle is blended with other ingredients in such dishes as *truffes sous les cendres*, a specialty of the Hotel Cro-Magnon in Les Eyzies. In this dish, according to Root, "large truffles are seasoned and spiced, each one sprinkled with cognac, wrapped in a thin slice of salt pork, and tucked under the ashes of the glowing embers in an open hearth." Other dishes peculiar to the Périgord include *tourtes de truffe à la périgourdine* (a pie filled with truffles and *foie gras* soaked in brandy); *tourain périgourdin* (an onion soup with tomatoes and egg yolk); *œufs en cocotte à la périgourdine* (eggs broken over a layer of *foie gras* and cooked in casserole); and a very elaborate dish which takes days to prepare, *poularde truffée à la périgourdine*, in which stuffed chicken is covered with truffle peelings, thus allowing the subtle flavor to insinuate itself gradually and properly into the fortunate fowl.

Or one can ask the chef to prepare "Neolithic Broth," after a recipe devised by Raymond Oliver, master of the Grand Vefour restaurant in Paris:

Scrub with dry hay or grass a hollow in the rock and fill it to a third of its capacity with spring or rain water. Allow a quart per person. By its side, where the wind cannot blow its ashes into the

broth, light a very hot fire. Heat round stones, preferably balls of sandstone, in its center. When they are very hot take one and drop it in the water. Remove it and replace with another and so on until the water boils.

Have a mat of twigs ready to cover it between operations. Prepare the vegetables; onions, beans, carrots, wild asparagus, beechnuts, peeled acorns, rue, nettles, dandelion, coleseed, and herbs. Add these to the water with salt and wild rose petals. You may also add the hips. Continue with the stones until the vegetables are cooked. Then add grated animal fat (such as mutton or kidney fat) and add just one hot stone to complete the blending of fat and liquid.

Eat with a scallop shell held with a wooden fork.

And as one imbibes either "Neolithic Broth" or the more prosaic specialties of Périgord, one can reflect—as I did, after a day in the caves, fortified by a *digestif* in the arbored terrace of the Hotel Cro-Magnon—that the Almighty, as shown by His placement of these splendid sites in this felicitous place, must surely be an archaeologist or a Francophile, or perhaps both.

Chapter Three

THE BOOK OF
THE DEAD

E G Y P T

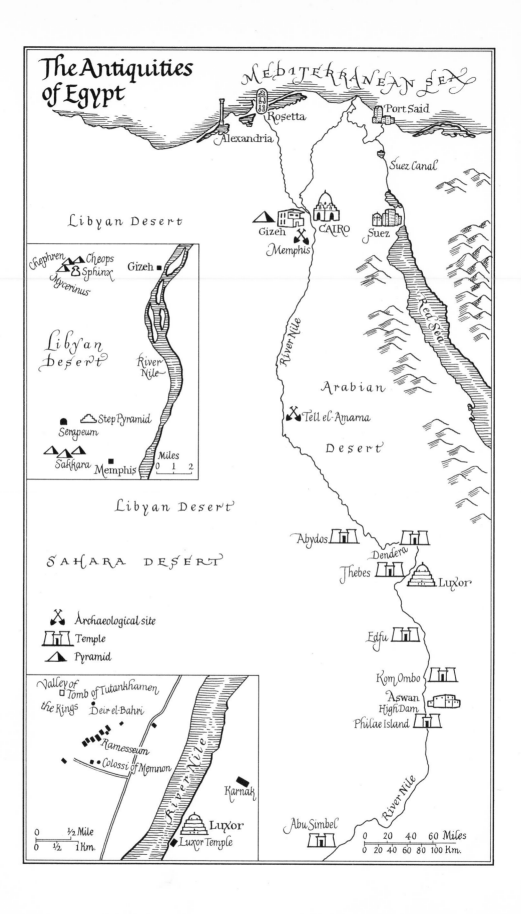

The Antiquities of Egypt

MEDITERRANEAN SEA

Rosetta

Port Said

Alexandria

Suez Canal

Libyan Desert

Gizeh

CAIRO

Memphis

Suez

Red Sea

River Nile

Chephren — Cheops
Sphinx
Mycerinus

Gizeh

Libyan Desert

River Nile

Step Pyramid

Serapeum

Sakkara

Memphis

Miles
0 1 2

Arabian

Tell el-Amarna

Desert

Libyan Desert

SAHARA DESERT

⚒ Archaeological site

🏛 Temple

△ Pyramid

Abydos

Dendera

Thebes

Luxor

Edfu

Kom Ombo

Aswan
High Dam

Philae Island

Valley of
the Kings
Tomb of Tutankhamen

Deir el-Bahri

Ramesseum

Colossi of Memnon

River Nile

Karnak

Luxor

Luxor Temple

0 ½ Mile
0 ½ 1 Km.

Abu Simbel

0 20 40 60 Miles
0 20 40 60 80 100 Km.

I

THE ENDLESS FRIEZE

I was yesterday; I know tomorrow.
The Book of the Dead

HISTORY IS WRITTEN on carbon papyri in Egypt. Once, to amuse myself, I wrote this summary of an Egyptian politico-military crisis in the manner of a slightly pontifical diplomatic correspondent:

> It is of course obvious why Mr. X, the ruler of Egypt, blundered so badly after he occupied Sinai with four divisions and advanced to the borders of Palestine. He overestimated his own power and forgot he was dealing with a European, not an Oriental adversary. He was lured into a trap by superior enemy intelligence, his armor was ambushed without cover and his entire army beaten in less than a week. Though the Egyptian regime may chose to ignore what happened on the battlefield, it will eventually be impelled to negotiate with the conquerors, even at the cost of angering its Syrian allies. If Mr. X had heeded my own earlier writings, the mood would be less lugubrious on the Nile today.

The year was 1286 B.C. or thereabouts, Mr. X was Ramses II, King of Kings, and his Indo-European opponents were the Hittites. I have simply summarized the Battle of Kadesh, the first major military engagement for which we have documentary accounts left by each side. It may be an augury that Kadesh ultimately led to the earliest known mutual non-aggression treaty—we even have parallel Egyptian and Hittite texts of the accord, dug up in sites a thousand miles apart.

Ramses II was a pioneer in another respect—he blandly rewrote history, converting a debacle into a triumph which his credulous artists commemorated in a thousand friezes almost covering the length of the Nile. A choice example can be seen at Abu Simbel, the temple which has been saved by the United Arab Republic with the help of an international UNESCO campaign. The first Big Lie is now a prime tourist attraction.

In rough outline, this is the story of Kadesh. Ramses was in the fifth year of his long reign when he came into conflict with the insufferable Hittites, an intruding Indo-European people whose capital was in Anatolia. Hittite warriors were annexing Egyptian client-states in Syria, and the challenge could no longer be ignored. The Pharaoh raised an army of 20,000 and advanced through Sinai to the northern border of Palestine. At this point the Hittites relied on guile. Two Bedouin agents, pretending to be deserters, stumbled into the Egyptian camp. They told Ramses that the Hittite King, terrified by the dread reputation of the Pharaoh, had ordered a retreat to the north.

The exultant Ramses then foolishly advanced into unscouted terrain, leading a column to Kadesh, in modern Lebanon. Here the Pharaoh caught two Hittite scouts, who, after being tortured, confessed the ruse. Ramses sent an urgent appeal for reinforcements, but he was already within the Hittite ambush. As a further unpleasant surprise, these Indo-Europeans had developed an improved weapon: their chariots provided room for two warriors as well as the driver. The obsolescent Egyptian chariot had space for only a single fighter.

The Egyptians were saved from massacre by three things: Hittite greed in looting, the chance arrival of Egyptian reinforcements, and the possible personal bravery of the Pharaoh himself. The evidence on the last point is somewhat suspect, since it consists of the Pharaoh's propaganda friezes in which he looms like King Kong, slaughtering whole regiments while his countenance remains in faultless profile.

In Hittite records it is plainly asserted that the Egyptians were defeated and that Ramses was forced to yield territory that his father had won. Treaties tell more than pictures. The agreement finally reached supports the Hittite version. The treaty defined spheres of influence, South Syria going to the Egyptians and the North to the Hittites; it provided for a defensive alliance; it even called for the extradition of refugees, carefully specifying that these were not to be treated as criminals on their return. In reviewing the evidence, Breasted offered this verdict on Kadesh:

> The immense superiority to be gained by clever manoeuvres masked from the enemy was clearly comprehended by the Hittite king when he executed the first flank movement of which we hear in the early Orient; and the plains of Syria, already at that remote epoch, witnessed notable examples of that supposedly modern science

which was brought to such perfection by Napoleon,—the science of winning the victory before the battle.

The same science has been more recently employed against Egypt. Yet, with a cold eye on facile parallels, it must be recorded that Kadesh was fought in the fifth year of the Pharaoh's reign. The peace that confirmed its outcome was not concluded until sixteen years later.

I went to Abu Simbel in 1964, drawn to Egypt by Mr. Khrushchev, who had come to dedicate the first stage of the Aswan High Dam. June is not the most agreeable month in Aswan. The air was like a gelatinous blanket, giving an illusion of quivering movement to the painted faces of Nasser and Khrushchev on the banner over the main street. Aswan itself is an odd hybrid, part spa and part boomtown, its divided personality expressed by the hovels of workmen and the domed tomb of the Aga Khan, both of which I could see from my room in the Cataract Hotel. The off-season mood in the hotel is best caught by a sign in the bar: DRINKING IS COMPULSORY.

By good luck, I was able to obtain a seat in the last but one of the hydrofoil boats that went to Abu Simbel before the temple was closed to enable salvage work to begin. My companions aboard the *Cleopatra* chanced to be Russian technicians on a holiday outing from their work on the Dam. (One of them had the splendid revolutionary name of Marat.) We drank vodka and chattered idly as the craft pressed into the wide blue ribbon of the

Abu Simbel: Temple Frieze Left, the Goddess Hathor and, right, the Goddess Isis flank Queen Nefertari in a temple consecrated to the favorite bride of Ramses II. (COURTESY UNESCO. PHOTO BY KEATING)

Abu Simbel When seen by early explorers, the temples were engulfed by sand, as in this print by David Roberts.

The temple as it was before being raised to its lofty new site above the rising Nile.
(COURTESY UNESCO. PHOTO BY LAURENZA)

Nile. On its banks we could see dozens of Nubian villages, like attractive collages of whitewashed mud and crockery. These had already been abandoned, and the inhabitants were resettled in new towns near Aswan, away from the rising waters that would flood their immemorial homes. Only Abu Simbel was to be saved at its old location, and in a few hours we saw the temple itself, its vast seated figures staring at the river with almost irritating self-satisfaction. Preliminary salvage work had begun. The temple was perforated by test borings, and the apron of sand at its base was piled high with cement bags.

We walked through the temple, the Russians and myself, dutifully inspecting the Kadesh friezes and the seated image of Ramses in the dim inner sanctuary. On impulse, I turned to a Soviet engineer and remarked quietly on the spiritual kinship between this cult-of-personality style and that found in art of the Stalinist period. A wary eye located the guide, who was out of earshot, and my fellow traveler murmured, "But in the Soviet Union we throw down the statues, and not to keep them forever."

It made me reflect, that remark, on how wrong Shelley was. His sonnet "Ozymandias" (the name is a corruption of User-Ma-Re, one of the praenomina of Ramses II) confidently concludes:

The Engulfing Nile Even before construction of the new High Dam, the seasonal rise of the river flooded the temples at Philae, such as this Pavilion of Trajan, on an island dedicated to the Goddess Isis. (COURTESY UNESCO. PHOTO BY LAURENZA)

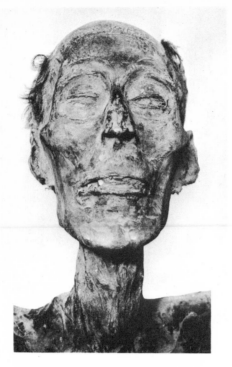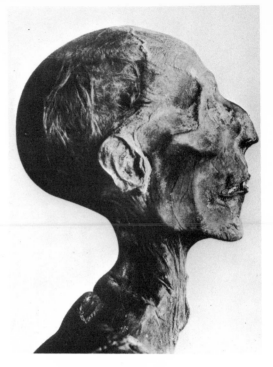

Ozymandias, King of Kings The Mummy of Ramses II, Shelley's Ozymandias, taken by G. Elliot Smith.

> "My name is Ozymandias, King of Kings:
> Look on my works, ye mighty, and despair!"
> Nothing beside remains. Round the decay
> Of that colossal wreck, boundless and bare,
> The lone and level sands stretch far away.

A comforting but misleading thought. In truth, almost too much remains of Ramses II, whose face and cartouche can be found from the Delta to Nubia. His name is far better known than that of the authentically great Thutmose III, who built the empire that Ramses so fecklessly diminished.

The King of Kings did better than immortalize his name—in itself an overriding goal among ancient Egyptians. His body too has been nicely preserved. In a room on the upper floor of the Egyptian Museum there is a unique morgue, still open to visitors in 1964, when a sign pointing the way said: TO THE MOMMIES. Here, as in a crowded surgery after an automotive disaster, repose the bandaged remains of nineteen Pharaohs and five of their Queens. Ramses II, a look of contentment embalmed on his face, sleeps regally as if he had died last week. In fact he was a contemporary of Moses, and his reign began before the fall of Troy.

One wonders what Shelley would have said about the international

A Tiara of Mummies All are in the Egyptian Museum, though their condition is not as perfect as in these photographs taken fifty years ago. The mummies are (a) Queen Taiouhrit, (b) Ramses VI, (c) the man "E," (d) Queen Notmit, (e) Ramses V, (f) Seti I, (g) Queen Anhâpou, (h) Ramses III. From G. Elliot Smith, *The Royal Mummies* (Cairo: Catalogue Général des Antiquités Egyptiennes, 1912).

campaign sponsored by the high-minded UNESCO to help a professedly social-
ist regime save Abu Simbel. Ozymandias in the process has become a phila-
telic celebrity along with Karl Marx, the British royal family, and John F.
Kennedy. At least thirty-one nations have issued stamps to support the
UNESCO campaign. The list makes interesting reading: Algeria, Argentina,
Congo (Brazzaville), Dominican Republic, Egypt, Gabon, Ghana, Guinea,
Ivory Coast, Kuwait, Laos, Lebanon, Libya, Mali, Mauretania, Monaco,
Morocco, Niger, Nigeria, Pakistan, Senegal, South Korea, Sudan, Syria,
Tchad, Togo, Tunisia, Upper Volta, Yemen, Yugoslavia, and the Vatican.

So much for Shelley.

II

THE PLUNDERED GARDEN

> *Antiquity is a garden that belongs by natu-*
> *ral right to those who cultivate and harvest*
> *its fruits.*
>
> CAPTAIN DE VERMINAC SAINT-MAUR,
> commander of the expedition that took
> from Egypt the obelisk now in Paris.

THE WORD *prestige*, it should never be forgotten, has as its Latin root *praestig-
ium*, a delusion. The Oxford Universal Dictionary lists these meanings: "1.
An illusion; a conjuring trick; a deception; an imposture. 2. Blinding or
dazzling influence; 'magic'; glamour; influence or reputation derived from
previous character, achievements or success."

The quest for prestige runs like a thread spun from fool's gold in the
loom of Egyptian history. The genuine curse of the Pharaohs was their
intoxication with prestige, an impulse that, regrettably, was supported by the
teachings of their religion and the structure of their state. The irony is that
the same impulse has prompted the looting of Egyptian antiquities; fool's gold
has an irresistible appeal.

Napoleon was the first to come. In 1798, when he was still only twenty-
nine, Bonaparte persuaded his government to approve a Middle East invasion
intended to cut Britain's lines to India. Also, he was not indifferent to the idea
of an Oriental empire, and, like Alexander and Caesar, he found Egypt
alluring. Once in Egypt, Napoleon easily subdued the Mamelukes, the mercenaries who had misruled the country for centuries. The future Emperor
also brought with him a Commission of more than a hundred French scholars.

"The time will come," wrote one of them, Etienne Geoffroy Saint-

Hilaire, "when the work of the Commission of Arts will excuse in the eyes of posterity the lightness with which our nation has, so to speak, thrown itself into the Orient." This hope was substantially realized with the publication, from 1809 to 1828, of the Commission's *Description de l'Egypte* in nineteen formidable volumes containing so many plates that 400 engravers were employed on the job. Napoleon himself corrected the preface to the work.

The French occupation brought immediate British reprisals. In 1799 Lieutenant Pierre Bouchard was building a defensive rampart near Rosetta in the Delta when his men chanced upon a black slab bearing a trilingual inscription. Bouchard had the good sense to grasp the importance of the Rosetta Stone. So did the British when they defeated the French shortly thereafter. The articles of surrender gave the victors as prizes of war the antiquities and specimens collected by the Commission. The French were rightly outraged. According to one account, Geoffroy Saint-Hilaire offered a reproach so elegantly insulting that one would like to believe he said it:

> Sooner than permit this iniquitous and vandal spoliation we will destroy our property, we will scatter it amid the Libyan sands or throw it into the sea. It is celebrity you are aiming for. Very well, you can count on the long memory of history. You also will have burnt a library in Alexandria.

The Rosetta Stone   The identical decree is repeated in hieroglyphics and demotic characters, and at the bottom in Greek. The British seized the trilingual stone from the French as a prize of war. (COURTESY BRITISH MUSEUM)

The English commander was taken aback, and the Commission allowed to keep its notes and specimens. The Rosetta Stone, however, was different. British prestige required its surrender. It went to the British Museum, inaugurating a century of Egyptology on the appropriate note of spiteful nationalism.

In 1806 Mohammed Ali, the Balkan soldier of fortune, became acknowledged as Pasha of Egypt. He was once implored to do something to protect threatened antiquities. "How can I do so, and why should you ask me," he replied, "since it is the Europeans themselves who are their chief enemies?" To some degree, zeal for knowledge inspired the plunder of Egypt. But the pillage was also a notorious form of status-seeking. A hall of Egyptian statuary, a trove of mummies, and an obelisk—these became a badge of sovereignty, much as a national airline is today.

The obelisk was deemed a special prize. According to tradition, Constantius took to ancient Rome the finest of the seven genuine obelisks still standing in the city. This classical precedent encouraged France to take an obelisk from Luxor in the 1830s and Britain to collect another from Alexandria in 1877–1878. America came last but not least, shipping in 1880 an obelisk to New York, where it has weathered more in less than a century in Central Park than it had in Egypt over several millennia. The spirit of the time was caught in a remark to Mohammed Ali by a French visitor in 1833: "Your Highness, I can see that it would be scarcely respectable, on returning from Egypt, to present myself in Europe without a mummy in one hand and a crocodile in the other."

National rivalry entered into the claims of scholarship. When the gifted Jean-François Champollion, after years of single-minded study, announced in 1822 that he had found the key to hieroglyphics, the English sourly observed that the Frenchman had benefited from the work of Thomas Young, who had already correctly guessed the meaning of isolated words. Yet credit for decipherment belongs securely to Champollion, who offered a coherent analysis of the entire language, proving its kinship to Coptic, and demonstrating that its picture symbols were phonetic. In one of the pleasantest episodes in all Egyptology, Champollion was able to visit Egypt before his death in 1832. Sometimes dressed in native clothes, the minuscule Frenchman clambered exultantly among the temples to whose walls he had restored the gift of speech. He had been only eleven when he first informed his parents that he would accomplish just this feat.

In the age of brigandage one figure stands out, or at least up: Giovanni Battista Belzoni, who stood at least six feet six inches tall. Belzoni had once been a circus strong man in London, and he turned up in Egypt in 1815 to promote an ingenious pumping machine that he claimed would make the desert bloom. Soon he was acting as an agent for the British in collecting

Kidnapping an Obelisk A contemporary photograph commemorates for posterity Yankee enterprise in uprooting from Alexandria the Obelisk of Thutmose III, which now stands in New York's Central Park. (COURTESY METROPOLITAN MUSEUM OF ART)

antiquities—managing at one point to outwit the French in securing for the British Museum an enormous head of Ramses II. The episode is said to have inspired Shelley to write "Ozymandias."

Belzoni was nothing if not direct. His work gangs hacked, shoveled, and battered their way into tombs. In recalling his entrance into one tomb, Belzoni nonchalantly related, "Every step I took I crushed a mummy in some part or other. . . . [In another passageway] I could not pass without putting my face in contact with that of some dead Egyptian [and] I could not avoid being covered with bones, legs, arms, and heads rolling above me." It was Belzoni who first cleared the sands from Abu Simbel, becoming the first modern to see the friezes of the Battle of Kadesh within, thus bringing together two splendid mountebanks in a strategic instant of time.

As the pillage continued, a salutary counterreaction set in. In 1858 the Frenchman Mariette was appointed Conservator of Egyptian Monuments, and at least the era of blatant thievery was over. Mariette himself excavated extensively, placing his best finds in the Egyptian Museum which he established. But the Newton of modern Egyptology was an Englishman, W. M. Flinders Petrie, who came as a youngster to Cairo in 1880 to test the theory of a family friend who claimed that the Great Pyramid was an occult computer that could foretell the Day of Judgment. Petrie found that the pyramid's base was seventy-one inches smaller than the figure required for the theory—an "ugly little fact," he later wrote, that killed "a beautiful theory." During a career that extended over seventy years, Petrie assembled thousands of such ugly little facts. He ranged through Egypt, Barbara Metz writes of him, "like a mythological dragon, gulping in raw material and ejecting it in the form of neat volumes which catalogued bones, stones, beads and pots."

Pots particularly fascinated Petrie, who learned to read their meaning much as Champollion learned to read hieroglyphics. He created a system of sequence dating that made it possible to decipher the soil of Egypt. He scorned hunting prizes for museums, which he dismissed in a spiky phrase as "ghastly charnel houses of murdered evidence." He redeemed the compromised honor of European scholarship in Egypt.

In 1922 one of Petrie's students, Howard Carter, finally realized what had long been a vain dream—he discovered a royal tomb that was virtually intact. But there is a neglected aspect of the famous story of the finding of Tutankhamen's tomb in the Valley of the Kings.

Carter and his noble patron, Lord Carnarvon, had been granted a concession to dig on condition that if an intact tomb were discovered the entire collection of objects would remain in Egypt. If the tomb were robbed, then its remains would be subject to division. It developed that thieves had once entered Tutankhamen's tomb, but they had taken only a few objects and had left the burial chamber intact. Should the entire collection remain in Egypt?

It was a nice question, since some special reward was in fairness due to Carnarvon, who had financed six years of fruitless search before the great find materialized.

On April 5, 1923, Lord Carnarvon died in Cairo, the victim of a mosquito bite or, as the press preferred, of the Pharaoh's curse. In the envenoming buzz of notoriety, the quick-tempered Carter and Egyptian officials began to quarrel. At one point Carter found himself prohibited from entering the tomb he had discovered. By this time the Carnarvon estate's claim for a division of the find was in an Egyptian court. Negotiations for a settlement ended instantly when Carter's lawyer, with excessive rectitude, claimed that the Egyptians had seized the tomb "like bandits."

The unfortunate remark caused an uproar, and Carter was permitted to resume work on the tomb only after a political assassination in 1924 caused a change of regime in Cairo. The unforgiving Egyptians vowed that because of the dispute not a single object from the Tutankhamen tomb would be allowed to leave the country. In 1961 the government relented a little, allowing a few pieces to be shown in the United States. Six years later a far larger sampling was shown in Paris, where the exhibition proved an astonishing success, drawing more than a million awed visitors. It was, everyone said, good for the prestige of Egypt and France, not to speak of the obscure teen-age monarch whose immortality was so splendidly assured.*

III

THE MIRAGE OF STONE

IN 1964 I HAD a pleasant luncheon in Cairo with Professor Ahmed Fakhry, a leading archaeologist and an authority on the Pyramids. We were dining in the Nile Hilton Hotel, from which one looks out on the green river as if from a bathysphere suspended from another planet. The Hiltonian atmosphere, with its vinyl purity and perfume of affluence, seemed all the more unreal since Mohammed Aly, then still known as Cassius Clay, was sitting at the next table.

I somewhat accusingly asked Dr. Fakhry why American tourists were so

---

* It is regrettably necessary to say a word about the "curse" that has such a magical effect on newspapers. "Believer in Pharaoh's Curse Killed," ran a *Daily Telegraph* headline on December 24, 1966. The London paper reported that Egypt's Director of Antiquities was killed in a traffic accident after agreeing to allow the Tutankhamen pieces to go to Paris. Yet of the ten principal explorers of the tomb, two were still alive forty years later and five others survived the find by an average of twenty years. This was not mentioned in the *Telegraph*, whose prose was vintage Boris Karloff: "Death shall come on swift wings to him that toucheth the tomb of the Pharaohs. So says the curse of Tutankhamen. . . ."

splendidly accommodated while Egyptian antiquities were so wretchedly displayed in the ancient and overcrowded Egyptian Museum immediately behind the hotel. I then learned that in the 1920s John D. Rockefeller offered to help build a new museum and research library, along with an endowment. The enormous figure of $10,000,000 was mentioned. But the condition was that the new museum would be administered by an international commission. This was considered unacceptable, largely because of nationalist feelings, aggravated at the time by the quarrel over Tutankhamen. The offer came to nothing; Rockefeller built his museum in Jerusalem.

A second chance developed after the Nasserite revolution when Philip Johnson, the American architect, volunteered to design at no charge a new museum to be located on the banks of the Nile. The site seemed ideal. "You are eating on it now," Professor Fakhry said a bit wistfully. "It was felt that a Hilton Hotel was more important for Cairo." He loyally added—surely there is weight to the point—that Egypt needs hard tourist currency as much as it needs a new museum.

Still, the atmosphere in the old museum curiously complements the collection. There is a smell of staleness, and the warmth of a hothouse, and the art it displays is likewise stale and warm—stale in its repetitiousness, and warm in its homely humanism. One longs for heresy, and one is refreshed to find it in an alcove on the ground floor that encloses the Ikhnaton collection from Tell el-Amarna. Whether Ikhnaton—aside from Nasser, the most controversial of all Egyptians—was really the first prophet of monotheism is subject for inconclusive argument. What is indisputable is that the art he encouraged at his new capital at Amarna (c. 1367–1350 B.C.) was at variance with the ossified modes of Egypt. He is the only Pharaoh who allowed himself to be depicted as ugly. His belly is a rubber sack, his hips are pear-shaped, and his chin is prognathous. In contrast, the women and children around him are rendered with sensual affection; Ikhnaton was indulgent to others but not to himself.

In looking at the Amarna collection, one wishes that Ikhnaton had been an abler politician, that he had somehow given continuity not only to his Aton cult but to the aesthetic standards he encouraged. One gets a drugged feeling in the museum as a whole, the feeling that all of ancient Egypt's creative energies were exhausted in an incredible formative spasm. The contrast is with Greek art as seen in the vivifying National Museum in Athens. There is a whole room of striding *kouroi*, the life-size statues obviously inspired by Egypt, each with shoulders thrown back and foot thrust forward. In the sixth century B.C. the *kouros* begins to move, as if liberated from the imprisoning pedestal. That second step is taken nowhere in the Egyptian Museum, save in the alcove devoted to the failed heretic-king.

The celebrated head of Nefertiti, Ikhnaton's queen, is not in the alcove.

The Art of Heresy Pharaoh Akhnaton and Queen Nefertiti present offerings to the Sun god, Aton, in a characteristic frieze from Tell el-Amarna, now in the Egyptian Museum. (COURTESY METROPOLITAN MUSEUM OF ART)

Taken from Egypt by Germans in still-disputed circumstances in 1912, it was first published in 1923 and then exhibited in the Berlin Museum. At one point the Egyptians tried to persuade Hitler to return the bust, and after the war American occupation authorities were pressed to recognize Egypt's claim. But to no effect. The one-eyed Queen is in a small museum in Dahlem in West Berlin. More than any other lost object, according to John A. Wilson, the American Egyptologist, "the head of Nefertiti represents to Egyptian nationalists the powerful exploitation of their assets by Western scholars."

The Pyramids of Gizeh are not so portable, for which the Egyptian Tourist Office can be thankful, since nothing else has drawn so many visitors to Cairo. From the top of the Great Pyramid, Napoleon is said to have assured his troops, "Forty centuries look down upon you!"—a story that has always seemed a little too pat to be true. More credible is the calculation that Bonaparte made about the Great Pyramid: that it contained sufficient stone to build a wall three yards high and one yard thick completely around France. The base of this monster is large enough (someone else has calculated) to hold St. Peter's, St. Paul's, Westminster Abbey, and the Cathedrals of Florence and Milan.

Such stuff has eternally fascinated tourists. Herodotus was told the exact amount spent for garlic and radishes eaten by the workmen who built the Great Pyramid; he scribbled it down for his *History*. The Gizeh Pyramids are an instance in which size alone has conferred prestige on otherwise monstrous objects. There is a pyramid on the Great Seal of the United States; the almost official newspaper in Cairo, *El Ahram*, means *pyramid* in Arabic; the only restaurant to be listed continuously with three rosettes since the

The Pyramids The smaller pyramid (foreground) shows the stepped style which prefigured the mountains of stone once faced with a smooth skin of masonry. (PHOTO AEROFILMS LTD.)

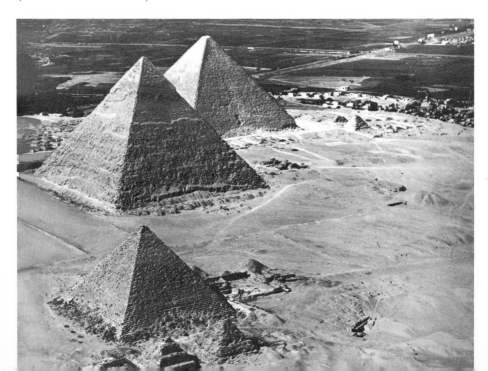

Guide Michelin was founded is the Pyramide in Vienne (though its name does not derive from the Gizeh pyramids).

I found them exhausting to look at and to walk around. Besides the three large pyramids, there are seven smaller ones, each trying to keep its nose above a lake of sand. It is as if architectural follies had multiplied. Close up, the Great Pyramid is ugly, its once-smooth façade hacked and mutilated but wholly indestructible. Nearby, like an impassive nanny to this absurd family, sits the Sphinx, her paws stretching to the ramshackle village of Kafr el-Haram and her face bathed nightly by the limelights of a *son et lumière* spectacle.

But one must suspend normal judgment. These are mirages in stone that have inspired innumerable variations on these lines of Byron:

> What are the hopes of man? Old Egypt's King
> Cheops erected the first pyramid
> And largest, thinking it was just the thing
> To keep his memory whole and hid.
> But somebody or other rummaging
> Burglariously broke his coffin's lid.
> Let not a monument give you or me hopes,
> Since not a pinch of dust remains of Cheops.

The sentiment is the common delusion of poets. It may be true—it is not wholly certain yet—that the tomb of Cheops (Greek for Khufu) was rifled 400 years after the end of his reign, which began around 2590 B.C. Yet the Pyramid achieved its larger purpose. The masonry of the Pharaoh's workmen was equal to the megalomania that ordained their task. Alone among the Seven Wonders of the Ancient World, the Great Pyramid survives, and its builder's name is on the lips of every illiterate dragoman who clings like adhesive to the tourists who see it. The final word, for a change, belongs to Kipling:

> Who shall doubt "the secret hid
> Under Egypt's pyramid"
> Was that the contractor did
> Cheops out of several millions?

Or, in soberer terms, I prefer the sound judgment of Herbert J. Muller in his *Loom of History:* "It is fitting that her [Egypt's] most enduring works remain the pyramids. They are the monuments to the majesty of her ideal, and to its basic absurdity; to the promise of her beginning, and to its curse."

For the true measure of the promise of that beginning, one must go not to Gizeh but to Sakkara, a unique blot of sand about twenty miles southwest of Cairo. In the scalped bareness of this landscape one finds the Step Pyramid, the first important stone structure known to history, designed by the first

Man's Oldest Edifice The Stepped Pyramid at Sakkara is the earliest known large stone structure built by man. The ornamental design of the surrounding courts show a surprising sophistication. (PHOTO ELIOT ELISOFON)

genius whose name still survives: Imhotep. Sakkara is an inaugural milepost on the road of human history.

Remarkably, Imhotep mastered not only the simple sums of his art as the first architect, but the calculus as well. The Step Pyramid is the opposite of primitive; it has a sophistication missing in its monster successors. This tomb is closer in spirit to Greece than to Gizeh. Imhotep's pyramid, to begin with, is not square but a series of terraced rectangles. At its base there is an enclosure that contains a stone simulacrum of the palace of the Pharaoh Zoser in nearby Memphis. The entrance colonnade has forty tapering columns which once supported a heavy roof painted on its underside in imitation of palm logs. Elsewhere—incredibly, this is the first known monumental building—there are false doors, fluted columns that anticipate the Doric style, and galleries decorated with blue faïence tiles. Many of these touches appear here for the first and last time in Egypt.

Apparently Imhotep was the overseer of works to the Pharaoh Zoser during the Third Dynasty, which began around 2700 B.C. Earlier kings had been content with burial in a *mastaba*, a rectangular-shaped tomb that derives its name from its resemblance to the brick benches still found in Arab villages. Imhotep's brilliant innovation was to stack the mastaba in stepped levels,

The Quest for Imhotep Professor Walter B. Emery of London University (right) examines a fresh find at Sakkara in his search for the tomb of the Adam of Architecture, the vizier Imhotep. (PHOTO ALFRED FRIENDLY)

approximating the pyramid shape. For his other ideas he had no known precedent whatsoever.

He was known to the Greeks, who identified him with Asclepius, god of healing, since Imhotep was a physician and a man of letters as well as an architect. In later dynasties Sakkara became a kind of Lourdes where pilgrims came for curative worship. They surely also paused to look at the Serapeum, a vast temple complex consecrated to the sacred Apis bull, whose carcasses were devotedly mummified and then stuck away in underground sarcophagi so big you can play a poker game in each. Mariette rediscovered the Serapeum in 1851; in visiting it today one feels it must once have resembled the Moscow Subway.

In our enlightened age Imhotep was for long dismissed as a mythical figure. His reality was first confirmed when his name was found inscribed at the base of a statue in the Step Pyramid enclosure. In 1956 the English Egyptologist Walter Brian Emery became curious about a few broken bits of pottery of the Graeco-Roman period which littered a patch of sand at Sakkara. He made a trial dig and in test pits found Third Dynasty remains and mummies of ibis birds, an offering associated with Imhotep. Emery returned in 1964 to begin a fresh series of major campaigns, and in clearing the galleries of an underground labyrinth he found an unknown catacomb crammed with statuary and thousands of embalmed birds, suggesting a temple to Imhotep. When he is not digging, Emery can be seen at the University of London, where he has succeeded to the chair once held by Petrie. When I visited him there recently, he told me he was convinced that he might yet find the actual tomb of Imhotep. Only of Egypt can one talk sanely of finding the burial place—and possibly even the mummy—of the Adam of architecture.

The Columns of Karnak Six men can lock arms around these indecently thick columns inspired, oddly, by the lotus. (FROM A LITHOGRAPH BY DAVID ROBERTS)

IV

LOOK ON MY WORKS!

CAIRO CAN SEEM a Sphinx with an inferior secret, the poorest as well as the biggest city in Africa. One slum has a density equal to 280,000 persons per square mile; a quarter of the city's inhabitants are under six years of age. The best one can say of it is to agree with Simonne Lacouture: "Cairo is a proud and verminous city, swarming and slow, full of cries and somnolence, rich and poor, living and dead."

It is good to escape to Luxor, where the plane glides into a landscape of Biblical serenity. Fields are green with clover and gold with sugar cane, and peasants resemble Sunday School illustrations of the story of Joseph. But from the descending airliner one already gets a sense of the immemorial priorities of Luxor, site of ancient Thebes. On the Nile's West Bank one sees the Valley of the Kings, with its forty royal tombs, and on the East Bank there are the temples of Karnak and Luxor, a veritable forest of masonry. But there is no bridge across the river. The imperial engineers never bothered to build one.

The tourist itinerary on the West Bank is fairly standard. A *felucca* takes one across the Nile, and the visitor is squeezed into an ancient Ford which scuttles like a rheumatic scarab from tomb to temple. Bored guides lead perspiring tourists through the musty royal tombs, ending with a stop before the faceless Colossi of Memnon. By the time one has finished seeing, on the following day, the temple of Karnak—big enough to hold six European cathedrals—one is not merely subdued. One is stupefied.

There is a reason, I suspect, for this. I was interested to learn that most New Kingdom Pharaohs tended to be short—the conqueror Thutmose III was only a bit over five feet tall. Thebes resounds with the bravado of the pint-sized. On murals each Pharaoh seems blown up, like the balloon figures in Macy's parade for children in New York. The gross columns of Karnak, so thick that six men can lock hands around each one, have overtones that might have interested Freud. Inscriptions have a locker-room flavor, such as this one by Ramses II about Kadesh:

> I dashed at them like the god of war; I massacred them, slaughtering them where they stood while one shrieked to the other; "This is no man but a mighty god; these are not the deeds of man; never has one man thus overcome hundreds of thousands!" I slew them all; none

The Temple of Deir el-Bahri A drawing by L. F. Hall shows the temple complex as it appeared in the time of Queen Hatshepsut. (COURTESY METROPOLITAN MUSEUM OF ART)

escaped me. . . . I caused the fields of Kadesh to be white with corpses, so that one did not know where to tread because of the multitude. I fought all alone and overcame the foreigners in their millions [*sic*].

Nevertheless, in this men's club the most visually interesting structure was built by a woman, Queen Hatshepsut.

Hatshepsut was in fact the first queen to rule in her own right, and as with some of her great successors on a throne—Cleopatra, Elizabeth I, and Catherine—her right to reign was in dispute, she manipulated the strong-willed men around her, and she left behind the suggestion of sexual scandal.

The conjectural dates of her reign are 1490–1468 B.C., but she apparently reached the throne while she was a regent during the minority of Thutmose III—who was her nephew or stepson or both or possibly even her husband. It is clear that she ruled as a Pharaoh for a generation, confounding the very language of her subjects since inscriptions show an uncertainty about the correct gender. In portraits she is often shown wearing the false beard of a king. Clearly, too, she was powerfully aided by a clique of courtiers, including one Senmut, whose swift rise suggests that his ascent may have led through the royal bedchamber.

The First Queen Hatshepsut, the earliest of great women in history, has the regal headdress of a male in this limestone statue. (COURTESY METROPOLITAN MUSEUM OF ART. MUSEUM EXCAVATIONS 1929. ROGERS FUND)

Her reign was tranquil. Her chief foreign venture was to send a trading expedition to the still-unidentified Land of Punt. She encouraged originality in the arts. Her mortuary, the temple of Deir el-Bahri, would be deemed a masterpiece anywhere, but in Thebes it is like coming upon a solitary fawn in a herd of rhinocerata. The temple is set against a sheer apricot-colored cliff and its fluted colonnades fix a visual horizon that harmonizes flawlessly with the setting.

Some Egyptologists believe the architect was Senmut, whose twenty titles included that of Overseer of Works. Plainly, Senmut was involved in the building, since he attempted to place his name and image along with those of the Queen in what had been exclusively a royal precinct. The effrontery was detected, and, seemingly, Hatshepsut herself ordered the removal of the disgraced courtier's impudent insertions. But the workmen who carried out the order were careless, and in a murky alcove one of Senmut's images can still be seen.

It is not known whether Hatshepsut was murdered or died naturally, but somehow Thutmose III finally claimed his birthright and turned with vindictive rage on the memory of the usurping Queen. Her name was effaced from her monuments, and the sarcophagus of the detestable Senmut was shattered into a thousand pieces. Thutmose was less interested in peace than war, and he conquered more land than any other Pharaoh. In the fullness of time the inscriptions he superimposed on the Queen's name flaked away. We thus know that the one original member of the Theban men's club was a woman.*

In Luxor perhaps more than anywhere else in Egypt, one realizes that everything about the country is eroded with age. Even the platitudes are rubbed and faceless coins. The oldest among them is that Egypt (as Herodotus said) is the gift of the Nile. But the gods drove a hard bargain. If the river feeds and clothes the people of Egypt, its cycles shape a seemingly indestructible political system. In this brilliant if eccentric book *Oriental Despotism*, Karl Wittfogel contends that the character of early Middle Eastern states was ordained by their preoccupation with large-scale irrigation. The scale of these projects required a pyramidal political system with a god-king at the top who ruled as a hydraulic dictator. In Luxor this generalization seems credible.

Here for five thousand years rulers have come and gone—Pharaohs, Greeks, Romans, Arabs, Turks, Mamelukes, British, and now Egyptian Socialists—yet in these fields, against the background of megalomanic masonry, the *fellahin* still works in the drowsy air as buffaloes turn the creaking wheels of the *sakieh*, a device for raising water used since the time of Thutmose and depicted in the tombs. His government is still highly centralized, he is still told that his rulers are infallible, and the country still has as its prime domestic concern a vast waterworks program.

* The heretic ruler Ikhnaton also built a large temple at Luxor, which is now being visually re-created in the most ambitious of all jigsaw puzzles. Ikhnaton's temple was dismantled after his reign, and its blocks used in later buildings. Some 25,000 decorated fragments from it have been found in the vicinity of Karnak. Each sandstone fragment has been photographed and coded, and an IBM computer is being used to match the parts. A team of Egyptian and American scholars hopes to be able to reassemble the temple on paper, and its inscriptions may throw more light on his puzzling religion. If so, it will be a literal example of *deus ex machina*.

The Colossi of Memnon   Both figures represent Amenhopis III and originally stood in front of his mortuary temple. The northern colossus is the vocal statue, who spoke at sunrise in classical times; his right leg is coated with inscriptions. (FROM A LITHOGRAPH BY DAVID ROBERTS)

With a touch of choler, Arnold Toynbee complains, "More than half of Egyptian history is a gigantic epilogue." Yet this very static quality has its fascination. Graffiti are the best proof. The timelessness of Egypt, the feeling that one is writing one's name on the scroll of perpetuity, makes the country a museum for the autograph collector. The names of Greek mercenaries are inscribed on Abu Simbel, a poem at the Colossi of Memnon recalls the visit of the Emperor Hadrian, and this Latin verse was once written by a medieval tourist on the casing stones of the Great Pyramid:

> Alone, alas! the Pyramid I see
> And can but weep, my brother, for thee.
> Upon the stone I've sadly carved thy name.
> The greatest Pyramid now knows the fame
> Of Annius Decimus who fought for Rome
> With Trajan, and returned in triumph home;
> Who e'en before his thirtieth birthday passed
> Was Pontiff, Consul, Censor too at last.

I cannot agree with the sanctimonious censure of Ernest Renan, who in 1865 said the greatest enemy of Egyptian antiquities was the English or American traveler: "The names of these idiots will go down to posterity since they were careful to inscribe themselves on famous monuments across the most delicate drawings."

No doubt the effect of these tattoos can be deplorable, but the impulse to scribble is honorable. The prestige of one's name and the desire for immortality led Pharaohs to build preposterous pyramids. Among the rest of us, in the humbler herd, immortal longings can also arise, the same desire to attach our name to a country that is like a trunk of eternity. It is better, anyway, than looting antiquities or uprooting obelisks for the greater glory of God, Queen, or President.

The Power of Prestige In the footsteps of all invaders, Scottish troops pose for the camera after they helped defeat Arabi Pasha in the Battle of Tell el-Kebir in 1882. (COURTESY RADIO TIMES HULTON PICTURE LIBRARY)

The Kartassi Kiosk A Roman temple moved to a new site above the High Dam at Aswan as part of the UNESCO salvage campaign. (COURTESY UNESCO. PHOTO BY KEATING)

Chapter Four

GODS' COUNTRY

ISRAEL AND JORDAN

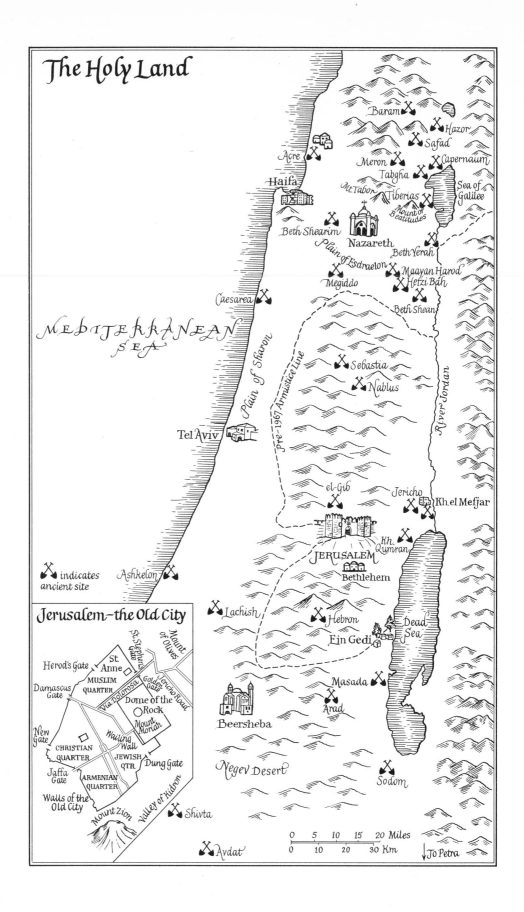

The Holy Land

MEDITERRANEAN SEA

Baram
Hazor
Safad
Acre
Meron
Capernaum
Tabgha
Haifa
Mt. Tabor
Tiberias
Sea of Galilee
Mount of Beatitudes
Beth Shearim
Nazareth
Beth Yerah
Plain of Esdraelon
Maayan Harod
Megiddo
Hefzi Bah
Caesarea
Beth Shean

Sebastia
Nablus
Plain of Sharon
Pre-1967 Armistice Line
River Jordan

Tel Aviv

el-Gib
Jericho
Kh. el Mefjar

Jerusalem
Kh. Qumran
Bethlehem

indicates ancient site
Ashkelon

Lachish
Hebron
Dead Sea
Ein Gedi

Masada
Arad

Beersheba

Negev Desert

Sodom

Shivta

Avdat

To Petra

0   5   10   15   20 Miles
0   10   20   30 Km

Jerusalem—the Old City

St. Stephen's Gate
Mount of Olives
Herod's Gate
St. Anne
Damascus Gate
MUSLIM QUARTER
Via Dolorosa
Golden Gate
Jericho Road
Dome of the Rock
Mount Moriah
New Gate
Wailing Wall
CHRISTIAN QUARTER
JEWISH QTR
Dung Gate
Jaffa Gate
ARMENIAN QUARTER
Walls of the Old City
Mount Zion
Valley of Kidron

I

THE DOUBLE-EDGED WORD

The Book and the sword came into the world together. HEBREW PROVERB

EVERY WRITER'S SECOND HOMELAND is Palestine. Washed by three seas, the Holy Land has a history shaped by three Books, each an Authorized Version. Here, *pace* McLuhan, the Message has always been the medium, and a single phrase worth more than a thousand images. "A word fitly spoken is like apples of silver in pictures of gold," says the Book of Proverbs. Yet, alas, when the author visits his Zion, he may be led to ask whether there isn't something to be said for illiteracy.

Once, for example, on a single day's drive through Israel I passed in rapid succession Biblical battlefields, Roman encampments, Crusader castles, Turkish parapets, British pillboxes, and the tanks and burnt-out trucks left over from three recent Arab-Israel wars. Like an outdoor Louvre of warfare, the landscape of the Holy Land visibly joins the Age of Joshua to the Age of Dayan. It is a countryside, I regretfully concluded, disfigured by the gunpowder of words.

Marshall McLuhan has perceptively pointed out that the Greeks believed their alphabet was invented by Cadmus, the King of Thebes who sowed the dragon's teeth which then sprang up as armed men. When combined with papyrus, the alphabet ended the priestly monopoly on knowledge and power and furnished the soldier with a potent new weapon. As Professor McLuhan writes in *Understanding Media*, "The alphabet meant power and authority and control of military structures at a distance." This insight can be applied to the Holy Land, where the alphabet became incandescent, inspiring prophets, forging nations, igniting insurrections, and dispersing armies to the most desolate corners of Gods' country, such as Masada, near the shores of the Dead Sea.

Masada is an incredible and ghastly place. I visited it in 1967, not long after what the non-Arab world calls the Six-Day War. The fortress is now comparatively easy to reach; from the town of Arad you take a jeep which thumps down a flint-bedded road until you reach the base of a Roman siege ramp which rises like a thick worm of earth to the flat crest of Masada. It was once an ordeal to reach the site. An early modern explorer was George Adam Smith, who wrote of the trip: "It is only when you come to it, as those who would attack it had come, through the waterless wilderness of Judea, that you feel its remoteness, its savage height, its fitness to turn whole armies of besiegers into stony despair. Masada is the Gorgon's head magnified to a mountain."

In 72 A.D. the Roman governor Flavius Silva came as such an attacker, leading the Tenth Legion, thousands of auxiliary troops, and a multitude of prisoners to hew whatever wood and draw whatever water could be found. His purpose was to lay siege to the last important garrison of rebels still holding out in the Jewish War, which had begun six years earlier. Jerusalem and the Temple had already fallen, and Flavius Silva was intent on wiping out some 970 Jews, most of them known to Rome as "Sicarii" or "dagger men," the most warlike faction of the fanatic Zealot sect. In a campaign lasting nearly a year, the Romans encircled Masada with a siege wall and constructed with slave labor a great ramp which rose a thousand feet to the walls of the fortified palace, originally built by Herod the Great, which commanded the top of the rock.

Masada: The Attackers　In this model, containing five thousand figures, the Roman Legions prepare to assault the fortress. (COURTESY JEWISH MUSEUM)

The fall of Masada is a grim epic. The Romans breached the outer wall, and the frantic defenders built an improvised barricade of earth and staves; when the battering ram smashed against it, the earth did not yield but became more tightly packed. The attackers then aimed fiery arrows at the inner rampart, and the staves began to burn. For a moment the wind carried the blaze into the faces of the Romans, and with wild shouts the Zealots exulted in their apparent delivery. But the wind changed, and the Romans returned at nightfall to their camp to prepare for the final attack at dawn.

With the end so obviously near, the Zealot commander Eleazar Ben Ya'ir called his followers together and in an impassioned speech urged the Zealots to choose death rather than surrender. "Let our wives die unabused," he pleaded, "our children without knowledge of slavery: after that, let us do each other the ungrudging kindness, preserving our freedom as a glorious winding-sheet." Lots were drawn, and the defenders first slew their wives and children and then each other. When the Romans burst into the citadel, they found the bodies and learned what had happened from two women and five children who had hidden themselves during the slaughter. The story was preserved by the historian Josephus, who has given what we have every reason to believe is an accurate account of Masada's fall.*

The somber dignity of the story is enhanced by the purgatorial starkness of its setting. From Masada's summit you can see the siege wall engraved in the desolation below, and beyond that the rectangular outlines of the Roman camps. About two miles away is the Dead Sea, a hard blue oval which stares upward like a basilisk eye. The site itself is well kept, well marked, and well visited; from 1963 to 1965 Masada was excavated by a team of Israeli archaeologists led by Yigal Yadin and assisted by an international corps of volunteers. The remains of the Herodian palace and fort have been painstakingly unearthed, and every meaningful fragment left by the defenders has been recovered, including a potsherd bearing the name Ben Ya'ir, patronymic of the Zealot commander and possibly the lot he himself cast in the suicide pact.

With quiet intensity Israeli guides relate the story of the siege, which you are likely to hear while sitting among grapefruit-sized pellets heaved up by Roman ballistae. My guide, who had taken part in the assault on the Golan Heights over Galilee in 1967, recited Eleazar Ben Ya'ir's speech (as

---

* Ironically, though Josephus is the sole source for this intensely patriotic story, he is generally regarded as a Quisling by Jews. Born Joseph ben Matthias in Jerusalem about 38 A.D., he died in Rome as Flavius Josephus, a Roman citizen. Originally he was a rebel commander in the Jewish War, but in ambiguous circumstances he surrendered and became an aide to Vespasian and Titus, the Roman commanders. Yet by his own lights he was faithful to Judea, believing that the war was senseless; he was proud of his Jewish heritage and esteemed even the Zealots for their courage. In his *Josephus* trilogy the German-Jewish novelist Lion Feuchtwanger has attempted to portray the apostate in a more sympathetic light. For a reasoned hostile account, see M. I. Finley's introduction to *Josephus*, a selection in the New American Library paperback series. High-school students in Israel from time to time hold mock treason trials of Josephus; he is invariably found guilty.

Cistern at Masada Carved from solid rock, this cistern provided the water that enabled the Zealots to withstand a Roman siege for nearly a year. (PHOTO ELIOT ELISOFON)

composed, in the manner of classical historians, by Josephus) and then concluded softly, "And now perhaps you understand why we say 'Masada shall not fall again.' "

And yet it is not the whole story, no matter how much one may respect the Israeli version of it. The Romans were indeed imperialists, who waged colonial wars with brutal ferocity. But the Zealots hated not only Roman imperialism and paganism; their detestation extended to the arts, tolerance, and humanism of the classical world. Herbert J. Muller says of the Zealots in his *History of Freedom in the Ancient World:* "They massacred not only thousands of Gentiles but many of their temperate fellow Jews, and eventually led the suicidal rebellions in Palestine at a time when Roman rule was growing mild, the rest of the Mediterranean was enjoying an era of peace hitherto unknown, and a Jewish sage observed that only the Romans kept the Jews from swallowing one another alive."

Through circumstances that might seem wholly incredible anywhere else, history has turned full circle, and it is the Arab who now resembles the Zealot. Poised upon the historic hills of Judea, the Palestinian Arab today looks down about the seaborn Zionist with the same implacable hostility that the ancient Hebrews, inhabiting the same mountains, felt for the intruding Philistines, Greeks, and Romans. Now as then, the Coastal Plain is dominated by Westernizing colonists, while insurgents in the hills fight a guerrilla war against what they regard as imperialism.

In the exasperated complaints among Israelis about Arab intransigence, one gets an authentic echo of the bafflement among the Romans about the Jews. Vespasian and Titus were astonished by the willingness of the Zealots to hazard the fall of Jerusalem rather than accept what seemed (to Rome) a sensible compromise.

The Arab guerrilla is likewise contemptuous of supposed realities, and his people, too, have seen the Holy City fall. Other paradoxes persist. Devout Jews could forgive Herod the Great his ruthlessness, but not his foreign birth and his fondness for Hellenic culture. The Arab nationalist will overlook the harsh feudalism of his rulers, but never tolerate any concessions to Israel. In a despairing appraisal of the history of the Holy Land, the theologian Kirsopp Lake was moved to observe, "As has always been the case in the East, the people submitted to extortion but rebelled against civilization."

As you look from Masada across the Dead Sea to the cliffs of Moab in Jordan, the thought occurs that the Israelis are romanticizing the very outlook that otherwise menaces their existence. By a formal cabinet vote, the Israeli government recently decided to rebury with full military honors the remains of twenty-seven bodies unearthed at Masada. (This was done not without misgivings among the Rabbinate, because of the uncertainty that all the skeletons were those of Jews, and because of the theological difficulty that

Masada: Three Finds Poignant relics unearthed by the Israeli excavation team include leather sandals of a curiously modern design, found near the skeleton of a young woman; the braided hair still attached to the scalp of a girl whose remains were found near those of a warrior; and a fragment of Ecclesiasticus, dating to the first half of the first century B.C., torn into shreds, like other parchments, by the conquerors. (PHOTOS BY YIGAL YADIN)

suicide is contrary to Jewish doctrine—but in the end the Rabbinate went along, and the bones were held to be those of martyrs of *Kiddush Hashem*, the Sanctity of the Lord.)

Each year Israeli recruits to the armored corps take their oath of allegiance on Masada. At the ceremony in 1963 Yigal Yadin declared that it was "thanks to the heroism of the warriors of Masada, as to those other links in the long chain of Israeli valor, that we stand here today as soldiers of the army of a youthful but ancient people. . . . The echo of our oath will be heard among the armies of our foes."

Still, seen in a different perspective, Israel's foes are closer in spirit to the defenders of Masada than to the democratic and Westernized state which Yadin personifies. Surely the Zealots would have understood the passions that impelled a distraught Arab in Los Angeles to murder Robert F. Kennedy on the first anniversary of the Israeli conquest of the Holy City. Like *zealot*, the word *assassin* also came into European currency as the name of a violent Middle Eastern sect.*

I put some of these objections to Yigal Yadin, the reconqueror of Masada, when I visited him in his book-cluttered study in Jerusalem. Yadin, of course, was Chief of Operations of the Israeli Defense Force in the 1948 Arab-Israeli War, and was later Chief of the General Staff before returning to his more tranquil calling of archaeology at Hebrew University. His manner still has the crispness of a soldier, and his sentences come out as if fed by gun-clip. "I understand your point," he said, "but there is a danger of applying the standards of one age to those of another. The Zealots must be understood in their context, not ours. I don't pretend they were in all respects admirable. But of their courage there can be no doubt, and that is important for us today."

The point is eloquent, but in Israel its force is vitiated by the tendency to judge the Romans as imperialists in the modern sense, making the Zealots patriots as well as religious fanatics. More than that, I found it impossible to picture Yadin himself as one of the "Sicarii"—he is too tolerant, good-humored, and alive to the lurking incongruities of history.

Such relativism would have been abhorrent to the Zealots, who were governed wholly by the Word of God, so much so that they were almost deterred from mass suicide because it was contrary to Jewish law. Their piety

---

* Though *assassin* derives literally from the Arabic for hashish-eater, the noun passed into European usage after the Crusaders encountered an Ismaili sect known as the Assassins, who were "thirsty for blood, kill the innocent for a price, and care nothing for either life or salvation," as a German priest advised Philip VI of France in 1332. See Bernard Lewis, *The Assassins* (London: Weidenfeld & Nicolson, 1967). Lewis relates that one trick of the Assassin leader, the Old Man of the Mountain, was to drug postulant killers and have them awakened in a palace whose delights accorded with the Muslim description of Paradise. The victim would then be told he was in heaven before being dispatched to earth to murder an offending prince—with the promise that if killed he would be borne by angels back to the same Paradise.

Masada's Reconqueror Soldier-archaeologist Yigal Yadin surveys the fortress during the 1963–65 campaign in which he was assisted by an international volunteer corps. (PHOTO ELIOT ELIOSOFON)

Masada Like the prow of a great ship, the citadel of Masada, fortified by Herod the Great, rises near the shore of the Dead Sea.

was inseparably joined to belief in a Sacred Text; among the important finds at Masada were fragments of Leviticus, Deuteronomy, Ezekiel, and the Psalms, as well as portions of the Book of Wisdom of Ben Sirach, an Apocryphal work. The Romans ripped these scrolls into shreds, as if they were part of the enemy arsenal. It was this communion with the Holy Writ that marked the Zealots apart from the Romans; Vespasian and Titus, however ruthless, did not contend that their wars served a divine purpose.

The orthodoxy of the Zealots was confirmed by a diverting episode during Yadin's campaign at Masada. At one point the excavators came upon a *mikva*, a ritual immersion bath. Its appearance caused a modest flurry in rabbinical circles. Was the bath *kosher?* Did its construction accord with exacting Jewish laws? A delegation of worried rabbis duly arrived at Masada. Led by an authority on *mikvas*, the party trudged up the arduous "snake path" on the citadel's eastern face, scorning the easier Roman ramp. Once aloft, the expert expressed interest only in inspecting the bath. He went into the pool, tape measure in hand, while Yadin and his colleagues looked anxiously on. His study completed, the rabbi announced with beaming face that the ritual bath was indeed *kosher*, "Among the finest seven times seven."

The story illustrates the special tension that envelops the spade in Palestine. Here rocks acquire a prophetic vocation, and the digger works amid a nervous audience. Not only do discoveries have a theological significance; the import is also political, since the Jewish claim to Israel is rooted in records of the past (during the Mandate period Zionists invariably appended an archaeological annex to their briefs). In Israel nearly everybody follows archaeological news with the passionate intensity others reserve for football scores.

The first question believers and non-believers alike ask is whether any given find accords with Biblical history. How could it be otherwise in the Land of the Book? In Palestine the spade does not simply excavate—it annotates.

II

DIGGING FOR THE WORD

> *Is not my word like as a fire? saith the Lord; and like a hammer that breaketh rocks in pieces?* JEREMIAH 23:29

THE LORD'S CLAIM is spacious, but amply sustained by the science of archaeology. Palestine is no bigger than Vermont or Sicily, yet in this small compass at least ninety-five sites have been excavated, and of these, twenty-five qualify as major digs. Homer is the only author who has rivaled the compilers of the Bible in prompting the moving of so much earth.

Fittingly, the single most important archaeological discovery in the Holy Land has been a library. With equal aptness, the acknowledged pioneer of the scientific Biblical archaeology was an explorer who studied not ruins but names. He was Edward Robinson, an American theologian who seized upon a single, brilliant, and unsuspected truth—that when all else changes, the root name of a place remains stubbornly the same.

Robinson arrived in Palestine in 1838, and at the time, though the land had been mapped by Napoleon's engineers, the location of many Biblical sites was obscured in a mist. In three months Robinson cleared up much of the haze, operating on this central principle: "to avoid as far as possible all contacts with convents and the authority of monks; to examine everywhere for ourselves with the Scriptures in our hands; and to apply for information solely to the native Arab population." The explorer's equipment included a German training in Semitic languages, the best maps available, and a brace of American pistols. In his swift foray Robinson was able to locate scores of lost sites, detecting in the Arab name el-Gib the Biblical Gibeon, in Beitin the Hebrew Bethel, in Kefir the city of Chepirah. Nearly all of his identifications are still accepted; few proved to be in error.

Accompanying Robinson was an American missionary named Eli Smith, whose Arabic was fluent. Near the Dead Sea the two travelers heard of a ruin known to the Bedouins as Sebbeh, located at the top of a lofty promontory. Robinson correctly guessed that this was "the site of the ancient and re-nowned fortress of Masada," adding scrupulously that the idea was first suggested by Smith. That Smith should have been the rediscoverer of Masada has its antithetical irony, since he is counted as a godfather of Arab national-ism—he brought the first printing press to Syria.

The merit of Robinson's method was rapidly acknowledged, and his technique was applied by British surveyors, including the future Lord Kitch-ener, in compiling the Palestine Exploration Fund map of 1880, which lo-cated 9,000 names in the 6,000 square miles of Western Palestine. By 1890 George Adam Smith was able to offer a convincing synthesis in his exemplary *Historical Geography of the Holy Land*. Adam Smith wrote in his preface: "We have run most of the questions to earth; it remains only to dig them up."

The proper way to dig was duly demonstrated in 1890 when the great English archaeologist Flinders Petrie drove six trenches through Tell el-Hesi in southwestern Palestine. The tell was the site of ancient Eglon and con-tained the layered remains of six cities. What impressed Petrie most was the tell's eastern face, which had been eroded by a stream leaving a gash that (he later wrote) "gives us at one stroke a series of all the variations of pottery over a thousand years."

In Egypt Petrie had been the first excavator to insist on the critical importance of getting the shape of pots classified in a chronology. At Eglon he showed that the same technique could be used in Palestine. His system was subsequently refined, providing an indispensable tool for mapping and dating the pot-littered Holy Land. An outstanding surface prospector is the rabbi-archaeologist Nelson Glueck (who in his clerical role delivered the benediction at President Kennedy's Inaugural). Glueck has located more than a thousand ancient sites in the Transjordan and the Negev, including what he believes to be the copper mines of King Solomon. "Wood disappears, stone crumbles, glass decays, metal corrodes," runs his paean to pots, "only pottery lasts forever."

But the Old Testament was not written on a pot, and for two generations it was a grievous disappointment to Biblical archaeologists that no parchment or papyrus turned up in such rich sites as Jericho, Megiddo, Gezer, Shechem, and Samaria. In the 1930s in the ruins of ancient Lachish a file of military correspondence was unearthed by the British excavator Leslie Starkey. The Lachish letters were in Hebrew and dated to the age of Jeremiah; however, they were written on ostraca.

Archaeologically, the Land of the Book seemed to be bookless. By 1939 Sir Frederick Kenyon, an eminent authority on Biblical texts (and father of the archaeologist Kathleen Kenyon), came to the distressing conclusion that it was improbable "that we shall ever find manuscripts of the Hebrew text going back to a period before the formation of the text which we know as Masoretic." (The Masoretes were rabbis who in the sixth century A.D. edited the text which forms the basis of the present Hebrew Bible.)

The misbehavior of a goat enabled Sir Frederick to live to see his pessimism confuted. The goat belonged to a herd being watched by a Bedouin boy during the summer of 1947. When the animal went astray, the boy pursued it up the limestone cliffs that rim the Dead Sea. It was hot, he was tired, and he lay down for a rest. His eye fell on a queer hole in the jagged escarpment. He threw a stone into the opening and heard a sharp ping that suggested the rock had struck pottery. That night he told another tribesman and the pair soon returned to the cave, squeezed into the crevice, and found the first seven manuscripts of the hoard known as the Dead Sea Scrolls.

This story has been disputed and embroidered, but seems authentic. There is no dispute that the first scholar to sense the immense importance of the scrolls was Dr. Elazar L. Sukenik, professor of archaeology at Hebrew University and father of Yigal Yadin. Sukenik first saw a fragment of one of the scrolls when it was handed to him on November 23, 1947, over a barbed-wire fence.

The fence had been put up by the British to divide the Jewish and Arab sectors of Jerusalem, and Sukenik had come to meet an Armenian dealer who had tipped him off about the find. The leather fragment the Professor saw fascinated him, but a trip to Bethlehem was necessary if he was to see more. Bethlehem was out of bounds to Jews. Should he risk the trip? His son Yigal Yadin urged him not to go, but Sukenik went—he was the sole Jewish passenger on the bus to Bethlehem. In the dealer's attic the Professor saw the scrolls. Sukenik's hand shook as he recognized their authenticity.

As the Professor returned to Jerusalem, the United Nations approved the partition of Palestine, and the next day the Arab-Jewish conflict became violent. Jerusalem was being shelled when Sukenik called a press conference to announce the discovery of the scrolls. When he recited the title of one work, *The War of the Sons of Light Against the Sons of Darkness*, correspondents were unable to hear it because a shell exploded. A journalist who was present told me that several colleagues fainted.

Sukenik, however, had obtained only three of the first seven scrolls. The others were sold to the Metropolitan-Archbishop Athanasius Yeshue Samuel of the Syrian Orthodox Monastery of St. Mark in Jerusalem. Though the bearded cleric sensed that his scrolls were important, he could arouse little interest in them. Then, on February 18, 1948, an American scholar excitedly told him he possessed a Biblical manuscript a thousand years older than any other extant. Eventually the Archbishop took the scrolls with him to the United States to seek a buyer, ultimately placing, in 1954, this advertisement in the *Wall Street Journal* (under the heading "Miscellaneous for Sale"):

THE FOUR DEAD SEA SCROLLS

Biblical manuscripts dating back to at least 200 B.C. are for sale. This would be an ideal gift for an educational or religious institution by an individual or a group. Box F. 206.

It happened that Yigal Yadin was in the United States when his attention was called to this curious notice. The Biblical scholar William F. Allbright had already told Yadin that the scrolls were on the market. Yadin immediately found an intermediary who had no connection with Israel and bid for the manuscripts. The final price was $250,000. The scrolls were secretly shipped to Israel, and have now been reunited with Sukenik's three in the Shrine of the Book in New Jerusalem. Professor Sukenik had already died in 1953, believing that the other scrolls were irrevocably lost to Israel.

Sukenik had rightly conjectured that more manuscripts would turn up along the Dead Sea—especially since the Bedouins had become aware of their commercial value. By 1956 in the area of the original find at least eleven scroll-bearing caves had been located. Cave IV yielded 400 different works, many of them lamentably rat-gnawed. An astonishing variety of other documents has turned up elsewhere. The discovery most important for Israelis was made by Yadin, who located in caves near Masada relics and letters of Simon Bar Kochba, leader of the second and last Jewish Revolt against Rome. Yadin used a mine detector to help locate the cache.

The use of the mine detector was appropriate to a place where archaeology is an extension of war by other means. General Yadin is in succession to a line of soldier-archaeologists that begins with Napoleon, whose officers searched for Biblical sites in 1799. The first scientific expedition down the Jordan River into the Dead Sea was led by an American naval officer, Lieutenant W. F. Lynch. The earliest authoritative maps of Palestine were compiled by British officers, who were also the first to examine systematically the sacred topography of Jerusalem. Field Marshal Lord Allenby carried into battle with him both a Bible and Smith's *Historical Geography*. Another British general, Sir Richard Gale, drew on his experiences as a commander in Palestine in writing *Great Battles of Biblical History*. Today, of course, every Israeli general seems to be either a professional archaeologist (like Yadin) or an amateur (like Dayan).

In the War of Independence Yadin drew on his knowledge of ancient roads to turn back an Egyptian attack in December 1947 at El Auja, just north of the border on the Sinai frontier. Two Egyptian brigades occupied the main roads, and Israeli commanders searched desperately for an attack route. Modern maps were of no help; it then occurred to Yadin to examine archaeological maps in the files of his father, Professor Sukenik. Yadin discovered a line tracing an old Roman road south of Beersheba; on December 17 Israeli engineers laid planks on the ancient thoroughfare, making possible a successful motorized attack on the Egyptian brigades, which took place at dawn on Christmas Day.*

Yadin was also involved in the inevitable interplay of sword and spade that occurred during the Six-Day War in 1967. On the second day of the fighting he was informed that an Israeli detachment, led by three officers, had descended on the Bethlehem home of an Assyrian Christian named Khalil Iskander Shahin, known to everybody as "Kando." For a generation Kando has been the middleman between scholars and Bedouins in gray-market bargaining over scrolls. At the time of the June war Kando was known to possess a scroll of impressive length which he was trying to sell for a suitably impressive price. Hence the arrival of the Israeli detachment.

"It was like melted chocolate when we found it," Yadin says of the scroll which Kando had hidden away for six years. I visited Yadin not long after he had announced the discovery of the Temple Scroll to the Israel Exploration Society at its first meeting after the unification of Jerusalem. Though his manner was laconic, his countenance glowed. "It's the longest yet found—8.6 meters—and the condition is not bad considering the way it was treated. By photographic techniques we can recover much that is missing."

The scroll deals with four subjects, Yadin explained, three of them

* This episode is fully described in Dan Kurzman's history of the War of Independence, *Genesis 1948* (New York: World, 1970).

concerned with the Temple and its rituals. The fourth subject is severely secular—the mobilization plans to be used in the event that "the land of Israel" is threatened with invasion. If the enemy force is a large one, the scroll advises, a third of the available manpower should be mobilized, with the remaining two thirds remaining on the land to protect cities and frontiers. If, however, "the battle be strong," then the king is advised to mobilize half the total strength while the other half remains in the cities. "This is precisely the mobilization formula we relied on two weeks before the outbreak of the June war," the soldier-archaeologist said, striving, without total success, to suppress unscholarly emotion.

As to Kando, Yadin will not discuss how the Temple Scroll was obtained and whether the dealer was paid for it. But the situation is well understood. If Kando is not mollified, there is a danger that he and his Bedouin suppliers will refuse to bring to Israelis any other scrolls which they find. As it is, the gray market is becoming blacker, and a Californian was reportedly sold a fake scroll for $100,000. It is feared that genuine scrolls will be torn into scraps and sold piecemeal to tourists, a prospect horrifying to scholars but curiously consistent with Palestine's tradition of turning divine revelation into an export commodity.

III

JERUSALEM THE GOLDEN

> *Pray for the peace of Jerusalem: they shall prosper that love thee.* PSALM 122:6

SEEN IN THE AFTERNOON LIGHT, the walls of Jerusalem are a warm honey color and the great gilt Dome of the Rock traps the rays of the receding sun. The best view is from the Mount of Olives; the Holy City seems an enchantment, a place of repose and boundless peace. A grotesque illusion! In fact Jerusalem the Golden has been sixteen times destroyed and seventeen times rebuilt. She has never known peace. She has been the source and symbol of more contention than any other city on earth. The Mount of Olives itself was the site of siege camps for attackers from Titus to Allenby.

Names, not sights, give a more authentic token of the haunting cacophony of Jerusalem. There are the Via Dolorosa, the Wailing Wall, and the Church of Our Lady of the Spasm. There is a gate called Golden and another called Dung. There is a Mount of Evil Counsel (once the place of residence of the British High Commissioner) and the Mount of Offense. Hebrew names form a throaty fugue: Ophel and Bethesda, Kidron and Absalom, Gethsemane and Golgotha. Proper names have a timbre of their own: Saladin Road, Hezekiah's Tunnel, Solomon's Stable, Robinson's Arch, and the King David Hotel—not to speak of Mandelbaum Gate, named after a Mr. Mandelbaum, owner of the building near what was once the sole link between Jordan and Israel. Since the Six-Day War the Mandelbaum Gate no longer exists, and the square next to it is now called "Square of the Central Command," after the Command that was in charge of the Battle of Jerusalem. (The old Suleiman the Magnificent Road was renamed Paratroopers' Road—the street plan of Jerusalem is an exegesis of military history.)

In the Holy City the word has become stone. Jerusalem is totally fascinating in her dissonances, her medley of peoples, her palimpsest of history, and her assurance that she is indeed the center of the world, as depicted on medieval maps. There is a reason for this cartographic convention. The Dome of the Rock encloses the sacred stone which Jews call *Even Hashettiva*, the Stone of the Foundation, because it was supposed to mark the precise center of the globe. On the same rock Abraham prepared to sacrifice his son Isaac, and from it Muhammed leaped straight into paradise mounted on a white charger. Gabriel put his hand out to stop the envious stone from following the Prophet. Guides show you the handprint.

The Dome of the Rock is on Mount Moriah, set on a flat esplanade as big as an airfield which marks the outline of the great Temple which Titus razed; all that is left of the Temple is the Western or Wailing Wall. On Friday afternoon the Wall is repossessed by the Guardians of the City, the inflexibly orthodox sect whose joy it is to pelt motorists who defy the Sabbath. Wearing long black coats and fur hats, the costume of Polish Jewry in medieval ghettoes, the Guardians herald the coming Sabbath with piping lamentations, their voices and sidelocks rising and falling in a threnody of sadness. They take with fierce literalness the Scriptural prohibition on making images, descending with fury on any tourist who mindlessly brings a camera.

Among her distinctions, Jerusalem is perhaps the only city where it is impolite not to talk about religion. At exasperating intervals it seems as if there is no other subject. In the spring the Holy City resounds with conflicting observances as the Jews mark Passover and the Christians celebrate Easter on different calendars. Always there is a continual round of processions, masses, festivals, services, attended by Christians and Jews in every hue and gradation of costume. Five times daily, all year, the *muezzin* sounds, summoning the faithful to their prayers in the third most holy of Muslim cities (next to Mecca and Medina).

This reverence for outward form can seem ostentatious. Edmund Wilson voiced a common plaint of visitors, that they are constantly confused as to whether to cover or uncover their heads in moving from one monotheism's place of worship to another. Natives are sometimes blunter in their views. I recall drinking cocktails in the lounge of the Intercontinental Hotel on the Mount of Olives while an Israeli journalist gave vent to his feelings.

"All religions disgrace themselves here," he began. "It is the law of Jerusalem. If the Christians believe that the Angel Gabriel will enter the Holy City through the Golden Gate, that is reason enough for the Muslims to seal it up. The Christians, for their part, can't agree among themselves on repairs of the dilapidated Church of the Holy Sepulchre, and the doorman is a Turk because no Christian could tolerate a member of a rival sect holding so important a job.

"When the Arabs controlled the Old City, they wouldn't let the Jews go to the Wailing Wall. When the Israelis took the Holy City, we immediately tore down Arab houses near the Wall and plastered the streets with signs in Hebrew saying 'To the Wall.' Mount Zion itself has the misfortune of being sacred to all three faiths. Before the Six-Day War you needed a special permit to climb from the supposed Tomb of David to the room in which the Last Supper supposedly took place, because David was buried on one side of the armistice line and Jesus dined on the other. Bah! Madness! Lunacy!

"But of course," he concluded, "there is no other place for a civilized person to live." *

Such is the atmosphere that envenoms the most unseemly of archaeological disputes, the Battle of the Two Museums. Scholars who are individually the best of men become crafty and pharisaical in this controversy over possession of the Dead Sea Scrolls.

The older museum is the Palestine Archaeological Museum, endowed in 1927 with a $2,000,000 benefaction from John D. Rockefeller, Jr. Facing Herod's Gate and located on the site of an old Crusader encampment, the museum is in an attractive if conventional building admirably decorated with the lettering and art of Eric Gill. Its important permanent displays include the sculptured skulls found by Kathleen Kenyon at Jericho, the Lachish letters dating to the age of Jeremiah, and the writing desks used by the scribes of Qumran to copy the Dead Sea Scrolls. A special room once enclosed a collection of the scrolls, among them a multitude of Scriptural texts and the renowned Copper Scroll, with its description of a fabulous treasure.

In 1967, on the second day of the fighting, a paratroop unit occupied the museum, and three Hebrew University scholars were dispatched by Yigal

* The same friend, in a recent letter to the author, had a further comment: "You might add a note on the recent reconstruction of the Wailing Wall area. The old Magreb quarter was leveled. Instead there is now a huge paved stone Piazza del Popole-type square. Following opposition from the Orthodox, the excavations at the base of the Wall have been discontinued. In recent months coin-operated explanation machines, replaying the truth for fifty agora, are available on the square. On the Sabbath the coin slots are blocked, and thus do not bring us into temptation."

Yadin to assure the safety of the scrolls. The war over, the museum was opened under Israeli auspices, an act of conquest ironically facilitated by the Jordanian government, which, a year before, had nationalized the institution, enabling Israel to seize it as enemy property, like the Intercontinental Hotel; had it been left as an international scholarly institute, it might still today be in private control.

The room exhibiting the scrolls was closed (some of the choicest, including the Copper Scroll, had been taken to Amman before the war broke out) and the Israeli government has been evasively Delphic about the status of the precious parchments. Father Roland de Vaux, the esteemed Dominican who has headed the international Rockefeller team studying the scrolls, has told journalists he is certain Israel will use the conquest as a pretext for abducting the scrolls. In an interview with the British journalist David Pryce-Jones, Father de Vaux used the regrettable word "Nazi" to describe Israeli tactics. For their part, the Israelis complain that Jews had been denied access to documents written by their own ancestors, that there has been an undue delay in publishing the scrolls, and that Gentile scholars lack the proper fluency in Hebrew.

As to the other museum—the Israel Museum and its adjoining Shrine of the Book—it was opened in 1965 thanks in good part to the energy of Teddy Kollek, the Mayor of reunited Jerusalem. As early as 1952 Kollek persuaded the government to donate a handsome site on a hill in West Jerusalem facing the Valley of the Cross, Hebrew University, and the new Knesset (Parliament) building. As chairman of the museum's board of governors, Mayor Kollek was instrumental in raising some $5,000,000 to build the museum, the shrine, and the Billy Rose Art Garden. Visitors are thus confronted with a complex of buildings and a variety of exhibits, ranging from Bronze Age burials to Mr. Rose's abstract art. The Israeli scrolls are in the Shrine of the Book, a well-intentioned effort to simulate in modern architecture the atmosphere of a cave; a long tunnel leads to a double parabolic dome in which the scrolls are shown in glass cases, the documents protected by a layer of helium gas.

The museum was shelled during the war. Its chief administrator, Yohannan Behan, frantically supervised the storage of exhibits as shells burst over the building. After the fighting his wife wrote to a friend in the United States: "Not a single object in the museum has been harmed—and the damage to the building can be repaired. . . . This letter goes off while we still wait word about our son, who is a paratrooper. Most of us are staggered by the enormity of our good fortune, this miraculous victory when we only dared hope for survival." Days later the Behans learned that their son had been killed; he had been in the paratroop detachment, I was told, that captured the Palestine Archaeological Museum.

Ultimately, as with all controversies, the Battle of the Two Museums intruded with elegant acrimony into the Letters column of the London *Times*. Hostilities commenced when John Carswell, Professor of Fine Arts at the American University in Beirut, demanded to know the precise status of the Palestine Museum and its scrolls. His question was directed to Sir Philip Hendy, retired director of the National Gallery in London, who had just accepted a new position as advisor to the Israel Museum. Sir Philip's reply was that the Palestine Museum was at last being run in accord with the wishes of its founder; it was open to visitors of every creed, and its once-effaced Hebrew labels had been restored to view.

Unsatisfied, Dr. Carswell resumed by asking whether Israel considered the museum and its scrolls to be Israeli property. Sir Philip rejoined by saying that the scrolls "will shortly have air-conditioning which is essential to their survival" and that attendance had risen fivefold in the first year after the museum was finally opened to all visitors, including Jews. Dr. Carswell pounced on the evasion, and in rebuttal brought up a new issue: the sad condition of the Armenian Church of St. Saviour on Mount Zion, near the old armistice line. The church, he wrote, after its occupation by Israel, was completely gutted, the altar wrecked, the tomb of fourteen patriarchs desecrated, and the building itself turned into an Israeli machine-gun post.

This brought a rebuking reply from the Armenian Patriarchate in Jerusalem, in which it was noted that the church had come under fire from both sides in 1948 and was in a no-man's sector of Jerusalem, therefore inaccessible to church authorities. Then a new belligerent, Richard E. S. Slotover of Jerusalem, joined in with this barrage:

> While on the subject of desecration of holy places in Jerusalem may I remind Professor Carswell of the latrines that were placed against the Wailing Wall by the Jordanians, of the synagogues that were torn down and used as stables, and of the old Jewish cemetery on the Mount of Olives through which a road was cut and from which tombstones were taken for use as building materials.

At this point I wanted to cry "Stop!" Why is it that so much bile emanates from a place so dominated by words and books and scrolls? Can the new world of cool visual media, which Professor McLuhan commends, be any less attractive than the irascibly verbal Holy Land? Are we wrong— "we" being writers, incorrigibly devoted to what is now called "the print media"—in believing that the written word is intrinsically more rational than the picture?

The answer, I think, is not quite. In the classical Hellenic world, with its magnificent visual arts and its very illiterate Olympian gods, slavery was regarded as a wholly natural institution, regrettable, perhaps, but certainly

not immoral. The notion of the equality of all men before God springs from
the Scriptures in the impassioned prose of the Prophets. The word cajoles,
persuades, and incites; can anyone name a revolution that was started by a
picture?

Even so, one wishes that in the Holy City this inscription could be
placed over the portals of each museum: "Ye see the distress we are in, how
Jerusalem lieth waste and the gates thereof are burned with fire: come, let us
build up the wall of Jerusalem" (Nehemiah 2:17).

IV

A SIEGE OF SITES

TAKING THE HOLY LAND as an entity, and ignoring armistice lines and political
boundaries, six ancient sites offer contrasting facets of an abnormally interesting archaeological past—Caesarea, Galilee, Megiddo, Jericho, Qumran, and
Petra—and in describing them I am conscious of how much else I am
omitting, and how selective and impressionistic my own comments are. What
follows, therefore, consists of notebook jottings and is not a *catalogue rai-
sonné:* put another way, these are modest footnotes to a literature of travel
whose breadth and richness is one of the secular prodigies of Palestine.

Caesarea is an hour's drive from Tel Aviv, and is probably the only
archaeological site in which you can drive a golf ball from a twentieth-
century green into a first-century hippodrome, uprooting Roman coins as
you chop out of the rough. This was Herod's city, consciously founded as a
Romanized counterweight to Hebraic Jerusalem, and as such it was regarded
with loathing by devout Jews. Riots and demonstrations were incessant; a
massacre here in 66 A.D. caused the outbreak of the first Jewish Revolt.
Subsequently it was a center of Christian learning until its conquest by the
Arabs in 639 A.D. The city was recaptured by the Crusaders in 1101, retaken
by the Saracens under Saladin in 1251, conquered again by Crusaders in 1251,
when St. Louis ordered the building of the walls that were overwhelmed in
1265 by the Mamelukes, whose Sultan Bibars took part in the sacking that
ended Caesarea's importance as a seaport.

The Crusader city is still recognizable in the surviving walls, and the
Herodian and Roman remains have been expertly landscaped and partly
excavated. Outstanding finds include the only known inscription that bears
the name of Pilate, who as Procurator had his official residence in Caesarea.

Amphitheater at Caesarea Concerts are again held in this Italian-restored amphitheater in the Roman capital of Judea. (PHOTO KARL E. MEYER)

As the outpost of Rome, the city symbolized to the ancient Hebrews what nearby Tel Aviv does to the modern Arabs—an alien city with blasphemous ways implanted by seaborn invaders. The Jews particularly detested the amphitheater, recently restored (by Italians) and used now for symphony concerts. Yesterday's pagan abomination is today's cultural amenity. Nudity also affronted pious Jews in Herod's time, but nowadays the admirable beach is frescoed with bikinis, and it is the Arabs who start riots when an Israeli girl, in occupied territory, saunters in a miniskirt.

Galilee can be reached directly from Caesarea in a half-day's drive, but I would recommend a detour by way of the walled city of Acre, north of Haifa, where Napoleon's dream of an Oriental empire vanished in defeat and where today it is possible to have a superb fish dinner in a restaurant enclosed by Acre's walls, affording a fine view of the scimitar-shaped shoreline.

As one approaches Galilee from Acre, the landscape palpably softens; depending on the season, the green hills are pricked with anemones, lilies, and thornbush thickets. The Sea of Galilee is freckled with fish and looks as clean as mineral water. Lightness, warmth, a feminine tenderness: these are the impressions one has of the place that provided the setting for the childhood and early ministry of Jesus.

Of the ancient sites, Capernaum is in every respect the most satisfying. The ruins of this synagogue are reached through a eucalyptus forest, and here

Capernaum Although the ruins postdate Jesus, the stones mark the site of a synagogue in which Christ is believed to have preached. Typical of the graceful architectural ornament is the filigreed palm tree.

one can readily believe is a place where Jesus preached, though the remains date from a period after His crucifixion. Capernaum has a Greek flavor—the filigreed lintels, the urn flanked by bunches of grapes, the menorah gracefully carved on a capital, all arrayed amid gentle and verdant foliage.

But, for all the outer tranquillity of Galilee, it has immemorially been a battlefield. Nearby are the waterless heights of the Horns of Hattin, where, on July 4, 1167, the decisive battle between Muslims and Crusaders took place. In George Adam Smith's biting summary, "A militant and truculent Christianity, as false as the relics of the True Cross around which it rallied, met its judicial end within view of the scenes where Christ proclaimed the Gospel of Peace and went about doing good." After June 1967 a new tourist experience, no less jarring in its incongruity, became possible. One could visit the Golan Heights and look across the Sea of Galilee to the hill on which tradition asserts Jesus preached the Sermon on the Mount, peering at it through a gun-vent.

Megiddo is best approached from Galilee by way of Nazareth, from whose hills one looks down upon the Plain of Esdraelon, a sight which prompted this magisterial passage in Adam Smith's *Historical Geography:*

> Esdraelon lies before you, with its twenty battlefields—the scene of Barak's and Gideon's victories, the scenes of Saul's and Josiah's defeats, the scenes of the struggles for freedom in the glorious days of the Maccabees. There is Naboth's vineyard, and the place of Jehu's revenge upon Jezebel; there Shunem and the house of Ilisha; there Carmel and the place of Elijah's sacrifice. To the east the valley of Jordan, with the long range of Gilead; to the west the radiance of the Great Sea, with the ships of Tarshish and promise of the Isles. You see thirty miles in three directions. It is the map of Old Testament history.

Proceeding downhill, one approaches the mound of Megiddo, the Armageddon of the New Testament, an ugly little hillock for which armies have bled for 4,000 years. Megiddo once commanded the trunk road that buckled together Egypt, Palestine, and Mesopotamia. Curiously, even today Megiddo seems an almost unavoidable crossroads in passing through this part of Israel. Here, by the way, Pope Paul entered Israel from Jordan during his Pilgrimage in 1963.

The mound itself encloses the remains of twenty cities, and it has been thoroughly ransacked by American, German, and Israeli archaeologists. There is a nice museum on the site, with a model of the Israelite fortress. Its gates were lined with iron, and its walls contained cavities to deflect the blows of siege rams. The extensive stables, once mistakenly attributed to Solomon,

View from Megiddo   The site of a thousand battles can be seen from the flat crest of this most formidable of Palestine fortresses. (PHOTO FRED CSASZNIK)

show that the defenders could strike back formidably with chariot armor. Megiddo's most imposing attraction is a shaft, 120 feet deep, joined by a tunnel 215 feet long. The tunnel led to a spring hidden by a turf-covered wall and thus supplied water during prolonged sieges. It is an unquestioned marvel of ancient military engineering.

The view from the top requires imagination. One must erase from sight the pastoral scenery, the fields sown with alfalfa, barley, and clover. One must mentally beat the plowshares into swords, populating the plain with this roll of armies: Egyptian, Israelites, Canaanites, Philistines, Babylonians, Assyrians, Persians, Greeks, Romans, Byzantines, Arabs, Crusaders, Mamelukes, Turks, and British—whose General Allenby chose as his title Viscount of Megiddo. More recently, in the 1948 Arab-Israeli war, a major battle took place nearby at Mishma Ha'Emek. A plump hummock of earth, Megiddo is the closest thing to the Hiroshima of archaeology.

Qumran involves a breath-catching descent from Jerusalem over a road with twenty hairpin turns, which also passes the Inn of the Good Samaritan (a police depot in recent times). One plummets 3,500 feet in thirteen miles and ends up in the bottom of the Great Rift caused when the earth dropped vertically 3,000 feet below the prevailing land level—the Rift runs like a

broken spine from northern Syria to the Gulf of Aqaba, clear across the Red
Sea to Kenya and Rhodesia. The same cataclysm created the Dead Sea,
around 1,300 feet below sea level, and near its shores are the ruins of the
monastery of Qumran, perched on a promontory. The landscape between it
and the gaunt Mountains of Judah is as featureless and indeterminate as the
dull colors that tint everything. When Edmund Wilson came here, a companion said to him, "Nothing but monotheism could come out of this. There's no
crevice for a nymph anywhere."

This is the area where a stray goat led to the discovery of the first Scroll
cave in 1947. Two years later archaeologists examined Khirbet Qumran—the
origin of the name is unknown—and found evidence that securely linked the
monastery with the cave library. The diggers were G. Lankester Harding,
then Jordan's Director of Antiquities, and Father Roland de Vaux, director
of the Ecole Biblique in Jerusalem. The excavation determined that Qumran
was first an Iron Age fort which was abandoned until a colony of Jewish
ascetics resettled it in the second century B.C. Seemingly destroyed in an
earthquake in 31 B.C., Qumran was then deserted until 4 B.C., when the monks
cleared the debris and restored the building. During the first Jewish revolt
(66–73 A.D.) the settlement was sacked by Romans. The monks assuredly had
advance warning, because they were able to hide their library before—it
seems likely—they themselves were slaughtered.

These dates are crucial because the monks were probably Essenes, and in

Tunnel at Megiddo Thanks to this impressive tunnel leading to a spring, the
defenders could withstand a prolonged siege—the gallery was 160 feet long and
60 feet below the top of the mound.

The Monastery of Qumran Amid this maze of walls and cisterns lived the ascetic monks whose doctrines anticipated some of the tenets of Christianity. The Dead Sea is a mile away.

important respects their doctrines anticipated those of Christianity. Though there are discrepancies, Qumran fits the description of the Essenes, the most ascetic of the three main Jewish sects, given by Josephus, Philo, and Pliny the Elder. Pliny is convincing: "To the west [of the Dead Sea] the Essenes live at a distance from the shore. . . . They are a people unique in kind, stranger than any others in the whole world: without women, renouncing all that is of Venus; without money, having only the society of the palm trees." The first scholar to make the double argument that the monks were Essenes and that their beliefs adumbrated Christianity was Professor A. Dupont-Sommer, whose thesis was at first either ignored or indignantly repudiated by most authorities. The idea is now a commonplace, though it was foreshadowed a century ago by Ernest Renan, who once remarked: "Christianity is an Essenism which has largely succeeded."

At the site itself one can make out the large rectangular room in which the monks probably debated where to hide the scrolls as the legions advanced. There are six large cisterns to store the infrequent rainwater, and seven smaller pools, presumably for baptisms, which the sect deemed important. A thousand potsherds were found in the kitchen, near the oven. What established the link with the scrolls was the discovery at Qumran of jars identical with those found in Cave I.

Jericho is not far from Qumran and makes a nice contrast with it. If life was too hard at Qumran, it was too easy at Jericho—at least, too easy to encourage metaphysics. Adam Smith says harshly of it: "No great man was born in Jericho; no heroic deed was ever done in her. She has been called 'the key' and 'the guardhouse' of Judea; she was only the pantry. She never stood siege, and her inhabitants were always running away." The softness was encouraged by abundance derived from year-round summer weather and a continuously watered great spring, the Fountain of Elisha. The succulence of Jericho's oranges and bananas is proverbial. Josephus, who lived well, called Jericho "a divine region" and "fattest of Judea."

Yet nobody suspected that Jericho was the oldest of all cities—certainly not Kathleen Kenyon, who began excavating here in 1952. Her aim was to find the famous walls, but in a splendid instance of serendipity she found that urban life apparently began in this oasis fleshpot. A deep trench in the ancient mound uncovered the remains of a Neolithic village which can be dated to about 7000 B.C., making it the oldest. Not even pottery had been invented at this early date, but the city founders knew enough to make a defensive tower, houses with packed-clay floors, and the sculptured skulls now to be seen in

A Jericho Skull   This is the finest of Neolithic skulls sculptured in plaster found by Kathleen Kenyon in her excavations at the oldest known urban settlement. The skull is now in the Palestine Archaeological Museum. (COURTESY KATHLEEN KENYON)

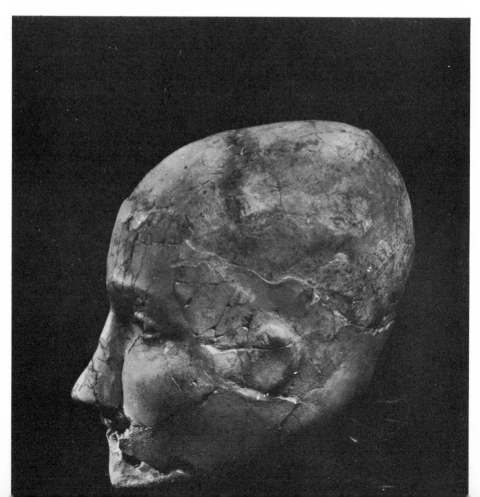

The Walls of Jericho Two views of the scarred hillock containing the remains of a score of cities, the earliest dating to the Neolithic era. But no walls have been found that can be ascribed to the time of Joshua.

Jerusalem. The celebrated walls of Joshua's time have so far escaped detection.

Jericho offers an admirable pretext for mound-clambering, and in a deep and clearly labeled pit one can see the great Neolithic tower. From the top it is also possible to view the new town of Jericho and the melancholy Arab refugee camp adjoining it. (In the 1967 war Jericho was true to its traditions —less than a tenth of the population, including the refugees, were found in the city when the Israeli forces entered it.)

Petra is more difficult to reach since the Six-Day War, for it is no longer possible to go, as I did in 1964, from Jerusalem. One presently goes to Petra from Amman or Aqaba, but in any case the trip poses nothing like the hazards routinely encountered by early explorers. Petra was rediscovered in 1812 by the Anglo-Swiss traveler J. L. Burckhardt, who was seriously menaced by hostile Bedouins; he advised future visitors to come "under the protection of an armed force," and the ruined city was not safe to visit until this century. All that has changed; in 1965 Petra drew 30,000 visitors, including children in perambulators. For miles around, the signposts read, TO PETRA ROSE-RED NABA-TAEAN CITY.

Petra's greatest modern debt is to an obscure Victorian parson, the Rev. John William Burgon, who won an Oxford prize in 1845 with verse that ended with this couplet:

> Match me such marvel save in Eastern clime;
> A rose-red city—"half as old as time."

The dating is inexact, but Petra is indubitably rose-red. As one turns off the Desert Highway at Ma'an, the white limestone gradually becomes pink. At a tourist hotel built within a cave, the visitor hires a horse which makes the slow descent through the Siq, a topless tunnel that coils downhill, its sheer sides as high as 200 feet. In 1963 a party of French tourists were drowned when a flash flood sent water roaring through the mile-long Siq, but a dam using ancient spillways now deflects rain. The slow horseback approach through this menacing canyon heightens the impact when one suddenly bursts upon the Treasury of the Pharaohs.

The visual effect is theatrical. The riders who precede one are pasted like black silhouettes against a flame-red temple carved from living rock in a style that can be called Arabo-Roman. As one continues past the Treasury and its enthroned urn, a vast plaza opens up and there is an entire city: streets and stairs, terraces of tombs and shops, and a large theater, all carved from rock streaked with white, yellow, ocher, and pink, like layers of Neapolitan ice cream. The place is totally desolate. One hears its silences.

In 1836 John Lloyd Stephens, later the rediscoverer of Maya civiliza-

Petra: The Treasury The temple which faces the entrance to the Nabataean city is depicted in one of the illustrations in David Roberts' magnificent *The Holy Land* (1849). Since this was drawn, the broken column has been restored and the façade has been pocked with Bedouin bullets, fired in the belief that a lucky hit would release a shower of gold.

tion, became the first American to visit Petra. He opened his Bible to Isaiah
34:12, 13.

> They shall call the nobles thereof to the kingdom, but none
> shall be there, and her princes shall be nothing.
> And thorns shall come up in her palaces, nettles and brambles
> in the fortresses thereof: and it shall be an habitation of dragons, and
> a court for owls.

"I would that the sceptic could stand as I did among the ruins of this city in
the rocks, and there open the sacred book and read the words . . . written
when this desolate place was one of the greatest cities of the world," Stephens
wrote.

Isaiah was referring to the Edomites, who founded Petra. But the ruined
city dates to the fourth century B.C., when the Nabataeans replaced the
Edomites. By all accounts, the Nabataeans were an inoffensive and clever
people who excelled at hydraulic engineering and at extracting tolls from
passing caravans. (Pliny says that a levy of twenty-five-percent toll was
exacted at Petra.) Unlike the Hebrews, the Nabataeans fused their culture
with Hellenism and became client-allies of the Romans. Ultimately Rome
conquered the Nabataeans outright—the traditional date is 106 A.D.—and the
Roman eagle was planted in Petra's main street. The Nabataeans did not
rebel; indeed, they had an almost cheerful fatalism about death. At Petra they
created a parfait necropolis in which tombs looked out upon a theater built
before the Roman conquest—a measure of the city's Hellenism. The Nabataeans had no Bible, no apparent sense of being a Chosen People. They
vanished completely as a cultural entity, becoming a footnote in Toynbee's
history, rather than an aggravating (to Toynbee) fossil like the Jews.

In a strange epilogue, a teen-age craze about Petra developed in Israel in
the 1950s. Youngsters deemed it a mark of virility to make a visit to the
ghostly city, and the craze persisted even though Jordanian patrols shot and
killed three Israelis. The aim was to have oneself photographed against the
ruins of Petra to prove (usually to girl friends) that one had made the
dangerous, clandestine trip. For months a pop song called "*El Hasela
Ha'adom*" (To the Red Rock) was at the head of the Israeli hit parade. In
Israel, a friend remarked to me, archaeology is not only the hobby of
generals, but part of teen-age culture. It is somehow right that a nation with
so precarious a future should have so pervasive a passion for the past.

Chapter Five
REALM OF LIGHT
GREECE

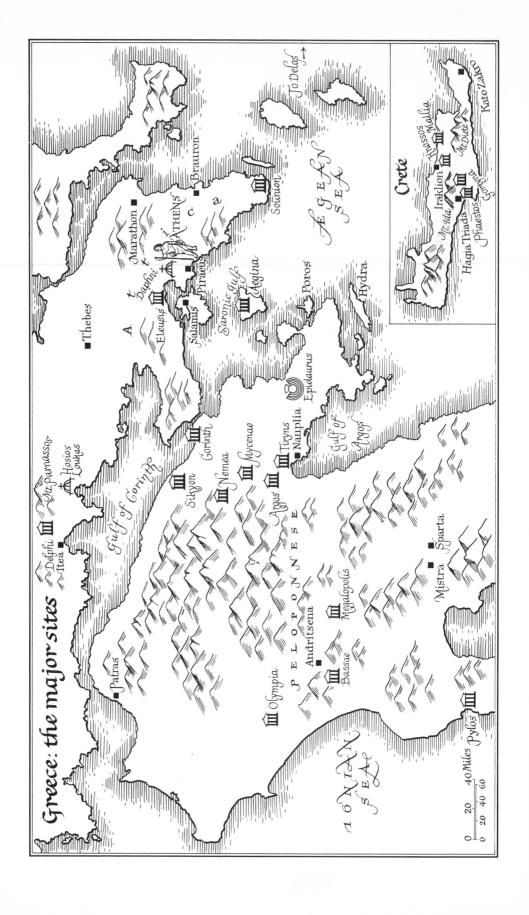

Greece: the major sites

Thebes

Marathon

Brauron

ATHENS

Daphni

Eleusis

Salamis

Piraeus

Sounion

Saronic Gulf

Aegina

Poros

Hydra

Epidaurus

Tiryns

Nauplia

Mycenae

Gulf of Argos

Argos

Nemea

Corinth

Sikyon

Gulf of Corinth

Hosios Loukas

Mt. Parnassos

Delphi

Itea

Patras

Olympia

PELOPONNESE

Andritsena

Bassae

Megalopolis

Mistra

Sparta

Pylos

IONIAN SEA

AEGEAN SEA

To Delos →

Crete

Knossos

Mallia

Mt. Ida

Mt. Dicte

Iraklion

Hagia Triada

Phaestos

Gortyna

Kato Zakro

0   20   40 Miles
0   20   40   60

I

ATHENA MASKED

Whatever deceives seems to exercise a magical enchantment. PLATO, The Republic, III

THE UNGUARDED EYE can be blinded by the splendor of classical Greece; without proper sunglasses, the landscape seems an Elysian vision, a detergent oasis in a blemished world. It can even appear as decorous as an English Sunday. Consider this passage by Gilbert Murray, in his day the most distinguished Hellenist at Oxford: "If you look at a Greek statue or bas-relief, or if you read an average piece of Aristotle, you will very likely at first feel bored. Why? Because it is all so normal and truthful; so singularly free from exaggeration, paradox, violent emphasis; so destitute of those fascinating by-forms of insanity which appeal to some faint element of insanity in ourselves."

Boringly normal? Can this apply, I wonder, to the Athenians, whom Thucydides described as taking no rest themselves and giving none to others? Is Greek mythology and drama free of exaggeration and violent emphasis? Can the suicidal Peloponnesian War be described without resort to paradox? And how did a people so destitute of interest in insanity provide almost the entire vocabulary with which we describe mental disorder—*maniac, phobia, paranoia, schizophrenia, complex,* and *psychiatrist* all being words of Greek origin?

In Plato's celebrated cave the prisoners could only see their own shadows cast upon the wall by the fire blazing behind them; unable to move their heads, they mistook their own images for eternal truth. The radiance of classical Greece has somewhat the same effect; it is the fire behind us, and we are apt to mistake our own shadows for the reality of Greece. So to Gilbert

Murray the Hellenic world could resemble an Oxford college: restrained, worthy, masculine, and dull.

One source, surely, of this prevalent view of Greece lies in the deceptive ruins which, ennobled by time, ennoble their creators. This is indisputably true of the Parthenon. Sponged by the ages, its Doric majesty is too chaste; its columns, mounted like honey stalks against an aqueous sky, are too austere. The effect, on most of us, is hypnotic—also a word of Greek derivation.

In truth, the Parthenon was a painted woman. Much of the temple was daubed with red, blue, and gilt; each carved figure was given a cosmetic coat, the hair tinted, the eyes whitened, the flesh rendered in pink or red; there were *rings* painted around the necks of columns. The Acropolis itself was thickly sown with slabs and statuary, creating (as Herbert Muller remarks) "a hodge-podge that makes Radio City seem a model of restraint." On all this the centuries have had a cleansing effect, rubbing away the colors, expunging the vulgarities, simplifying the litter. Time has wiped away the exaggerations and violent emphasis, putting an alabaster mark on Athena.

Part of what is masked is the political purpose of the Parthenon, which was frankly intended by Pericles to serve as propaganda for Greek democracy. Built in an astonishingly short period—its sculpture was completed in only fifteen years—the Parthenon was debated continuously in a free assembly, in which Pericles was repeatedly reproached for extravagance. But Pericles felt, so Plutarch asserts, that during a period of Athenian naval ascendancy the people at home should "take their benefit from the public funds no less than the crews and the garrisons and the expeditionary forces." Plutarch goes on to describe the Athenians at work:

> The raw materials were stone, bronze, ivory, gold, ebony, cypress-wood, and to fashion and work them were the crafts: carpenters, moulders, coppersmiths, stone-workers, goldsmiths, ivory-workers, painters, pattern-weavers, workers in relief. Then there were the men engaged in transport and carriage, merchants, sailors, helmsmen by sea, and by land cartwrights, and men who kept the yokes of beasts, and drovers; rope-makers, flax-workers, shoemakers, roadmakers and miners.
>
> And each craft, like a general with its own army, had its own crowd of hired workers and individual craftsmen organized like an instrument and body for the service to be performed; so in a word, the various needs to be met distributed and spread prosperity through every age and condition.

Meticulous accounts were kept, showing the cost of the Parthenon, its cult statue, and the Erechtheum nearby; archaeologists have pieced together many of these tablets, and they show that citizens, slaves, and resident aliens

The Stoa of Attalus All that survived of the ancient market can be seen above, but the modern reconstruction is scrupulously based on known architectural facts and is not conjectural. (PHOTO AGORA EXCAVATIONS)

were given equal pay for equal work. Regrettably, this appealing frieze of crafts collaborating in the most sublime of public works tends to be blotted out by the temple's denuded loveliness. We need to be reminded that the Parthenon could never have been built by a cabal of colonels.

To recover more fully a sense of the audacity of classical Athens, one must descend the slopes of the Acropolis to the site of the ancient Agora, with its untidy litter of stones, its squat little temple, and its incongruously new Stoa of Attalus, which stretches diagonally across it like a huge white bar of carved soap. For all its homely clutter, this is a precious eminence in the topography of freedom. The Agora was for a thousand years the civic and commercial heart of Athens. Its refuse is the debris of democracy.

For several decades the rubble has been sifted by Homer A. Thompson, a mild-eyed scholar who is director of the Agora campaign sponsored by the American School of Classical Studies in Athens. There is hardly an unearthed pebble that Homer Thompson has not devotedly appraised. On my last visit to Athens I talked with Professor Thompson about everything from the novels of Mary Renault ("I prefer Plutarch," he said dryly) to the habits of Greek workmen. He told me he once asked an expert if garrulous digger what he, the workman, would do after the excavation season ended. "No problem," was the reply, "I'll call up the Prime Minister and he'll find me a job. You see, we're both from the same city." And somehow the workman penetrated the ministerial switchboard and a job was duly found for him.

This unshakable sense of fraternity among citizens of the same city has an appealing antecedent in a choice find made by American excavators—a handful of hobnails and a scrap of pottery that recalled to life Simon the Shoemaker.

Simon lived in the Athens of the fifth century B.C. and is known through a number of anecdotes. "I wish I were a shoemaker in ancient Athens," a friend remarked to Plutarch, "so that Socrates would come and sit beside Pericles in my house and chat with him." Reputedly, Pericles was so taken with Simon that he invited the cobbler to join the statesman's political circle. Simon declined, saying he valued his freedom of speech more. Once Alcibiades met Socrates in Simon's shop, and the philosopher asked sharply: "Do you despise that shoemaker?" Alcibiades shrugged. "The people of Athens are just such people," Socrates chided. "If you despise this one, you despise all."

These stories were told centuries after the lifetime of Socrates, and it was not certain that Simon existed. A few years ago, in the southwest corner of the Agora, archaeologists found a heap of hobnails, some bone eyelet rings, a whetstone, and a drinking cup that could be dated to the third quarter of the fifth century B.C. On the black cup the name "Simon" was scratched. The

A Shoemaker's Legacy   The hobnails, the bone eyelets, and the inscribed cup were found in the Agora and appear to confirm the historicity of Simon the cobbler, the friend of Socrates. The finds are now in Agora Museum. (PHOTO AGORA EXCAVATIONS)

cup can be seen in Case 38 of the Agora Museum; Simon is surely unique among the shoemakers of antiquity because his name and hobnails have eluded oblivion.

The Agora Museum is housed in the reconstructed Stoa of Attalus, which has been criticized as an antiseptic American intrusion. "We didn't build it as a stunt," Homer Thompson said, with a slight note of asperity. "We needed a place to store our finds. We've got more than seventy thousand catalogued items, not to speak of a hundred thousand coins. Our excavations have documented five thousand years of Greek history, and there's not an item we cannot produce in minutes."

Most of these finds date from the thousand years in which the Agora flourished before it was abandoned in the fifth century A.D. "You will find everything sold together in the same place in Athens," the poet Eubolos wrote. "Figs, witnesses to summonses, bunches of grapes, turnips, pears, apples, givers of evidence, meddlers, porridges, honeycombs, chick-peas, law-suits, beesting-puddings, myrtle, allotment machines, irises, water-clocks, laws, indictments."

Americans have moved a mountain of earth to retrieve what is imperishable on this list, including the allotment machines for choosing jurors and the water clocks for setting a time limit on Athenian eloquence. John D. Rockefeller, Jr., provided three fourths of the $4,000,000 cost. When work started in 1931, the twenty-five-acre site was covered by 360 modern houses, and in places the blanket of earth was forty feet deep. All this was exhumed, and after the war it was decided to rebuild the Stoa of Attalus. The reconstruction is not conjectural. Identical materials were found to match the known remains: the blue Hymettus marble for the steps, Pentelic marble for the columns, gray Piraeus limestone for the walls, and even roof tiles of the same Attic clay. The building now provides space for archives, offices, workshops, and a museum. (It also duplicates an important classical function—it provides shade.) *

As we walked through the museum, Homer Thompson was talking about the singularity of classical Athens. "Over the years we have accumulated the names of twenty thousand *individuals* who lived in Athens, because each had played some part in civic affairs. You could not compile a directory like that anywhere else in the ancient world." He recalled a famous passage from the Funeral Oration of Pericles: "We alone regard a man who takes no interest in public affairs not as a harmless, but as a useless character. If few of

---

* The Stoa of Attalus was one of six in the ancient Agora. Stoic philosophy takes its name from the Stoa Poikile, or painted Stoa, which the American School is now excavating thanks to a $1,000,000 grant from the Ford Foundation in 1967. Regrettably, this will entail demolition of the street now used by blacksmiths, fittingly called Hephaestus Street. The excavations will take a decade, and when completed the whole Agora will have been unearthed and landscaped.

Ballots for Banishment These four are among thousands of ostraca found in the Agora and used in the custom of ostracism. Clearly legible are the names of Aristides, Themistocles, Cimon, and Pericles, the first three of whom were ostracized. (PHOTO AGORA EXCAVATIONS)

us are originators, we are all sound judges of policy."

I was gently guided to a case containing a clutter of broken pottery. Each fragment had a name scratched on it, sometimes with an expletive added, such as "Themistocles—out with him!" These were the *ostraca*, or potsherds, used in the practice of ostracism. More than a thousand of these pottery ballots have been unearthed in the Agora dig.

The Athenian distrust of personal power made democracy a form of Greek roulette. In the time of Pericles the ruling Council of Five Hundred was selected annually by lot from among some 45,000 male citizens who were responsible for around 250,000 persons living in Attica (120,000 of them were slaves). But the decisions of the Council could be overridden by the Assembly, a meeting of citizens in the open-air forum known as the Pnyx, not far from the Agora. There was, to be sure, a Board of Generals whose members tended to be aristocrats and whose tenure could be continuous. Yet the Assembly could reject the wishes of the Board, and the Generals would then be obliged to carry out a policy they had opposed.

On top of all this there was ostracism, a system devised in the sixth century B.C. which in practice meant that Athens periodically sent its ablest citizens into exile for the offense of being too able. It worked in this fashion. Each year the citizens would decide if a vote of ostracism should be held. If a majority of a quorum of 6,000 felt it should, the Agora was fenced off into ten enclosures, one for each of the city's tribes. The voter then entered the enclosure of his tribe carrying an *ostracon* on which he had scratched the name of the citizen he regarded as the worst menace to the state. If more than 6,000 potsherds were voted, the citizen who led the poll was ordered into exile for ten years. He was given ten days to leave town, but did not lose his citizenship or property.

At least eleven Athenians, most of them distinguished, were banished, including Themistocles, the victor at Salamis. The best-known story about ostracism is preserved by Plutarch: the story of Aristides the Just, who met an illiterate farmer who wanted help in scratching the statesman's name on a pot because "I am sick of hearing him called 'The Just.'" Aristides, whose rectitude does seem excessive, wrote his own name on an *ostracon* and prayed that no calamity would befall Athens that would require his presence—he was in fact recalled after three years in exile.

Plutarch describes how the practice ended with a bad joke. During the Peloponnesian War in 417 B.C. the Assembly was divided into two factions, one led by the cautious Nicias and the other by the impulsive Alcibiades. A demagogue named Hyperbolus started a campaign against both men, reasoning that if either were banished, then he might prove a match for the survivor. But Nicias and Alcibiades were alerted to the plot, and the rivals secretly cooperated to turn the vote against Hyperbolus himself. When the pots were counted, the demagogue's name led the rest. Athenians were at first amused and then scandalized. Ostracism was deemed a dignified custom, and it was debased by its use against the son of a slave like Hyperbolus. A poet wrote:

> The man deserved the fate, deny who can:
> Yes, but the fate did not deserve the man.
> Not for the like of him and his slave brands
> Did Athens put the sherd into our hands.

It was the last instance of ostracism.

What can one make of this extraordinary custom? The ardent Hellenist George Grote contended that ostracism enabled the Athenian democracy "to grow from infancy to manhood without a single attempt to overthrow it by force." The Swiss historian Jakob Burckhardt is more severe: "In all the history of the world, mediocrity has never again displayed a similar flash of genius; it barricaded itself behind popular feeling. Thus ostracism was applied as soon as a man began to gain public confidence, a thing the state ruled out in principle until it blindly accorded this very confidence to the demagogues."

An even more drastic political step was sanctioned by Athenians. Homer Thompson led me to the inscribed base of the monument that was the most prominent in the ancient Agora: the statue of the Tyrannicides, Harmodios and Aristogeiton, who in 514 B.C. killed a putative tyrant. In what other city would assassins have pride of place in the civic center? Not far away, in the arcade of the Stoa, I saw an inscribed tablet with this decree, enacted by the citizens of Athens in 336 B.C.: "If anyone rises against the people with a view to tyranny, or join in establishing tyranny or overthrow the People of Athens or the democracy of Athens, whoever kills him who does any of these things shall be blameless."

Where else would it be conceivable for such an edict to be passed and posted? To ask the question is to suggest the audacity of Athens. As the Corinthian envoy warned the Spartans before the start of the Peloponnesian War:

> You Spartans have never tried to imagine what sort of people these Athenians are against whom you will have to fight—how much, indeed how completely different from you. An Athenian is always an innovator, quick to form a resolution and quick at carrying it out. . . . While you are hanging back, they never hesitate; while you stay at home, they are always abroad; for they think the farther they go, the more they will get, while you think that any movement may endanger what you have already. [Thucydides, translated by Rex Warner]

In the moment of its glory Athens was a noisy, uninhibited, smelly, crowded, discordant place. The Acropolis was crammed with statuary, and the Agora was a jumble of buildings. It was a place so jealous of power and so devoted to democracy (despite the anomaly of slavery) that it lost the Peloponnesian War because strategy was dictated by the vicissitudes of the popular Assembly. The Athenians invented the drama, they evolved whole schools of philosophy, wrote the first histories and treatises on politics—they were briefly radioactive, throwing off particles that disturb the world still. Whatever they were, they were hardly like the schoolroom Greek with his plaster gaze. The spare beauty of the Greek ruins conveys a Hellenism with the humanity rubbed out.

II

THE EGG OF NEMESIS

> *Archaeologists all the world over owe a debt to Schliemann of Troy; the German poets owe none.*
>
> E. M. BUTLER, The Tyranny of Greece over Germany

THE GREEK SOIL nurtures myths with the same fecundity with which it nurtures wildflowers: the anemones, asphodel, and oleander that brightly mottle the bare hills in spring. Of the modern myths, the best surely is that of Schliemann of Troy. I would like to tell the familiar story in a slightly different way, beginning with the guest book in the hotel La Belle Hélène in blood-ridden Mycenae.

Recently I had a pleasant lunch under the mulberry tree on the terrace of La Belle Hélène, which lies about a mile below the ancient citadel. I chatted with Orestes and Agamemnon, the brothers who run the hotel, and they told me, as they have told so many others, about their grandfather, who was one of Schliemann's workmen. We also talked about Aristotle, the old man who had shown me around Mycenae on a previous visit. They pointed to a nearby house which had a curtained window. "He is there," said Orestes. "It is his time to die."

I asked Agamemnon if once again I could look at his hotel's guest book. It had an almost morbid fascination for me. In its tattered pages one finds the names of three not obscure wartime visitors: Goebbels, Goering, and Heinrich Himmler.

Why had they come here? A persuasive answer, I believe, can be found in the pages of *The Tyranny of Greece over Germany* by a Cambridge don, Eliza Marion Butler. Miss Butler writes: "Greece has profoundly modified the whole trend of modern civilization, imposing her thought, her standards, her literary forms, her imagery, her visions and dreams wherever she is known. But Germany is the extreme example of her triumphant spiritual tyranny. The Germans have imitated the Greeks more slavishly; they have been obsessed by them more utterly, and they have assimilated them less than any other race." (Miss Butler's book was published in 1935; it was quickly put on the Nazi index.)

What the Germans did, Miss Butler contends, was to invent a wholly fictitious classical Greece peopled by superhumans, a kind of Hellenic Reich. They did it with little knowledge of, and often little genuine interest in, the reality of ancient Greece. Typically, the process began with Johann Joachim Winckelmann (1717–1768), the homosexual son of a cobbler, whose most famous essay was based on the study of a plaster cast of Laocoön. Though this Hellenistic sculpture is assuredly more remarkable for its passion and anguish, Winckelmann found in it "noble simplicity and serene greatness." This first effort at systematic appreciation of classical art had an abiding influence on the German poets: Goethe, Schiller, Lessing, Herder, and Hölderlin all in varying degree propagated the notion of a flawless Greece, as did Romantic poets everywhere, though arguably with less rapturous intensity.

Goethe's case is especially interesting because he had a chance actually to visit Greece during his Italian journey. He made uneasy excuses for avoiding the trip. Of the failure of a single German poet to go to Greece Miss Butler remarks: "Had they seen with their own eyes its wild, titanic landscape and experienced its sometimes menacing moods, they would perhaps have recognized that tragic element in Greek poetry and thought which they resolutely ignored and eliminated from their conception of a golden age of Greece."

To be sure, poets of other countries likewise succumbed. But, writing in 1935, Miss Butler cautioned that the Germans were unique "in the ardor with which they pursue ideas and attempt to transform them into reality. . . . If most of us are victims of circumstances, it may be truly said of the Germans as a whole that they are at the mercy of ideas."

Her thesis forms the backcloth for my retelling of the myth of Schliemann of Troy.

Unlike the poets, Heinrich Schliemann wanted not only to see Greece but to dig up its heroic past. He was absurdly single-minded. In his old age he lived like a Homeric demigod, in a severely furnished mansion in Athens, with classical texts at one elbow and a stock ticker at the other. His visitors were greeted by Bellerophon, the porter, or Telamon, the footman. Elsewhere in the house were the Schliemann children, Andromache and Agamemnon, and their nurses, Danaë and Polyxena. Working in the yard was the gardener, Calchas. All the names, of course, were chosen by Schliemann himself. In conversation he would talk with certitude about everything from Homer to the local laundry service, which he found execrable, so much so that he shipped all of his shirts by express steamer to London for a washing. He was, in short, as much self-made myth as self-made man.

Of the elements in the myth, the most problematic is the celebrated story that as a boy in a Mecklenburg parsonage in Germany he announced to his father that he would dig up the walls of Troy. Schliemann tells the story in the autobiographical introduction to *Ilios*, published in 1880 when he was already famous. Somehow he had overlooked it entirely in an earlier sketch inserted in *Troy and Its Remains* (1875) when he was just beginning to become known.

Nor is it certain that his overriding motive in accumulating a fortune was to fulfill this supposed childhood pledge. He liked to put it this way: "I loved money, indeed, but solely as the means for realizing the one passion of my life —to find Troy." Indisputably, he acquired a merchant's fortune, thanks to his gift for languages and his speculative instincts during the Crimean War. But Troy? One looks in vain for references to the childhood ambition in the published correspondence for this period. One finds instead a demonic uncertainty and poignant unhappiness. At one critical point Schliemann came close to settling permanently in Indianapolis, Indiana (he had become a U.S. citizen while in California during the Gold Rush). The Hoosier State is a long way from the wine-dark Aegean.

My impression is that Schliemann was a sleepwalker, and it could be as true to say that Troy found him as the other way around. During his forties he became bored with business, his first marriage was a failure, and he was wandering like Odysseus in search of home, wife, and purpose. He found all three in Greece, where, fittingly, he began his explorations with a visit to Ithaca in 1868. Thankfully, Indianapolis was forgotten (he returned to the city only to get a divorce). He wrote to the Archbishop of Athens asking for help in choosing a young bride: she had to be Greek, poor, pretty, and affectionate. He was rewarded with a photograph of Sophia, who fitted all the specifications and also loved the classics. After an eccentric courtship, which included a classical quiz, he married the seventeen-year-old girl when he was forty-seven.* He finally began planning his long-deferred siege of Troy. His life was acquiring shape and purpose, and it was perhaps only

---

* Schliemann's questions were: "Can you recite a passage of Homer?" "What were the dates of Hadrian's visit to Athens?" "Would you like to go on a long journey?" Sophia passed easily.

"*The Mask of Agamemnon*" Upon discovering this golden mask at Mycenae, Schliemann instantly announced that its features were those of the leader of the Greeks at Troy; in fact it was the visage of an unknown Mycenaean ruler. The engraving is from Schliemann's *Mycenae*.

human that he retrospectively imposed a pattern on a sleepwalking past.

From 1870 to 1873 his gang of workmen drove a deep trench into the mound of Hissarlik, the hill in Turkish Asia Minor that Schliemann correctly insisted was the true site of Troy. With that instinct for finding gold that marked him as a merchant, Schliemann found a shimmering hoard that he promptly dubbed "The Treasure of Priam." His success at Troy was even more sensationally crowned at Mycenae in 1876, where in a single short campaign he found five graves heaped with gold. He announced he had found the tomb of Agamemnon and his companions. His enthusiasm led him to publish his results immediately: a virtue. Against this there were his admitted deficiencies: the frenzied tempo of his digging, his Odyssean cunning in dealing with officials, and his habit of linking every find to a hero in Homer.

At Troy his faults led him to destroy much of the city he was so intent on finding. To his astonishment, his shoveling at Hissarlik unearthed not one but nine cities (later work showed that in all there were fifty-seven layers of occupation in this single mound). He wrongly assumed that the Homeric city would be near the bottom, and thus burrowed through Priam's city to the much earlier settlement which yielded the treasure. The "Treasure of Priam" was actually in Troy II, dating back to 2500–2200 B.C., or about a thousand years before the Trojan War. Ultimately, and reluctantly, Schliemann conceded he was mistaken; by this time Troy VIIA, the Homeric city, was mostly in a pile of rubble heaped up by its discoverer.

At Mycenae there were other ironies: Schliemann unwittingly stumbled into an unknown continent of the past. In looking for Homer's heroes (which scholars insisted was a waste of time), Schliemann found Mycenaean civilization (which scholars had never known existed). His experience prompted Sir Arthur Evans to dig up Knossos in Crete, exposing to light still another and even more mystifying pre-Homeric civilization, the Minoans.

This achievement by Schliemann more than cancels out the ellipsis in his biography, his admitted defects as an excavator, and his vain idiosyncrasies. "The glory of discovering Troy and making it known to the world is his," writes Carl Blegen, Schliemann's more scholarly successor at Hissarlik, "and his fame was fairly won."

Of all the major countries in Europe, the Germans were the most reluctant to acknowledge Schliemann's greatness. In Britain, Schliemann's visits were processions of triumph. He was befriended by Gladstone, who wrote a long preface to the book on Mycenae, and his amateur pluck made him a popular hero. The same amateurism annoyed German scholars, especially since they had decreed with mistaken confidence that the Homeric stories were mere myths. Schliemann's lack of formal education was almost an

Schliemann at Mycenae The great excavator sits in the foreground beneath the Lion Gate; within, Schliemann found the gold-filled tombs in the Grave Circle. (COURTESY GERMAN ARCHAEOLOGICAL INSTITUTE, ATHENS)

The Acropolis from the Air Greek archaeologists have tidied up the litter around the Parthenon. At the tip, at the upper left, is the terrace from which King Aegeus flung himself when he saw the black sails on the ship bearing home his son Theseus, the Minotaur-slayer. (PHOTO BY ROTKIN, P.F.I.)

affront; to be proven wrong was bad enough, but by a largely self-taught businessman . . . ! Yet one German grasped the importance of Schliemann's work: the eminent pathologist Rudolf Virchow.

Virchow was endowed with many of the qualities that Schliemann so conspicuously lacked and envied. He was suave, possessed formidable learning, and had an aristocrat's contempt for money-grubbing. He championed Schliemann to the extent of contributing an elegantly written preface to *Ilios*. One passage is interesting. In discussing the finds Virchow warns that the claims of poetry and reality must be brought into judicious accord: "We must not sever the story of the gods from men."

In 1879 the pathologist made a visit to Troy, where Schliemann was at work on a new campaign. On a pleasant day the two friends went for a walk around Mount Ida, from whose heights Zeus had watched the Trojan War. Virchow noticed that his companion was morose and distracted and asked why. Schliemann explained that he was worrying about his death and what to do with his Trojan finds. Virchow astutely avoided obvious salesmanship. He plucked a flowering blackthorn and gave it to the reconqueror of Troy, saying, "A nosegay from Ankerhagen." After this reference to Schliemann's boyhood in Germany, nothing more was said. In returning to the camp, Virchow risked putting the unspoken decision in words: "Of course they should go to the German nation. They will be cared for, and you will be honored for giving them. It is all very simple. With your permission, I shall speak to Prince Bismarck about it."

The negotiations were intricate and awkward, and the bargain that was finally reached took account of the snubs Schliemann had received in Germany. He was to get a special letter of commendation from the Kaiser, membership in the Prussian Academy of Sciences, and (most important of all) honorary citizenship of Berlin, something that had been bestowed only on Bismarck and Von Moltke. It was further agreed that the Trojan finds would be displayed in a Berlin museum that would bear his name in perpetuity. Accordingly, the collection was shipped to Germany, and Heinrich and Sophia went to acquire his honors. It was his meridian.

At the same time, and entirely unwittingly, Schliemann had provided another gift to the Germans—he had publicized the queer symbol he had found at Troy and Mycenae which he called a "suastika." His earliest published mention (in *Troy and Its Remains*) has curious overtones: "All that can be said of the first settlers [of Troy] is that they belonged to the Aryan race, as is sufficiently proved by the Aryan religious symbol met with in the strata of their ruins (among which we find the *Suastika*)." The symbol fascinated Schliemann; he repeatedly refers to it in books and letters; once he wrote Renan to ask what it meant. In *Ilios* he inserted a seven-page essay on the swastika by the Oxford Orientalist Max Müller, whose language had the

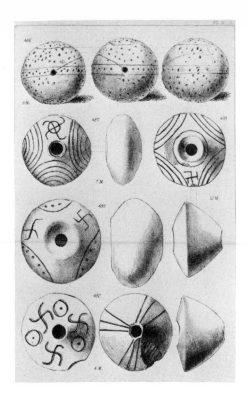

Schliemann's Swastikas   A few of the illustrations in *Troy and Its Remains* (1876) depicting the swastika which Schliemann found on Trojan spindle whorls.

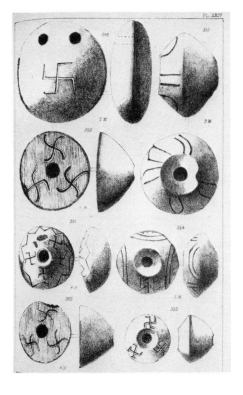

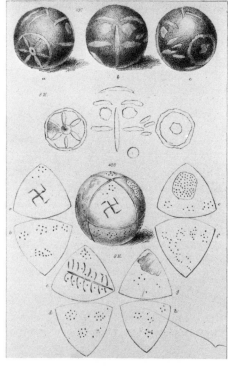

portentous obscurity that would appeal to a racial mythogogue, as indeed it did.

The Nazis turned around the swastika symbol that Schliemann had popularized, just as they turned inside out the romantic Germanic conception of Greece, enlisting Olympus into the Thousand-Year Reich. A careful reading of Schliemann's frequent use of *Aryan* shows that he intended the word in its old, precise, and reputable sense—as a description of peoples, whether white or brown, who spoke an Indo-European language. (See his explicit definition in *Troy and Its Remains*, London, John Murray, 1875, pp. 101–102.) There is no evidence of racial obsession in Schliemann's writing. On the contrary, in a letter written from New Orleans in 1867 he protests "the *downright falsehoods*" spread about Negro freedmen in the American South, who morally and intellectually "stand much higher than their former tyrants and present calumniators." He was impressed by Black Reconstruction legislatures in Mississippi and Louisiana, saying he regretted "that I was myself not a Negro to speak as they did" in speeches that employed graceful gestures.

These were not the characteristic sentiments of the masters of Germany who brought on World War II. As the swastika spread over Europe, the Schliemann collection in Berlin was carefully hidden. Much of the pottery was placed in Lebus Castle on the Oder River, other finds were stored in a mine and beneath the Berlin Museum, while the "Treasure of Priam" was packed in a bunker below the Zoo. The Russians demolished Lebus Castle, and in the sack of Berlin the gold in the bunker simply vanished. One theory is that the gold was melted down and sold; another is that it was taken by the Russians under heavy guard. All that is certain is that in the fall of the Third Reich the gold of Troy disappeared for a second time as a city was sacked.

So ends the myth of Schliemann of Troy, as rich and bizarre as anything conjured by the Greek imagination. At the risk of sounding a bit portentous myself, I must add as a pendant the interesting parentage of Helen of Troy. There are varying accounts, and Robert Graves gives one that was widely accepted: "Some say that Zeus once fell in love with Nemesis and pursued her over the earth and over the sea. Though she constantly changed her shape, he violated her at last by adopting the form of a swan, and from the egg she laid came Helen, cause of the Trojan war."

Who would have thought that the old god had so much blood in her? *

---

* There is an arresting passage in Gladstone's preface to *Mycenae:* "But there was in ancient poetry, a Destiny stronger than the will of the gods. To me, on this occasion, Dr. Schliemann is the vice-regent and organ of that Destiny." (The honorific "Doctor" is a reference to the degree awarded to Schliemann by the University of Rostock after he submitted an autobiography written in classical Greek.)

III

THE ROBES OF PROTEUS

"FOR A FOREIGNER," wrote Nikos Kazantzakis in 1937, "the pilgrimage to Greece is simple, it happens without any convulsions; his mind, liberated from sentimental entanglements, leaps to discover the essence of Greece. But for the Greek, this pilgrimage is fraught with hopes and fears, with distress and painful comparison. . . . Merciless questions arise to lash our brains. How were so many wonders created, and what are we ourselves doing? Why has the race become so debased? How can we carry on once more?"

Like all Greeks, Kazantzakis is too kind to foreigners. Making the pilgrimage is not always quite so simple. A case in point is Henry Miller, who hugged the whole country, past and present, in his not unformidable embrace. "In Greece, one has the conviction that *genius* is the norm, not mediocrity," he exclaimed in one cadenza in his admirable *Colossus of Maroussi*. Miller goes on: the landscape is the "most satisfactory, the most wondrous" that the world has to offer. The Greek cosmos is "the most eloquent illustration of the unity of thought and deed." And so forth.

Yet Miller raises a problem which he ignores. He lived in Greece for nearly a year in 1939, during the Metaxas dictatorship, which is never mentioned. The Greek writer Mimica Granaki reproaches him: "You managed to climb all 999 steps of the fortress of Nauplia, without hearing the groans rising from its dungeons. Today they are empty, sure enough. Their inmates are elsewhere." Miss Granaki was writing before the Colonels took over in 1967.

As a political writer, I cannot pass in silence over the same question. I find it disheartening that some argue that the modern Greeks are mongrel Levantines who are getting the government they deserve. The point should be met head-on. Nobody who is familiar with the spirit of classical Greece could doubt for a minute that he is in the same country when he visits Athens. I know of few places where there is less forelock-touching, where taxi drivers do not expect to be tipped, and where argument is so obviously the national sport. If Greeks find it hard to make democracy work, it is because they dislike admitting that anyone is truly fit to govern them—see Thucydides, *passim*.

For long and dark centuries the Greek lands were occupied by Turkish conquerors who had a different language, culture, and religion. The Greeks retained their religion, their outlook, and their language, the latter in such undefiled form that it differs less from classical Greek than modern English does from Anglo-Saxon.

Circumstances change, but the Greeks remain the same, their outer form altered, like Proteus, while the inner spirit is unconquerably unchanged. Whether one should visit Greece while that spirit is momentarily fettered is a matter on which honorable persons can differ. But before describing the pleasures of Greek travel, I should like to make my own view plain. I could not feel comfortable as a private visitor in a Greece where it is deemed a seditious provocation to recite the Funeral Oration of Pericles.

IV

THE EYE OF APOLLO

> *No flushful tint the sense to warm—*
> *Pure outline pale, a linear charm.*
> *The clear-cut hills carved temples face,*
> *Respond, and share their sculptured grace.*
> HERMAN MELVILLE

IDEALLY, one should approach Greece with the stealth of a ship, as the ancients did, and not with the abruptness of a jetliner. This can be done by taking the overnight ferry that embarks from Brindisi in Italy and glides through a spangling sea, docking at Corfu, passing Ithaca, and disembarking at Patras, where there is a welcoming bustle at the quay, as if each arrival were an unexpected benison. One should make careful advance arrangements for hiring a car; once blanket-sized documents have been signed, one should head up the coastal road toward Olympia.

The best month is May. Greece is graced with a profusion of wildflowers; she has three times the number of floral species found in Britain, though she is only a third as large. As one approaches Olympia, the countryside is a spare vista of spiky hills brocaded with flowers and cloaked with olive trees. Otherwise, the colors scorn brightness, as if too much display would blur the crystal light.

In a few hours Olympia materializes, the main street a dusty mingling of souvenir shops, restaurants, and children. One thus begins where Greek history started, since the ancient calendar had as its earliest fixed date 776 B.C., when the first games were held. One also begins on sacred neutral ground; wars were interrupted to permit the games to continue. Officially held in honor of Zeus, the games were abolished in 393 A.D., and the last recorded victor known to history was a Persian boxer from Armenia—to the end, Olympia was hospitable to foreigners.

Since 1875 the site has been excavated by Germans, who have done a characteristically thorough job (there was a special burst of activity in 1936, when Hitler wanted something to turn up to help promote the Berlin Olympics). The great Temple of Zeus has been bared, along with the gymnasia, the hostels, and the stadium. With a little imagination, one can visualize how the games were run, where the athletes lived, and what the workship was like in which Phidias made the colossal statue of Zeus, one of the Seven Wonders. The statue is long vanished, but archaeologists have dug up some of the actual molds used by Phidias to make it.

A small museum on the site documents the mutability of taste. Victorians expressed unanimous admiration for the statue of Hermes by Praxiteles, and dismissed as semi-barbarous the mutilated fragments from the pediments of the Temple of Zeus. "Is there a single figure in either of these pediments that deserves to be called beautiful?" dejectedly asked Sir James Fraser. Yet now the Hermes seems blandly vapid, and it is the pediments which catch the eye.

The figures on the East Pediment illustrate the story of Pelops, the King of Elis on the peninsula that bears his name. Pelops was suitor to the daughter of a king who had been warned by an oracle that his death would be caused by his son-in-law. So the king devised a chariot race in which all suitors would surely be killed. Pelops was fourteenth in line, but he cannily bribed the king's charioteer, Myrtilos, into putting a wax linch-pin in the monarch's chariot. In the race the king was thrown and killed by his collapsing chariot, but afterward Pelops declined to pay the promised bribe—some say it was first claim to his bride's favors—to Myrtilos. Instead, Pelops drowned the charioteer, who gasped out a curse that fell on Pelops' House of Atreus, eventually dooming Agamemnon at Mycenae.

In their present smashed state the figures on the East Pediment, which show the start of the fateful race, have acquired an added intensity. The same is true of the jagged sculptures on the West Pediment, which depict that battle between the Centaurs and the Lapiths. There is an innovative vigor in the figures, as if the sculptors had worked with lava. One is not surprised to learn that scholars believe that these carved figures probably constitute the earliest attempt to show emotion on the human face.

Otherwise my own memory of Olympia is serenely pastoral. Not far from the ruins I waded in the Alphaeios River, which Shelley inaccurately calls a "brackish, Dorian stream." In fact the river has a surgical cleanliness, and I was not surprised to learn that Hercules diverted it to clean the Augean Stables. As I was sitting on the bank, two Greek youths hove into sight. They were mounted bareback on black stallions and burst down the river like

Art of Olympia These women were on the West Pediment of the Temple of Zeus, which depicted the battle of Centaurs and Lapiths. Scholars assert that Olympia's pedimental figures constitute the earliest attempt by sculptors to portray emotion on the human face. (PHOTO ALISON FRANTZ)

emanations from a frieze. We exchanged greetings and the older boy, who was eleven, told me his name was Platon. With a jaunty farewell the youngsters vanished down the pebbly river, becoming only a fragrant memory, a wildflower pressed in an Olympian album.

Bassae, a temple high in the Arcadian wilderness, was unreachable by road until 1959, and even now involves a vertiginous climb around sheer-sided hairpin turns. Suddenly, without warning, the temple appears in the solitude—a temple that faultlessly combines the Doric, Ionic, and Corinthian orders in a design attributed to Ictinus, the architect of the Parthenon. Once sacred to Apollo, Bassae had its oracle and priests, but now reposes, in self-sufficient splendor, in undefiled isolation (it also once had its pedimental friezes, but a century ago they were stripped and carted off to the British Museum). Because of its remoteness, one can visit Bassae without hearing anything but goat-bells; although the trip requires a detour from Olympia over bad roads, one would be foolish, if time permits, not to make it.

The next goal is Nauplia, a pleasant seaport town in the Argolid that provides an excellent base for a trip to Epidauros. Dedicated to healing, Epidauros was the Lourdes of classical Greece; the ruins of the Temple of Asclepios—only the foundation and an adjoining guest house can be seen— still possess a medicinal calm, drowsy with the hum of bees in a soft eiderdown of shrubs.

Nearby, a small museum contains tablets that attest to the god of medicine's efficacy in curing lameness, baldness, migraine, gout, barrenness, pinkeye, lice, dropsy, worms, dumbness, ulcers, and other like afflictions. Case-

Theater of Epidauros A whisper uttered in the orchestra can be heard in the topmost tier of the best-preserved of Greek theaters. (PHOTO ALISON FRANTZ)

histories have their own charm. A dog's lick cured a blind eye, the bite of a sacred goose mended a gouty toe, and a woman, pregnant for five years, gave birth here to a son, only to see him run to the river and wash himself. Or there is the child who dreamed that Asclepios asked him what the boy would give for a cure. "Ten knucklebones," the boy replied, and the god laughed and the boy awoke to find himself well.

But Epidauros is most famous for its theater, the best-preserved in the Greek world. Some 12,000 persons could fill its seats; the acoustics are so perfect that the chink of a drachma in the circular orchestra can be heard in the topmost tier. Scholars assert that this excellence was achieved by placing hollow jars under the seats, creating what is in effect an infinite baffle. Built in the fourth century B.C., the theater is now used again for a summer festival; Epidauros still provides the therapy of drama.

It is only a short drive from Nauplia to Tiryns, the Palace of Hercules, a compact fortress built of huge blocks that commands the road to Argos and Mycenae. Homer's "well-girt Tiryns" dates to 1400 B.C. and retains a Bronze Age grimness. Within is a posthern that has been used for centuries as a sheep pen, and the rubbing of wool has given a sepulchral gleam to the hard blocks that wall the tunnel. Still, for all its severity, Tiryns could not have been entirely cheerless; it had so lighthearted a reputation that the Oracle at Delphi was asked by the Tirynthians how they might become more solemn. They were told to cast a bull into the sea for Poseidon and to do so without laughing. All children were ordered from sight as a poker-faced procession led a bull to the sea. But a wayward child appeared as the sacrifice was about to be made; he was angrily waved away. "What," the boy shouted, "are you afraid I shall knock your bull over?" There was an eruption of laughter, and, according to one historian, Tiryns had to abandon hopes for achieving solemnity "until all smiles stopped together."

Beyond is Mycenae, and the approach to Agamemnon's citadel is deceptively cheerful, even in May, when the poppies bloom blood-red. One ascends a road lined with eucalyptus trees, wheeling upward past a small village and by tobacco fields. But the great fortress broods in a mortuary chill from the moment one enters it, passing under the vast Lion Gate with its unnerving heraldic crest of faceless beasts.

My first guide was the old caretaker Aristotle, who was resolutely indifferent to the finer points of archaeology. As I approached the Inner Grave Circle, he assured me that Mycenae had been built by Perseus in 2200 B.C. His arm pointed to a mountain, and he intoned dramatically, "The mountain is now called Hagios Elias, but the old name is Arachnaion. You can look as far as the sea from its top, and that's where Clytemnestra had the

watchmen posted to tell her when the Trojan War was over. One day the
great signal fire was lit, and she knew that Agamemnon was returning. With
her lover Aegisthos she plotted to murder him. Now follow me." He hobbled
briskly to the palace living-quarters higher up. "What does this look like?" he
demanded. "Like a bath? Bravo, it *is* a bath, and here Agamemnon was
murdered. Look around for a while, and we'll visit the gate through which
Orestes fled. . . ."

One surrenders to the stories, only half attentive to the prosaic fact that
the walls in their surviving form date to 1350–1300 B.C., and that the graves
found within them were dug around 1550 B.C., or 300 years before the
Trojan War, meaning that Agamemnon could not have been buried there.
Nor is there any scientific basis for the traditional ascriptions given the
beehive tombs outside the wall, the so-called Tomb of Clytemnestra and
Tomb of Aegisthos. Still, though archaeology may explain Mycenae, the
myths vivify it, and so perfectly does the setting accord with Atreid gloom
that during a visit one shrugs away the bloodless iconoclasm of science.

The road continues to Corinth, passing Nemea, where Hercules slew the
Lion and where an excellent, robust red wine (Sang d'Hercule) can be
bought at roadside stands. At a picnic one can consider the melancholy

Corinth: Temple of Apollo This is the ancient city as it was before archaeologists
began digging, as shown in an engraving in Wordsworth's *Greece* (1853).

history of Corinth, a city consecrated to Aphrodite and devoted to pleasure. Corinth was razed by the Romans in 146 B.C, rebuilt by Julius Caesar, devastated by an earthquake in 375 A.D., more thoroughly demolished by Alaric the Goth in 395 A.D., struck by another earthquake in 521 A.D., plundered by the Normans in the twelfth century, and, after a series of further conquests, was flattened by still another earthquake in 1858—a chronicle of disaster that moralists may find comforting.

In the old city, excavated by Americans since 1897, one wanders through the rubble, passing the columns of the Temple of Apollo and entering a city planned on Roman lines. The goal is the Fountain of Peirene, named for a nymph whose sorrowing tears for a murdered son formed the stream (others say the water appeared when Pegasus, just captured by Bellerophon, stamped an angry hoof). There are six basins of trickling water, linked to a capacious underground reservoir. Pausanias, the Baedeker of the classical world, wrote of the fountain: "The spring is ornamented with white marble, and there have been made chambers like caves, out of which the water flows into an open-air well. It is pleasant to drink, and they say the Corinthian bronze, when red-hot, is tempered by this water. . . ."

The fountain eluded modern discovery until an American remembered this passage a half-century ago. He was a member of the excavation staff, and on an impulse decided to explore the well in the garden of the house in which he lived. He clambered down, found running water and a passage which led to a "chamber like a cave" and rightly guessed he had found Peirene. The excavators had been living on top of it.

From Old Corinth one continues around the coast past the Corinth Canal and the site of ancient Sikyon en route to the ferry that sails to Itea, the port of Delphi. Not only was Delphi the spiritual center of ancient Greece; it was also believed to be the geographical center, or navel, of the earth. The navel itself was proudly exhibited in the sanctuary—an egg-shaped rock inscribed "GES" or mother earth (a later copy can be seen in the local museum).

Originally Delphi was sacred to the Mother Earth religion, personified in a Python, but it was with Apollo's conquest of the serpent that the sanctuary became important as a place of prophecy. By the early classical period the Pythian Oracle was already enthroned in Delphi, and pilgrims were thronging the shrine. They found themselves in an eyrie furrowed in the slopes of Parnassos, overlooking a churning gorge and the contorted crags of the Valley of Pleistos, the very reverse of the anodyne blandness of Olympia.

A favorite story concerns a forgotten German scholar named Otfried Müller who denied that Apollo was a sun god. While exploring Delphi in 1840 he was afflicted with sunstroke, became fevered and died. "Strangers," the priests would warn pilgrims before they drank Castilia's waters, "when

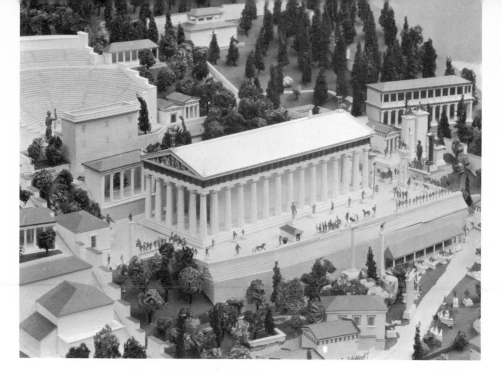

Delphi Restored   The gaudy clutter of Greek temple architecture is suggested in this reconstruction. The Temple of Apollo, in which the Oracle spoke, is in the foreground; below are the smaller temples built as offerings by Greek cities. (COURTESY METROPOLITAN MUSEUM OF ART. DODGE FUND, 1930)

you enter Apollo's sanctuary, be pure in mind. You may be pure if you but drink the waters of this stream. But the seas of the world cannot wash clean a mind that is evil." So great was the repute of the Oracle that history could be influenced by Pythia's advice, most propitiously when a warning that Athens needed "walls of wood" was interpreted by Themistocles as a call for a powerful navy. There were exacting conditions for eliciting a sound prophecy. A goat was sacrificed, and the creature had to respond in the approved manner; as Plutarch writes: "No oracle is given if the victim does not tremble and shake throughout its whole body, right to the extremity of its hooves, while it is dedicated. . . . It is necessary that all its members shiver and shake together with a rattling noise. Without these signs it is declared that the Oracle does not function and Pythia is not introduced to it."

The Oracle flourished with Greece and fell silent with the advent of Christianity. In 362 A.D. Julian the Apostate tried to give Pythia a voice as part of his effort to revive paganism. The Emperor sent a doctor named Oisbasius to Delphi, and the emissary heard these words:

> Tell the King the fair-wrought house has fallen.
> No shelter has Apollo, nor sacred laurel leaves.
> The fountains now are silent; the voice is stilled.

Beginning in 1893, French archaeologists have enabled the Oracle to address us again. The Sacred Way has been cleared, and the Treasuries donated by grateful city-states excavated and some of them restored. The Temple of Apollo has assumed a recognizable shape, and a theater and a stadium have been uncovered in a condition good enough to be used for drama and games. A wealth of statuary has come to light, including a bronze charioteer who in his godlike pride seems the incarnation of Apollo. Delphi is a sanctuary again.*

The road winds downhill from Delphi, leading to Thebes, passing the crossroads at which tradition asserts Oedipus unwittingly murdered his father. Thebes is ancient in name but modern and unlovely in appearance; its inhabitants have been quarreling with Greek archaeologists who have been tentatively digging for the Palace of Cadmus in a downtown section of the city. Some inscribed tablets have been found which suggest that Thebes was among the earliest Greek cities to acquire writing—consistent with the legend that the dragon's teeth sown by Cadmus were the alphabet.

From Thebes one proceeds to Athens, the School of Hellas.

Initially, Athens can be a shock. There is pitifully little left of the Athens that Byron knew, the Levantine village from which he wrote in 1811: "I am living in the Capuchin Convent, Hymettus before me, the Acropolis behind, the Temple of Jove to my right, the Stadium in front, the town to the left; eh, Sir, there's a situation, there's your picturesque!" During centuries of Turkish occupation Athens dwindled into a huddle of buildings around the Acropolis, and even this remnant was badly smashed during the Greek wars of independence. When Christopher Wordsworth, the nephew of the poet, visited Athens shortly after it had become the capital in 1834 of newly independent Greece, his report was depressing: "The town of Athens is now lying in ruins. The streets are deserted; nearly all houses are without roofs. . . . The least ruined objects are some of the ruins themselves."

The reconstruction began under Otto, first modern King of the Hellenes and son of Ludwig I of Bavaria: as a consequence, the style of the new public buildings was Germanic neo-Hellenism. Private buildings of uncertain pedigree sprang up around boulevards and great squares. Athens retains a boom-town atmosphere because it has grown by spasms; from a village of around 10,000 it has become a swollen metropolis of nearly two million with suburbs that spill over an eighty-square-mile plain. It is aggressively eclectic, a mélange of blinking neon lights in Constitution Square, honky-tonk tavernas on the crumbling Plaka, boulevards that seem Bavaro-Parisian, and modern buildings in a dozen borrowed styles, one of them being what is perhaps the

---

* An odd modern pilgrim was the American poet George Cram Cook, founder of the Provincetown Playhouse and discoverer of Eugene O'Neill. In 1922 Cook turned to his wife and said, "It is time to go to Greece." He lived at Delphi for two years, dressing himself in a shepherd's cloak, and then died at fifty-one. He is buried high above the modern village, overlooking the theater; his story is told in *The Road to the Temple* by his wife, Susan Glaspell.

most tasteless of Hilton Hotels. Where in all this jumble is Pericles? What is left of Athens, Ovid asked centuries ago, but the name?

There are the people. They are recognizably Athenian in temper—furiously energetic, so much so that even while sitting in the café the Athenian must click the orange lozenges of his worry-beads. Motorists drive as if they were in a state of war, resentful of the traffic lights only recently installed, each car with a daemon at the wheel. Another trait is the refusal of any Athenian to regard himself as anyone else's inferior. "The Greeks are all traders in some degree," Byron's friend John Hobhouse wrote in 1809. "This circumstance, together with the Turkish oppression, and the want of hereditary dignities, occasions a kind of equality between them. . . . When a rich, or, in other words, a great man meets an inferior in the street, he not only returns his salute, but goes through the whole round of those complimentary rituals which are always usual upon a casual encounter, and prefatory to any other conversation."

In appearance the Athenian is Levantine seasoned with Phidias—the variety of physical types is partly due to the influx of darker refugees from Asia Minor following the transfer of a million and a half Greeks from Turkish-controlled areas in the 1920s. "As to the question of their descent," said Lord Byron, "what can it import whether the Mainotes are the lineal Laconians or not or the present Athenians as indigenous as the bees of

Athens: The Olympieion Once the largest temple in the city, the Olympieion was built by Hadrian; its Corinthian bulk affords a Roman contrast to the Parthenon beyond. (PHOTO AEROFILMS LTD.)

Byron's Parthenon Another view from Wordsworth's book; the nephew of the poet came to Athens not long after Byron and saw the Parthenon as it was left by Lord Elgin and the war with the Turks.

Hymettus, or as the grasshoppers to which they once likened themselves? What Englishman cares if he be of a Danish, Saxon, Norman, or Trojan blood, or who, except a Welshman, is afflicted with a desire of being descended from Caractatus?"

As a city Athens is also the Levant seasoned with a touch of Phidias. However unprepossessing the modern metropolis, the Acropolis is always there, lovely in all its aspects. One of the delights of the city is to stalk the Parthenon from different vantages. Seeing it from the ruins of the Olympeion, the enormous temple built by Hadrian, one glimpses a montage of Greek grace and Roman pretension. From the Pnyx, where the Assembly debated, the Parthenon takes on a different guise as a barque heading toward us on the horizon, like the ships one can also see distantly in the Aegean. From the orchestra of the Theater of Dionysos (not to be confused with the Odeum of Herodes Attikos, where plays are still performed) one looks up at a Parthenon shielded by the steep face of the Acropolis, seeing it from the stage where Sophocles was originally performed. Looking up from the Hephaesteum, the temple Byron knew as the Temple of Theseus, one sees a diagonally placed Parthenon bisected by the violet Acropolis Rock. From the monument of Philopappus there is a panoramic view of the entire Acropolis

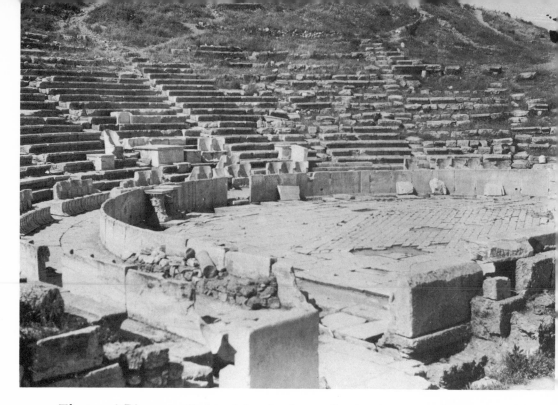

Theater of Dionysos Sheltered by the Acropolis, the theater marks the site of the earlier stage in which the classic dramatists had their premières. The throne-like chairs were for judges at dramatic festivals. (PHOTO AEROFILMS LTD.)

—the two theaters, the beautifully shaped Propylaea or ceremonial entrance, and the Erechtheum, with its slender Ionic columns so cunningly juxtaposed with the Parthenon's heavier Doric. Or as one drives from Athens to Eleusis, the cluttered site of the sanctuary where the Mysteries were performed, one sees the Parthenon from a distance, like a beacon indicating the solar center of the Greek universe.

By degrees the city of Pericles can be found in the crevices of the modern metropolis, literally so at the Cerameikos, the ancient cemetery (which has a choice museum) in an excavated crater near the Diplyon Gate to the city. In the midst of a jumble of modern buildings one unexpectedly comes upon the Tower of Winds, an ancient water-calendar, or Hadrian's Library (Athenians were voracious library patrons, a trait suggested by this inscription found in the Agora: NO BOOKS CIRCULATE. OPEN FROM SIX A.M. TO TWELVE NOON).

And, finally, there is the National Museum, a chalice of the Greek spirit. The best place to start is in its galleries which display the *kouros* statues. This was a style of sculpture invented by the Egyptians and transfigured by Greek artisans. In the chronologically arranged display there is a Pygmalion effect. In the earliest forms the striding statues are stiff and Egyptoid, then gradually the limbs become more supple and the faces acquire a smile of lyric delight— in Greek the same word is used for *delight* and *statue*. A sixth-century B.C.

statue of Kroisos from Anayssos approaches us with disarming charm, despite this poignant inscription below him: "*Stand and mourn by the tomb of dead Kroisos, whom furious Ares slew when he was fighting in the front line.*"

The museum encloses a thousand examples of the kinetic creativity of Greece—the Brancusi-like abstractions carved in the Cycladic islands, the virile Mycenae reliefs wrought in gold, the roomfuls of decorated vases with their sportive gods and Sybaritic feasts, the coins embossed with mythological beasts. Especially unforgettable are the figures in bronze which have acquired a green patina, like the statue of Poseidon (or is it Zeus?) hurling an invisible trident. The god's blank eyes have an imperious impartiality, and his body is so perfectly balanced that one can envision him walking on waves. In fact he was fished from the sea along with others in the matchless collection, and it is to sea that we head on our final two journeys.

Boats go every morning from Piraeus, the port of Athens, to Aegina, the fair-sized island across the Saronic Gulf. One disembarks in the modern town of Aegina, boarding a bus which goes to the other side of the island, to the Temple of Aphaia. The island was once celebrated for its merchants and pirates, and the Aeginetans are credited with introducing the first coinage into Europe. However, the Athenians detested Aegina, which Pericles sneeringly dismissed as "the eyesore of the Piraeus." In 431 B.C., at the beginning of the Peloponnesian War, Athens, having already sacked Aegina and razed its

Temple at Aegina Poised dramatically over the Saronic Gulf, the temple was sacred to the islanders, who were rivals to Athens. The pedimental sculptures were stripped a century ago and sold to the King of Bavaria, and must now be seen in Munich. (PHOTO KARL E. MEYER)

walls, occupied the island, expelled the population, and resettled it with Athenian colonists.

Yet, despite successive disasters, the island's noble Doric temple remained relatively intact, and its surviving pedimental sculpture rivaled the Parthenon's. In 1811, in the high tide of romantic Philhellenism, two young Englishmen and two Germans sailed from Piraeus to claim these sculptures—on the way the party drank wine with Lord Byron, who was then aboard a British naval transport moored in the Gulf. On Aegina the four enthusiasts paid the islanders £40 for the temple's treasures, dug out of the earth sixteen statues, and had them boxed and shipped in stealth to Zante, off the western shore of Greece, where they were put up for auction. The Englishmen hoped to obtain the marbles for the British Museum, but the English bid never reached Zante and the haul went to Prince Ludwig of Bavaria for 10,000 sequins. The masterworks, which are carved in a style transitional from the Archaic to the Phidian, wound up in Munich, where they have pride of place in the Glyptothek.

There was a characteristic postscript. Prince Ludwig's marvelous acquisition was dismissed as "primitive," a word used by Goethe himself in shrugging off as merely interesting these superb figures (as we now judge them) of archers, warriors, goddesses, and athletes. When Canova, the famous sculptor, was asked by Lord Elgin to restore the Parthenon figures, he replied that it would be sacrilege "to presume to touch them with a chisel." But the Danish neo-classic artist Thorwaldsen saw nothing blasphemous about using his chisel to "improve" the Aegina statuary.

Its European pillagers mistakenly concluded that the Aegina temple belonged to Zeus; we now know it was sacred to Aphaia, a nymph who had Zeus as a father and who was a favorite of Demeter's. Greek archaeologists have restored and strengthened the temple's columns, and have also set in their old place the original pedimental sculptures, made earlier than the Glyptothek marbles, which were miraculously rediscovered in the earth nearby. It is pleasant to visit, and from the temple's hilltop site one looks out on an effervescent sea and around to fields dotted with asphodels.

Sounion, the last stop, is more Odyssean in its appeal. The fifteen surviving columns of a temple which stood on this promontory over a seacoast near Athens are not as impressive as the Temple of Aphaia. But the setting has a compulsive sorcery. At dusk, when the big tourist vans leave, the sea acquires violet menace; the slender columns of the Temple of Poseidon become the masts of a vessel outlined against a brilliant sky. We who stand within it share the exultation of the ancient seamen who knew that when they saw the silhouette of Sounion they were back in Greek waters.

Yet at Sounion one can again reflect on the deceptive power of ruins.

Sounion The surviving columns of a temple believed to have been dedicated to Poseidon are embossed on an Attic sunset in this fine photograph by Roloff Beny, a specialist in ruins, who comes close to being the Piranesi of the camera. (From *A Time of Gods: A Photographer in the Wake of Odysseus*, London: Thames and Hudson, 1962)

Lord Byron, whose carved name is still visible on one of the columns, wrote these too familiar lines:

> Place me on Sunium's marbled steep,
>   Where nothing, save the waves and I
> May hear our mutual murmurs sweep:
>   There, swan-like, let me sing and die.

If Byron had been at Sounion during the Periclean Age, he might also have heard the crack of a lash and clatter of chains. Not far from Sounion are the hills of Laurium, honeycombed with the mines whose silver, lead, zinc, and manganese helped enrich Athens. In these tunnels, seldom more than a yard high, archaeologists have found the rings driven into the walls to chain the slaves and felons who dug for ore. Sounion's loveliness cannot efface the fact that Athens in its glory accepted as natural the servitude of slaves.

But surely the Greeks themselves would have preferred us to take an unsentimental view of their world, which had marvels enough. There is a verse appropriate to Sounion, this passage from Sophocles:

> Numberless are the world's wonders, but none
> More wonderful than man; the stormgrey sea
> Yields to his prows, the huge crests bear him high;
> Earth, holy and inexhaustible, is graven
> With shining furrows where his plows have gone
> Year after year, the timeless labor of stallions.
> The lightboned birds and beasts that cling to cover,
> The lithe fish lighting their reaches of dim water,
> All are taken, tamed in the net of his mind;
> The lion on the hill, the wild horse windy-maned,
> Resign to him; and his blunt yoke has broken
> The sultry shoulders of the mountain bull.
>
>   [*Antigone*, translation by Dudley
>   Fitts and Robert Fitzgerald]

Chapter Six

REALM OF POWER

ITALY

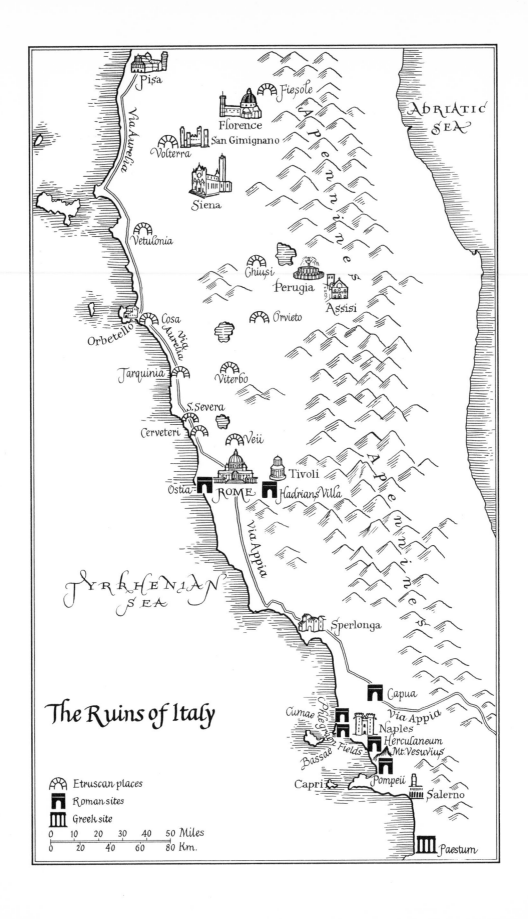

The Ruins of Italy

Pisa
Fiesole
ADRIATIC SEA
Via Aurelia
Florence
San Gimignano
Volterra
Siena
Apennines
Vetulonia
Chiusi
Perugia
Assisi
Cosa
Orvieto
Orbetello
Via Aurelia
Tarquinia
Viterbo
S. Severa
Cerveteri
Veii
Tivoli
Ostia
ROME
Hadrian's Villa
Apennines
Via Appia
TYRRHENIAN SEA
Sperlonga
Capua
Via Appia
Cumae
Naples
Phlegrean Fields
Herculaneum
Bassae Fields
Mt. Vesuvius
Capri
Pompeii
Salerno
Paestum

Etruscan places
Roman sites
Greek site

0 10 20 30 40 50 Miles
0 20 40 60 80 Km.

I

A CONTAGION OF ROME

Time makes all things worse.
DEMETRIUS, Fragment, c. 415 B.C.

IT IS IMPOSSIBLE to be indifferent to Rome. "At last for the first time I live," wrote Henry James, who went "reeling and moaning through the streets in a fever of excitement." A century earlier Boswell was "seized with enthusiasm" when he saw the ruins of Rome, so much so that he began chattering in Latin to his startled companion, a Mr. Morison. "He laughed a little at the beginning," Boswell noted in his diary. "But we made a resolution to speak Latin continually during this course of antiquities."

Goethe was easily enraptured. "Everything is just as I imagined it, yet everything is new," he reported to his friends in Weimar. "I have not had a single idea which is new or surprising, but my ideas have become so much more firm, vital and coherent that they could be called new." After three weeks in Rome, Byron succumbed to ruin-melancholy, a mood that elicited whole stanzas of *Childe Harold*, this being the message:

> There is the moral of all human tales;
> 'Tis but the same rehearsal of the past;
> First freedom, and then glory—when that fails,
> Wealth, vice, corruption, barbarism at last.

Moralizing about the ruins is surely the most prevalent spectator sport in Eternal Rome since the Christians closed the Colosseum. In joining in, one must modestly emulate Goethe; there is nothing new or surprising that can be said on the subject. I venture these thoughts simply because they are not so commonly expressed: that the Roman ruins are ugly, that their effect on Italian politics in our times has been mischievous, and that classical Rome was a better place than its remains would ever lead one to guess.

Save for the Pantheon, Hadrian's Villa, and perhaps the Colosseum, there is little that is visually pleasing among the Roman ruins. There are two reasons for this. Most of the remains date from the later period of the Roman Empire, when taste was debased. The second reason is a simple structural fact. The Greeks built of stone and used no mortar; the Romans favored brick and concrete. On his deathbed Augustus boasted that he had found Rome a city of brick and left it a city of marble, but the change was achieved chiefly by putting a stone facing over the humbler brick. Most of the marble on the ruins was plundered long ago by Renaissance popes and princes. The great sites—the Palatine Hill, the various forums, Nero's Golden House, and the massive baths—are clumps of brick and a few forlorn columns. Denuded of their shrubbery, they have lost the charm found in Piranesi prints. Without their ornament, they are brute assertions of Roman power.

As such, ruins can be a dangerous intoxicant. In *Pleasure of Ruins*, Rose Macaulay writes: "To be surrounded by great ruins is seldom safe; they have a singular effect on the mind. The Romans, always thus surrounded, were never safe, and life for them was an unsteady affair. To live among all that strange broken grandeur was more than any but equable spirits could endure tranquilly, and few Romans have had equable spirits."

Two of the maddest episodes in Italian politics are connected with the power of ruins over the Roman imagination, the first being the rise of Cola di Rienzo, who in 1347 proclaimed the Restoration of the Roman Republic, styling himself "Nicholas, severe and merciful, deliverer of Rome, defender of Italy, friend of mankind, and of liberty, peace and justice, tribune august." *

Cola was the son of an innkeeper and a washerwoman, and as a youth he was obsessed with the grandeur of antiquity. He was among the first to copy down the inscriptions on the ruins. A superlative orator, he took to declaiming to the Roman people about their vanished glories: "Where are now these Romans? Their virtue, their justice, their power? Why was I not born in those happy times?" It was a period of confusion in Rome—the Papal See was then in Avignon—and Cola actually managed to install himself as a Roman Tribune, disclosing that his goal was to unite Italy and Europe under his leadership. He had a preference for making speeches from a balcony. He liked clothing his followers in brilliant costumes. His reign lasted seven months, ending when Roman nobles grew weary of his ranting and overthrew him. During a vain attempt to regain power, Cola was killed by a

---

* Cola was more modest than the Emperors. The half-mad Commodus began his messages to the Senate this way: "Pacifier of the Universe, Invincible, the Roman Hercules, Pontifex Maximus, Holder of the Tribuncian Authority for the eighteenth, Imperator for the eighth, Consul for the seventh time, Father of his Country, to consuls, praetors, tribunes and the fortunate Commodan Senate, Greetings!"

Roman mob, which strung him up by his heels and left his body hanging on a public square.

Benito Mussolini, Cola's spiritual heir, was no less infatuated with the Roman past. After seizing power, the Duce became Italy's most generous patron of archaeology. He ordered construction of the Via dell'Impero (now Via dei Fori Imperiali), a grandiose boulevard linking the Colosseum to his own Palazzo Venezia, with its famous balcony. A map of the ancient Empire at its greatest extent was proudly displayed near the Roman Forum. The nearby forums of the various Caesars—Julius, Augustus, Nerva, and Trajan—were exhumed at prodigious expense. The Duce himself was personally on hand when Lake Nemi was partially drained to raise up a well-preserved ship built for Caligula (the Nazis wantonly burned the ship in 1944). Archaeologists were under orders to dig up the Augustan Altar of Peace in time to celebrate the bimillenary of the Emperor's birth on September 23, 1938. The deadline was met. More than 600,000 cubic yards of earth were moved at Ostia to prepare the old Roman port for an exhibition that was to have been held in 1942. So ravenous was the Duce's appetite for ruins that when a high fence was placed around excavations at Largo Argentina, in the center of Rome, the popular belief was that Mussolini had secretly dragged some old stones to the site to fabricate a ruin.

The dictator commemorated the conquest of Ethiopia in imperial style, by building a forum. The Foro Mussolini has been renamed Foro Italico, but the sixty-five statues of muscular athletes, the three stadia, and the Fascist inscriptions can still be seen. One of the slogans repeated many times on the pavement reads:

> MANY ENEMIES
>
> MUCH HONOR
>
> MANY ENEMIES
>
> MUCH HONOR

Other slogans say more simply: DUCE DUCE DUCE DUCE, while underneath a picture of happy Fascist workmen there is this sentence: ITALY FINALLY HAS HER EMPIRE.

Like Cola, Mussolini changed the calendar to conform to Roman style. Luigi Barzini records that only three days before he himself was strung up like Cola, the Duce proudly inscribed a photograph he gave to a journalist: "Anno XXIII E.F.," or Year 23 of the Fascist Era. But the Duce's benefactions to archaeology are now officially forgotten, like the Fascist era itself. His name does not appear in a single guidebook to any of the ruins bared to glorify his regime.

Ancient Rome cannot be judged by Mussolini's pathetic attempt to revive it, nor should it be judged by its ugly remains. One could be forgiven

sion that the classical Romans did little but bathe, watch the
of gladiators, and dwell in palatial depravity. The qualities that are
imirable in Rome could hardly be deduced from the ruins—the belief
v, the universal temper of mind, and, above all, what Pliny called "the
pendous majesty of the Roman peace." Greek cities in the Imperial system
vere not wholly insincere in expressing fulsome thanks for the essential
mildness of Roman rule in an era of unprecedented peace. Roman citizenship
was prized precisely because the citizen enjoyed genuine rights, and it was
ultimately extended to everyone in the Empire (save, of course, women and
slaves). In the celebrated verdict of Gibbon, the human race was most happy
during the reign of the Four Good Emperors, Trajan, Hadrian, Antoninus
Pius, and Marcus Aurelius. As Gibbon asserts, "The vast extent of the Roman
Empire was governed by absolute power, under the guidance of virtue and
wisdom. The armies were restrained by the firm but gentle hand of four
successive emperors whose character and authority commanded involuntary
respect."

But there is little poetry in Roman power. The ruins are the relics of a
people who were not architects so much as engineers, not poets but soldiers
and lawyers, not creators but imitators. They were very like Americans, who
face the same risk that posterity will judge their civilization by the ruins of
the Pentagon while the Declaration of Independence is lost somewhere in the
rubble.

II

ROMAN PLACES

> *Look around: you see a little supper room:*
> *But from my window, lo! great Caesar's*
> *tomb!*
> *And the great dead themselves, with jovial*
> *breath*
> *Bid you be merry, and remember death.*
> MARTIAL, Epigrams, II:59

ROME, a city that lives in the shrouds of its greatness, is a place where it is
difficult to ignore archaeology. The Romans have learned to cohabit with
their past, which provides a distinctive backdrop for a mingling of activities:
eating, singing, whoring, pocket-picking, homosexuality, and the noisy mat-
ing of cats.

Thus, it is possible to dine by candlelight near the place where great
Caesar was felled by twenty-three dagger wounds. He was murdered not in
the Forum, but at the Theater of Pompey, whose buried entrance now forms

The Roman Forum Looking to the Capitoline. In the foreground of this engraving (c. 1810) is the Arch of Titus, on whose jambs is depicted the Triumph celebrating the sack of Jerusalem. Cattle for centuries were a bucolic fixture in the Forum.

a grotto for the restaurant di Pancrazio at 92 Piazza del Biscione. Every summer opera is performed in the Baths of Caracalla, an innovation begun under Mussolini in 1937. Prostitutes loiter hopefully among the tombs in the old Appian Way, as their sisters did in classical times. Pickpockets are a well-known menace in the Colosseum, which was also recently colonized by homosexuals, who took over two sections of the Amphitheater for midnight meetings. Cats show a marked preference for the Pantheon, and there was a scandal a few years ago when the Department of Fine Arts and Archaeology threatened to reduce their numbers. The newspaper *Messaggero* commented sharply: "Let the Ministry be warned that animal lovers are found not only abroad, and in Italy they are not limited to 'dear, kind-hearted ladies' and to a few 'obsessed' souls, but are an immense if invisible army."

I have the impression that Romans are more devoted to the cats than to the ruins, whose ubiquity has bred a certain contempt. As a result, Rome is declining and falling still, and one must hurry to look at it while there is yet something left.*

Some Roman ruins gape from craters, some resemble a bomb-site, and some of the most memorable are seldom included in the standard tourist itinerary. In the last group are the Ara Pacis Augustus, or Altar of Peace of

---

* Even the Appian Way is in peril. Incredibly, developers are proposing that the most famous of Roman roads should be lined by apartment complexes, while preservationists are urging that the Appian Way become a six-mile-long recreational park. If the commercial pressure prevails, no doubt one can expect a Quo Vadis Supermarket to mark the place where St. Peter paused in his flight from Rome.

The Roman Forum Looking to the Tarpeian Rock, from which traitors were flung. The Column of Phocas (right) preserves the memory of an otherwise totally obscure and reputedly wicked later Emperor, now remembered solely because of this phallic souvenir. (PHOTO CURTIS BILL PEPPER)

Augustus, and the Pyramid of Cestius, which overlooks the tiny graveyard in which Keats and Shelley are buried.

The Altar is on the Via di Ripetta, near the Augusteo, the mausoleum of the Emperor, and its recovery is one of the feats of archaeology. The existence of the Altar was long known because fragments of it had come to light in earlier centuries, but the greater part of it was buried in muddy earth far below immovable modern buildings. A gifted excavator, Giuseppe Moretti, Rome's Curator of Antiquities, froze the mud so that the buried slabs could be painstakingly retrieved without weakening the substructure of nearby buildings. Copies were made of fragments owned by other museums, and the whole Altar put together and housed in an ugly concrete shed of Late Fascist style (building this and clearing the Augusteo in 1942 were Mussolini's last ventures in archaeology).

The Altar was dedicated in 13 A.D., and was clearly intended to improve the Imperial image; its principal frieze shows Augustus and his circle walking in a dignified procession to celebrate the Pax Romana. Its classical spirit, graceful and severe, is Augustan in the best sense, and in the Altar one finds the *gravitas* that is missing from the bloated ruins left by later Emperors. Yet it is propaganda nonetheless. One would not guess from this Altar of Peace built in the Field of Mars that the Julio-Claudian dynasty excelled in conspiracy, poisoning, and madness.

Across Rome, near the Porta Ostiense, is the Pyramid of Cestius, which I mention for reasons that are unashamedly romantic. To visit the Pyramid and the small cemetery that adjoins it is to return to Piranesi's Rome, when vines still softened the indestructible ruins. The Protestant Cemetery is entered through a gate which, as it clangs shut, closes out the roar and fumes of the Roman traffic. A miscellany of people are interred in this graveyard set aside in the eighteenth century for the non-Catholic dead, including Goethe's only son, August; Gramsci, a founder of Italian communism; and Shelley and Keats.

When Shelley visited the cemetery in 1818, he was deeply touched by its solemn beauty, the sun shining on its bright grass, and the whisper of wind among the trees that have overgrown the tomb of Cestius. "One might, if one were to die, desire the sleep they seem to sleep," he wrote to a friend of the tranquil dead. In four years Keats was buried there, to be joined in 1823 by Shelley in the shadow of the "one keen pyramid with wedge sublime" (Shelley's phrase in *Adonais*).

The pyramid was built as a tomb for Caius Cestius, a thoroughly obscure praetor and tribune who died sometime before 12 B.C., when Egypt and its symbols were very much in the Roman mind. The pyramid was spared because it happened to be joined to the Aurelian Wall built some four centuries later. It has scant architectural or historical importance and its

The Pyramid of Cestius In the shadow of the "keen pyramid with wedge sublime" lie the graves of Keats and Shelley in a cemetery which preserves the mood of fragrant decay in this Piranesi print.

location next to the cemetery is a miraculous accident. The result is a place where poetry, not power, for once has the final word.

For a whiff of Rome's power, one must go to the Colosseum, the Forum, and the monstrous baths. The Colosseum was the Roman counterpart of an American cultural center: a building financed by the socially ambitious whose touchstone was cost and quantity. Begun by the soldier-emperor Vespasian and completed by his son Titus, the amphitheater is as much a pile of imposing statistics as imposing stone. It could seat up to 45,000 persons who in a single session might witness the slaughter of 11,000 beasts and the combat of 5,000 pairs of gladiators. Chroniclers record that the millennium of the city was celebrated in 240 A.D. with the extermination of 30 elephants, 10 elks, 10 tigers, 10 wild lions and 60 tame ones, 10 hyenas, 19 giraffes, 20 wild asses, 40 wild horses, one hippopotamus, one rhinoceros, plus the combat of 1,000 pairs of gladiators. In 281 A.D., on the occasion of a triumph, 100 magnificent lions were loosed in the amphitheater, and were followed by 100 lionesses, 100 leopards from Nubia, 100 leopards from Syria, and 300 bears. The resulting roar was said to have shaken the building to its foundations.

Even as a ruin the Colosseum has yielded impressive statistics—it was once famous for its 420 varieties of flora, many unique in Italy to the amphitheater itself. The plants were ripped out in 1871, leaving the arena like a deserted and decaying slaughterhouse.

The gladiatorial matches continued from 80 A.D. until at least 405, and the last recorded animal spectacle was in 523. In few places does one have a better sense of the wastefulness of the Empire; one could have built a hundred Parthenons with the money needed to stage the games. Other statistics are suggestive. Estimates of the population of Rome at the height of Empire range from 600,000 to 2,000,000. The needs of this population were met by 11 great public baths, 856 private baths, 1,152 fountains, 11 aqueducts, 190 granaries, 254 flour mills, 28 libraries, 3 theaters, 2 circuses, 2 amphitheaters, 4 schools for gladiators and 2 arenas for naval shows. The city itself was divided into 423 districts, served by eight bridges over the Tiber, entered through 37 gates in the Aurelian Wall, provided with 8 parks, 11 forums, 10 basilicas, 29 major thoroughfares and countless smaller streets, and adorned with 36 marble arches. The Empire probably died of urban thrombosis as much as anything else.

Standing at the center of this sprawling city, and of the Empire itself, was the Roman Forum, which became a pathless waste by the tenth century

The Fora of the Caesars   Julius Caesar's Forum is in the foreground and Trajan's in the background; both were excavated during the ruin craze of the Mussolini era. (PHOTO CURTIS BILL PEPPER)

and which is now a shadeless archaeological site scooped from the covering earth. This is where tradition asserts the city was founded in 753 B.C., here were located the Tomb of Romulus, the Umbilicus Urbis Romae (marking the imaginary center of the city), and the Golden Milestone, on which distances to great cities in the Empire were inscribed. Here also were the Senate, the Rostra, and the Temple of Vesta, in which the six Vestal virgins lived. Over the Forum loom the Capitol, the Tarpeian Rock, from which traitors were flung, and the decaying palaces on Palatine Hill. But in their present desolate state none of these gives more than a faint echo of Rome before the Fall. There are two exceptions—the Arches of Titus and Severus. Sculptured in the jambs are the Legions, the sinews of the Empire, and on the Arch of Titus the soldiers can be seen carrying in triumph the seven-branched menorah of the Temple in Jerusalem, which Titus sacked.

Here is the incarnation of Roman power: unawed by alien gods, visible or invisible, turning the holy relics of the Temple of Solomon into flashy spoils for a triumph. One is reminded of Gibbon's half-admiring summation: "The various modes of worship which prevailed in the Roman world were all considered by the people as equally true; by the philosopher as equally false; and by the magistrates as equally useful."

When foreign religions ceased to be useful, they were put savagely in their place, providing fresh material for gossip in the baths. The baths are the most unappealing relics of Roman power. Their scale is absurd. In the Baths of Diocletian, 3,000 Romans could refresh themselves in three immense pools, the *calidarium, tepidarium,* and *frigidarium*—and this was only one of eleven great public *thermae*. Even as a looted ruin the Baths provide ample space for a large church and an enormous museum. (Pope Sixtus V demolished a fifth of the baths with gunpowder blasts in 1586–1589, using the brick for a villa for his sister and a chapel.)

The other survivor, the Baths of Caracalla, was nearly as big, the central block measuring around 118,000 square yards as against 130,000 square yards at Diocletian. The lofty main entrance inspired the design of the now-demolished Pennsylvania Station in New York, and the ruins enclose the world's largest opera stage (the platform occupies 270,000 square feet, spacious enough to hold the Houses of Parliament). In this depressing immensity —the Baths as a whole are a mile in circumference—the human scale is lost. One pictures fat, waddling men being toweled by slaves, doing their ablutions in a canyon of fake marble. Eleanor Clark, in her admirable *Rome and a Villa*, puts it justly: "Nobody loves the ancient Romans anywhere, though they may feel bound to respect them, but it is in the baths that you love them least." *

---

* A final statistic: The baths and fountains of Rome were fed by eleven aqueducts with a total length of about 350 miles which, according to the engineer Frontinus writing in 97 A.D., could supply 97 *billion* gallons a year. The figure has been dismissed as absurdly high, but no

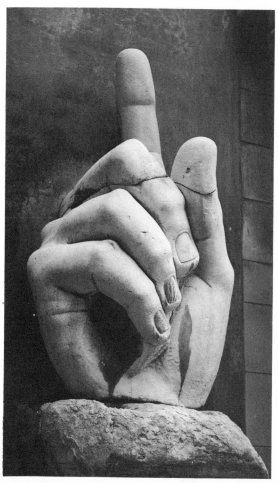

Pieces of Constantine The finger and head of the Emperor are now in the courtyard of the Palazzo dei Conservatori at Campidoglio. The fragments survive because Constantine's conversion gave his relics a certain immunity from Christian plunderers. (PHOTOS CURTIS BILL PEPPER)

There is little that is lovable, intimate, or personal among the monumental ruins of Rome, but the shadows play less heavily on the ruins left by Hadrian. Spanish-born and despised in his lifetime as "the Greekling," Hadrian has a hexagonal fascination. The historian Aurelius Victor asserts that the Emperor was an expert in song, lyre, and medicine; he was a geometer, a painter, and a sculptor in bronze and marble "second only to Polycletus and Euphranus." He had an astonishing memory, a supple wit, and limitless energy. He ruled for twenty-one years, and in the end he wished he were dead.

His memoirs, alas, have been lost, but some poems survive. Once a friend named Florus sent him these lines:

> I don't want to be a Caesar
> Sauntering among the Britons
> Lying low among the Germans,
> Putting up with Scythian winters.

To which Hadrian replied:

> I don't want to be a Florus
> Sauntering among the taverns,
> Lying low among the cook-shops,
> Putting up with fat mosquitoes.

The Emperor was unconventional in his curiosity, which made travel an obsession. He was Roman in his impatience with the Jews, whom he destroyed as a nation. He was Greek in his skepticism, his devotion to beauty, and in his passion for Antinoüs, his Bithynian favorite. He was thoroughly complicated and has not implausibly been called the first modern man.

Among his skills, Hadrian was a master architect, with the ability to make the sky, the water, and the forest an integral part of his plastic vision. Consider his masterpiece, the Pantheon. For centuries this unique structure, the oldest standing roofed temple, was ascribed to Agrippa, the son-in-law of Augustus, who was the first great builder in the Imperial era. In 1892 a French expert found that the Pantheon was made entirely of brick stamped with dates within Hadrian's reign. The confusion arose because an earlier temple had existed on the site, and in replacing it Hadrian followed the modest Roman custom of inscribing the name of the original builder on the portico, where it can still be easily read.

Only the exterior of the Pantheon is unprepossessing. Within, Hadrian

---

one doubts that the capacity of this waterworks matched modern urban standards. In describing the aqueducts, Frontinus strikes the authentic Roman note: "With such an array of indispensable structures carrying so many waters, compare, if you will, the idle Pyramids or the useless, though famous, works of the Greeks!"

Hadrian's Villa The swans quicken the spectral melancholy of the Canopus, a finger of water inspired by the temple on the Nile which Hadrian built to preserve the memory of his lover Antinoüs. (PHOTO CURTIS BILL PEPPER)

fused Greek taste with Roman engineering to create an interior that is (in Shelley's words) "the visible image of the universe." He opened a great eye in the dome, making the sky itself part of the design. Clouds roof the temple, and the sun stamps a moving circle of light on the walls. The interior is almost a perfect circle, with a diameter equal to its height, and the dome is ingeniously built with a crown of light pumice that increases in thickness as it descends to concrete supports. The Pantheon is both durable and felicitous. Even the Renaissance Popes could not bring themselves to employ their crowbars and gunpowder against it (though for a while it was "improved" with two bell towers, known as the asses' ears).

If the sky infiltrates the Pantheon, the artful use of water and landscape enchants the sprawl of ruins in Tivoli, twenty-five miles east of Rome. Hadrian apparently began this villa when he became Emperor in 117 A.D. and work continued on it until his death in 138. Though ravaged by time, looters, and the Holy See, enough remains on the 750-acre tract to convey an impression of an Emperor whose life was a restless search for a defining style: it is an epiphany of stones, shrubs, and cunningly deployed water.

Scholars venomously dispute the names of the buildings. One authority asserts that Tivoli contains copies of the Lyceum, the Academy, the Prytaneum, and the Painted Stoa, all of which Hadrian had admired in Athens. My own guidebook is a collection of dubieties, referring to "the so-called libraries," "the so-called palace peristyle," and "the so-called Praetorium." But no matter: the labels are only a convenience, and Tivoli's patina is mellower through the mist. Among the intensely personal buildings is the "Maritime Theater," a circular colonnade planted on a moated island which the Emperor reached over a drawbridge when he wanted seclusion. It is a geometer's delight, presenting in a tiny compass a diversity of views, none of them displeasing (it was restored by an Italian tire manufacturer, who saw in its shape a resemblance to his product). The island is the epitome of discreet civility, like a Haydn quartet.

A sadder place is the Canopus, a long finger of water framed by a colonnade and leading to a half-domed grotto. Scholars are in accord in seeing in this a copy of the Canopus, a celebrated sanctuary to the god Serapis near Alexandria. It was built late in Hadrian's reign, and is almost surely connected with the memory of Antinoüs, who was drowned in the Nile. The Canopus has been capably restored by Italian archaeologists, who have had copies made of the Greek statues once found here and removed elsewhere. Swans glide in the lagoon, their whiteness matching the spectral reflection of the pensive statuary. In this solitude one can almost hear the swans breathe and feel the pain of Hadrian, alone and ill, waiting to die, writing these lines:

Hadrian's Tomb   There was originally a hillock crowning the tomb which the Emperor designed for himself and which later became the dungeon and papal fortress known as Castel Sant'Angelo, the name recalling the miraculous appearance of the Archangel during one of Rome's many calamities. (PHOTO CURTIS BILL PEPPER)

Animula, blandula, vagula,
Hospes comesque corporis
Quae nunc abibis in loca,
Pallidula, rigidam nodula?
Net ut soles dabis jocos.

O blithe little soul, thou, flitting away.
Guest and comrade of this my clay,
Whither now goest thou, to what place
Bare and ghostly and without grace?
Nor, as thy wont was, joke and play.
[*Translation by A. O'Brien-Moore*]

When he died, Hadrian's ashes were placed in a mausoleum begun before his death and inspired by a similar tomb built by Augustus. Known for centuries as Castel Sant'Angelo (because a statue of the Archangel Michael crowns it), Hadrian's tomb is inseparably linked with the fall of Rome and its rebirth as a modern city. Now a stumpy turret on the banks of the Tiber, the tomb was originally crowned by statuary and a tumulus of trees. The statues were used as weapons against the Goths in 537; the Romans threw them down on the attackers, so that shattered marble limbs were mixed with real severed legs and heads, a grisly picture. Later the tomb became a papal prison, then a fortress, and finally a military museum. From its parapets Cellini claimed that he killed the Constable of Bourbon, commander of the siege of Rome in 1527. It is a gloomy place, filled with grim passages, but from its summit there is a magnificent view, vindicating Hadrian's choice of site. Looking out on the Eternal City, upon a skyline that blends a hundred borrowed styles, one reflects that Rome has paid a price for its universalism. Rome is more cannibal than creator, a voracious consumer of the wealth and ideas of others. Even the cultivated Hadrian was, in the final analysis, an inspired eclectic who spent a lifetime shopping elsewhere for an identity.

The Roman Forum Looking toward the Palatine Hill. The Forum was excavated decades ago, but no one has yet solved the problem of how to landscape it attractively. (PHOTO CURTIS BILL PEPPER)

III

ETRUSCAN TRACES

The Etruscans are not a theory or a thesis.
If they are anything, they are an experience.
D. H. LAWRENCE, Etruscan Places

IF THE ROMANS ARE SEVERELY JUDGED because of the ruins they left behind, the Etruscans, whom the Romans extinguished as a people, benefit from exactly the same condition. Hardly anything remains of the homes and temples of the Etruscans; their literature has been wholly lost; their language and origins are imperfectly understood. What does survive are the tombs, and it is these that provide most of the material evidence for their civilization. If the Etruscans live in our imagination, it is because they died with such style.

What tombs they are! Treasures from them are gathered in the Villa Giulia, an old Roman estate that has been cunningly converted into an Etruscan museum. How can anyone dislike this people after seeing the life-size terracotta of a husband and wife, found in Cerveteri? The couple repose on their sarcophagus and amiably beckon to us to join their invisible feast in Etruscan heaven.

Authorities, modern and ancient, with a few distinguished exceptions, believe that the Etruscans migrated from Asia Minor to Italy, where by 700 B.C. they occupied much of Tuscany and Umbria. They came briefly to dominate Rome; a revolt against the last Etruscan king, Tarquin the Proud, c. 510 B.C. led to the founding of the republic. From this point, as Rome expanded, the power of the loosely federated Etruscan cities waned. By the time of Augustus the Etruscans were already overwhelmed and assimilated, their language almost a memory.

The Romans tend to be spiteful in their references to their defeated rivals: the Etruscans, they said, were obsessed with superstitious divinations, allowed women too many liberties, were untrustworthy and given to gluttony. But it was also admitted that the Etruscans had charm, that they were devoted to good living, the dance and music. In a third-century A.D. work on zoology, the Etruscans were credited with such skill on the Tuscan pipe that pigs, stags, and dogs were enraptured by the music. The piper, writes Aelian, "avoids so far as possible regular melodies and loud sounds and plays the sweetest tone the double pipe can produce. In the silent solitude his airs float

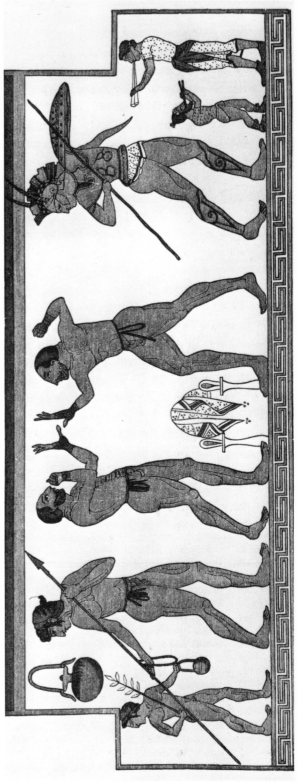

Etruscan Murals at Chiusi Wrestlers, horse racers, and monkeys enliven this characteristic mural in Tomba della Scimmia; boxers and dwarfs adorn the facing mural in the same tomb. The engravings are from the pioneering work by Dennis, *Cities and Cemeteries of Etruria.*

up to the tops of mountains, into gorges and thickets, into all the retreats and breeding-ground of the game." The animals were irresistibly attracted and then trapped.

Regrettably, the Etruscans cannot speak for themselves because, of the 10,000 extant texts, most are short inscriptions and the known vocabulary consists of only about 120 words. In 1964 a bilingual inscription was discovered at Santa Severa, a tiny seaside resort thirty miles north of Rome. The inscription was on two gold tablets used to dedicate a temple to the goddess Astarte, the Ishtar of the Bible. The contents were a surprise: the roughly parallel texts were in Etruscan and Punic, the language of Carthage and the Phoenicians. This was a line of contact that scholars had hardly suspected, and its implications are a matter of recondite debate. But the tablets do little to fill a tantalizing void caused by an absence of texts.

One would like to know more about Etruscan religion, which was an exotic variant of Greek beliefs. Among the curious gods in their infernal demonology was Tuchulcha, with the face of a vulture, the ears of a donkey, and armed with snakes. They believed in eight super-divinities, each of whom could throw thunderbolts; all were subordinate to Tinia, who was equipped with three red thunderbolts, one so potent that it could be tossed only if the other gods agreed. There was also the fatalistic Etruscan fascination with the nail. The driving of a nail was seen as an acceptance of destiny, and in some temples the passing of a year was observed by a "year-nail" hammered into the wall.

The Etruscans were devoted to haruspicy, the art of the soothsayer in forecasting the future by examining the entrails of animals. A bronze liver survives in which each part of the model organ is marked with an inscription to help the haruspex divine its meaning. They could not have been wholly foolish in their beliefs because a seer foretold that Etruscan civilization would perish at just about the time it did. With a cheerful fatalism, the Etruscans vanished, leaving only a Cheshire smile behind.

"Museums, museums, museums," erupted D. H. Lawrence, "object lessons rigged out to illustrate the unsound theories of archaeologists, crazy attempts to coordinate and get into fixed order that which has no fixed order and will never be coordinated! It is sickening!" The Etruscans are in complicity with the Lawrentian view, because their remains have no fixed order. Each of their cities is distinctive in its art, its burial customs, and its flavor, however unified by a common vivacity.

"City" is a misnomer, since little survives but the graveyards. For example, Cerveteri, site of ancient Caere, has a burial area covering a thousand acres, triple the size of the city itself. Of the actual city almost nothing is left,

Tomb of the Reliefs, Cerveteri Homely houseware make this a tomb of immeasurable documentary importance. The onlooking skeleton in this engraving, also from Dennis, is regrettably not visible today.

since domestic buildings were made of perishable wood. But the necropolis has almost an urban flavor to it. Burial mounds were favored in Caere, and it is pleasant to walk among these humps of earth, some topped by holm oak or olive trees, the hillocks like dwellings set among grassy thoroughfares.

In Caere's most important tomb, the Grotta Bella, the sense of a living presence is intensified by stucco reliefs showing all the implements needed to make a banquet for the dead. It is a little like a fallout shelter, complete with bunks carved in the walls for the now-vanished bodies. All around, in painted relief, is the homely kitchenware: ladles, axes, spits, knives, coils of rope, jugs, and pots. It is the grave of a good consumer and a hopeful gourmet.

North of Cerveteri, past Santa Severa, where the parallel texts were found, lies Tarquinia, which used to be Corneto until Mussolini restored its ancient name. The necropolis of Tarquinia, the mother-city of Etruria, is wholly underground, and its graves are painted with the murals that more than anything else have fixed our image of the Etruscans. The paintings show the delights of an afterlife without the formalized solemnity found in Egyptian tombs. The gaiety is almost shocking. The Tomb of the Boar Hunt was visited in the nineteenth century by George Dennis, an English savant and pioneer Etruscologist. He studied the banqueting scene, in which a female of

The Pleasures of Death Carved on their sarcophagus, this blithe couple illustrate the lighthearted Etruscan view of death, which scandalized the Romans and captivated D. H. Lawrence. (COLLECTION BOSTON MUSEUM OF FINE ARTS)

exquisite beauty throws her arms around a lover while guests quaff wine. "Can this be a resting place of the dead?" asked Dennis in his *Cities and Cemeteries of Etruria.* "Can these scenes of feasting and merriment, this dancing, this piping, this sporting, appertain to a tomb?"

The same question prompted the Romans to dismiss the Etruscans as licentious; for his part, Lawrence was totally captivated. He found phallic symbols everywhere in Etruria ("Here it is, big and little, standing by the doors, or inserted, quite small into the rock: the phallic stone!"). In fact, as best as can be determined, the Etruscans were rigorously monogamous, and differed most notably from Greeks and Romans in the social equality permitted women.

Yet in visiting the painted tombs of Tarquinia one does get an impression of an appealing frivolity that contrasts with the severity of Republican Rome. Only a short drive from Tarquinia are the ruins of Cosa, a Roman frontier town with bastions hard as a fist. Here one vividly sees the contrast. Reached by a hike up the hill from the pleasant seaside resort of Ansedonia, the ruins are desolate—the loudest sound is a cowbell—and the view of the Tyrrhenian Sea is exhilarating. Cosa has a mile and a half of rugged walls, with eighteen towers spaced a bowshot apart. Here one senses what the loosely federated, individualistic Etruscan cities were up against.

To go from Cerveteri and Tarquinia in southern Etruria to Volterra and Chiusi in northern Etruria makes one even more aware of the fissiparous

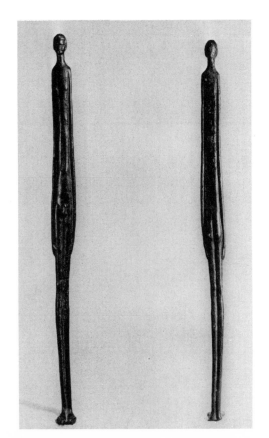

Volterra's Stick Men These votive bronze statues are in a style which anticipates Giacometti. (COURTESY ETRUSCAN MUSEUM, VOLTERRA)

vitality of the vanished race. Volterra is thirty-one miles from Siena, poised on a hill in a Tuscan setting. In narrow streets in the walled citadel workmen grind away at the local alabaster, making souvenirs and chess sets. The same material was used by Etruscans, many of whom were interred in cinerary chests of a uniform type, each with a sculptured top showing a contented Etruscan lying with his left hand on a pile of cushions, his right hand holding a round bowl. The Volterra Museum is packed with such casks, but it also contains bronze figures with stick-like legs that uncannily resemble the sculpture of Giacometti. Elsewhere in the city the Etruscan traces have been rubbed away, like the three featureless faces that gape blankly above the Porta dell-Arco, once the gate to the ancient walled city.

Chiusi, which can be reached on an easy side trip on returning to Rome via the Highway of the Sun, has not only an excellent museum but several fine tombs. The best is the Tomb of the Monkey, showing a wrestling match and horse races, with a monkey looking on enigmatically, as if to referee. Another burial place, The Tomb of the Two Chariots, is the only one with a hinged door in it, and on its frieze a score of Etruscans are taking part in funereal games, the chariots posted next to cypress trees. A virile athleticism lingers in Chiusi, once Clusium, the city of Lars Porsena, whose soldiers fought Horatius at the bridge.

The museum displays another variant of the Etruscan burial—funeral urns capped by a stylized face, with arms frequently doubling as handles. In going through the Chiusi Museum, with its rich array of urns, masks, and busts, one is led to puzzle at the strangely uneven quality of Etruscan art. It has been expressed well by Massimo Pallotino, the pre-eminent authority on the Etruscans:

> Achievements of the highest quality are cheek by jowl with much that is second-rate, coarse grained: a pitiless and pedantically gruesome realism with a completely metaphysical world of fantasy: patient, unimaginative imitations of Greek designs with flashes of an inspiration which is completely anti-classical. And all this is found in the same period, in the same place, even in a single monument if not in a single object. . . . There is something at the root of Etruscan art which we cannot understand.

The last sentence is telling. No one is more pitiless than Professor Pallotino in scourging the romantic notions of Etruria, the outlook purveyed in such telltale words as *enigma* and *riddle*. But, confronted with Etruscan art, even he confesses that there is something at its root which cannot be understood. For all his ill-mannered spleen and intuitive raptures, Lawrence strikes a chord in insisting that the Etruscans are not a theory but an experience.

The dilettante and the collector have been ineluctably attracted to the Etruscans since an eccentric Scots baronet named Sir Thomas Dempster wrote the first modern systematic study of the vanished race after a visit to Italy in 1616–1617. A lawyer, Sir Thomas never got around to publishing his illustrated manuscript; it appeared as a book a century later when Etruscomania had begun to spread. By the nineteenth century the Etruscans were so fashionable that Dennis' two thick and learned volumes were a best-seller in London.

The result has been disastrous for the Etruscans. Demand for Etruscan works has been so intense that producing forgeries has long been a profitable Italian industry—at one time the Metropolitan Museum of Art placed a bogus figure of an Etruscan warrior in a place of honor near the entrance, where it remained for thirty-odd years until proven a fake. Worse than the forgers have been the grave-robbers who have plundered the tombs with ignorant rapacity.

"We have too many ruins, and not enough public money to take care of them," says one of Italy's remarkable men, Carlo Maurillo Lerici, founder of the Lerici Foundation, whom I have mentioned in Chapter One. A falcon-eyed engineer whose specialty was aerial prospecting, Lerici retired in 1955 and turned his talents to archaeological exploration, developing new techniques for locating and photographing Etruscan tombs. In one five-year period he found as many painted tombs as had been discovered in the past century and a half. But he had to cope not only with grave-robbers but with the hostility of officials paid supposedly to protect the ancient sites. In some zones of the province of Grosseto, which is plagued by treasure seekers, Dr. Lerici has reported, "The Polytechnic team did not even receive the authorization of the local representative of the Department of Antiquities to carry out a survey—let alone excavation. Incredible but true."

When I visited him, Dr. Lerici said he was undiscouraged. Sooner or later, he feels, the government must realize that Italy's monuments help attract some thirty million tourists a year and that adequate care is simply a sensible investment. But, despite Dr. Lerici's eloquence, there is little sign of change, with melancholy consequences not only for the Etruscan remains but also for Italy's prime antiquarian treasures, her buried cities.

House of the Poet, Pompeii Typically sumptuous, this villa is built around an atrium; the name is based not on any find but on the house's association with a character in Bulwer-Lytton's novel. (COURTESY RADIO TIMES HULTON PICTURE LIBRARY)

IV

CITIES IN ASPIC

There is nothing that the earth has hidden,
but Time shall bring forth into sunshine.
HORACE, Odes

OSTIA, POMPEII, AND HERCULANEUM are the unrivaled miracles of Italian archaeology, unique places where one can see classical life clearly and, more than anywhere else, see it whole. They are like fully provisioned galleons, manned by a crew of ghosts, that have somehow glided into a modern harbor. Sometimes the ghosts are even corporeal. A century ago the ingenious excavator Guiseppe Fiorelli discovered a technique at Pompeii for pouring hot plaster into the cavities left by decomposed bodies in the Vesuvian ash. When the crust was chipped away, death casts materialized of humans frozen in a final agony, and the sight of them brings out the Bulwer-Lytton in the most resolute anti-romantic.

Writing of the famous eruption, Goethe said, "Many a calamity has
happened in the world, but never one that has caused so much entertainment
to posterity as this one." It is entertainment of an unnerving kind. There are
the children of Paquius Proculus, trapped and forgotten in their playroom.
There is the beggar found at the Porta di Nuceria, carrying an alms sack but
wearing sandals of unbeggarly high quality. There is the woman wearing
costly jewels, obviously not a prostitute, lying among the bodies in the
gladiatorial barracks. There is the steward Erotus, who calmly waited for
death, holding his master's seal. Less calm was the dog next to his owner in
the House of the Vestals—the man died first, and his flesh was devoured by
the ravenous animal. So clear are some of the casts that even pubic hair can be
seen, in one case shaved in a semicircular form, as in classical statuary.

Each of the cities has its special character. The first which I visited was
Ostia, the ancient port of Rome. At the time, I was a student traveling
through Europe, and my guide was Paul MacKendrick, one of my teachers at
the University of Wisconsin. As we drove out to Ostia, I had only the
vaguest inkling of what I might see, certainly not anticipating that I would
encounter the very marrow of the past.

We walked down the cobbled main street, passing Ostia's snack shops,
theater, and forum, and then threaded obliquely through side alleys until we
reached the steamroom of a small public bath. On the wall there was a

Ostia: Aerial View   The ancient port of Rome is near the modern port—Leonardo
da Vinci Airport—and adjoins a popular bathing beach. Here the Tiber can be
seen in the background; the roofed building is a museum. (COURTESY RADIO TIMES
HULTON PICTURE LIBRARY)

Canine Pompeii Preserved in its death agony, the dog is one of the many living creatures whose forms have been re-created by pouring plaster into the hollowed cavities in the volcanic blanket. (COURTESY RADIO TIMES HULTON PICTURE LIBRARY)

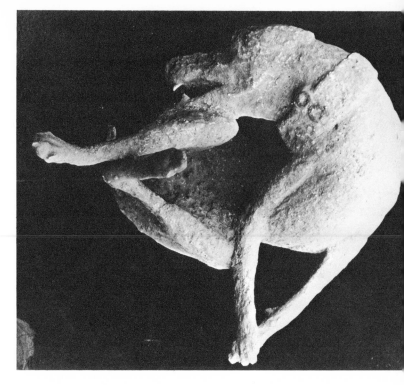

A Pompeian Street Rutted by cartwheels and therefore slippery during rain, the street considerately provided steppingstones for a dry crossing. (COURTESY RADIO TIMES HULTON PICTURE LIBRARY)

cartoon of the Seven Sages of Antiquity, including Socrates and Thales, each squatting in a homely pose, while couplets beneath confided the connection between constipation and intellectual life. With a flourish of his pipe, Mac-Kendrick translated the Latin, which revealed resources for profanity unsuspected in the classroom. We continued to the Square of the Corporation, where seventy trades were represented in stalls floored with a mosaic suitable to each calling. Then we wandered to a block of apartments, some with shops on the ground floor and three stories of balconied flats above. They were identical in form with the tenements one sees in every Italian city; the centuries were telescoped with dizzying abruptness, and the dead streets swarmed with noisy life.

Ostia was preserved thanks to malaria and the engulfing sand, the first contributing to its decline as a port of Rome and the second sealing in the buildings of a city where some 50,000 persons once lived. Excavations began in the eighteenth century, accelerated in the nineteenth, reaching a furious tempo in our time when Mussolini wanted the city bared for a 1942 exhibition that was never held. Guido Calza, a gifted digger, was put in charge, and his scrupulous principle was: "Better to brace than repair; better repair than restore; better restore than embellish; never add or subtract." He succeeded in moving 600,000 yards of earth, exposing seventy acres of a city that is now three-fourths uncovered.

Pompeii and Ostia are as unlike as Cannes and Cherbourg, but an unblushing love of money unites the port of Rome and the resort south of Naples. In the vestibule of a merchant's house in Pompeii an inscription says SALVE LUCRUM (or HAIL, PROFIT!) and the phrase was the municipal maxim. To visit Pompeii is to enter the world of Trimalchio, who at one point brags in the *Satyricon,* "By the favor of Mercury, I have built me this house. It was a mere cottage, as you know, and now it is a temple. It has four dining rooms, twenty bedchambers, two noble porticoes, a storeroom in the upper floor, a chamber in which I sleep myself, a sitting-room for this viper [his wife], a porter's lodge, and accommodations for a hundred guests." The description accurately fits Pompeii's larger villas, which loom among the cramped homes of tradesmen like islands of money.

Salve lucrum! Scores of Pompeii's inhabitants died because they tried to lug their wealth away as hot ash poured down on the city in the eruption of 79 A.D. The same materialism prompted the Bourbon rulers of Naples to loot the art of Pompeii when the city was rediscovered in the mid-eighteenth century. But with the era of modern excavation, beginning in 1860, more probity prevailed, and it is thanks to the tireless work of Italian scholars that Pompeii's most perishable treasure has been salvaged—the graffiti.

It is fascinating to puzzle out these inscriptions, which bleach in the sun along ghostly streets, with the cone of Vesuvius always visible in the back-

Pompeii: The Small Theater The smallest of the theaters in the city, this Odeon was once canopied and used for comedy and concerts. (COURTESY RADIO TIMES HULTON PICTURE LIBRARY)

ground. We thus know that only sneak thieves favored Vatia for the aedileship, that a girl named Attike priced her charms at two *asses* (an *as* was worth 2.5 American cents), that Serena had had enough of Isidore, and that in a certain wine shop undrinkable slops were sold ("May you, landlord of the devil, die drowned in your piss-wine"). Advice is offered: "Love and the cough cannot be hidden." Power is mocked: "Augustus Caesar's mother was only a woman." Beggars are warned: "There is no room here for loafers, move on without stopping." Debts are recorded: "Faustilla owes me fifteen *denarii* plus nine *asses* interest." And the impulse to scribble is amiably derided: "I wonder, wall, that you do not go smash, who have to bear the weight of all this trash." Vesuvius preserved the buildings, but the inscriptions pickle Pompeii's humanity. Its materialism, thankfully, was seasoned by irreverence, and even discarded lovers knew how to sign off with style: "Farewell, my Victoria, and wherever you go, may you sneeze sweetly."

The third buried city, Herculaneum, is an ugly gash in the slums of the modern town of Resina. Pompeii was covered by ash and pebbles, but Herculaneum, closer to the volcano, was drowned in sixty feet of hot muddy lava, preserving, as a result, wood furniture and even libraries. Yet unfortunately, because excavation is difficult, only a small part of this wealthier and smaller city has been uncovered, while all but a third of Pompeii has been dug

up. Thus it is entirely possible that the complete works of Sophocles lie
embedded in rock-hard lava beneath the city of Resina.

As long ago as 1754 scrolls were found in Herculaneum, the only
classical Italian site that has yielded manuscripts. One villa contained 1,800
works, of which two thirds, disappointingly, turned out to be the writings of
an obscure Epicurean philosopher named Philodemus. Excitement over the
find prompted Wordsworth to write:

> O ye, who patiently explore
> The wreck of Herculanean lore
> What rapture! could ye seize
> Some Theban fragment, or unroll
> One precious, tender-hearted scroll
> Of pure Simonides!

But for a hundred years no effort was made to find pure Simonides. At the
turn of this century the English classicist Charles Waldstein said imploringly:
"Herculaneum is the one site above all others which ought to be excavated."

Herculaneum: Aerial View A square crater dug from the center of a living city,
Herculaneum is better preserved than Pompeii because it was buried in harder
volcanic material in which wood and paper can survive. It is conceivable that
the missing plays of Sophocles lie under one of the modern houses at the upper
left. (COURTESY PHOTOCIELO ROME)

He proposed that the city be uncovered through an international campaign, but nothing came of his suggestion, and little was done at Herculaneum save for a spurt of digging during the Mussolini period.

After World War II, Cyril Connolly suggested in the pages of *Horizon* that an allied war memorial in Italy could take the form of an Anglo-American campaign to unearth classical sites, most notably Herculaneum. His suggestion was welcomed by Dr. Umberto Zanotti-Bianco, musician, archaeologist, and anti-Fascist, who for years had tried to arouse interest in the site. Yet Dr. Zanotti-Bianco ruefully wrote Connolly that "in this tragic postwar period in which our greatest anxiety is to secure shelter for the many deprived of it, it would be more unthinkable than ever to demolish a great part of the densely populated town of Resina."

The period of postwar privation is over. Herculaneum is still largely undug. Recently an American author, Joseph Jay Deiss, concluded a book on the city with this reflection: "Antiquity is Italy's greatest natural resource, and Herculaneum is the richest of all finds. It seems incredible to discover a buried treasure and not dig it up." In the long run, no doubt, the Italians will get around to exhuming the greater part of the most perfectly preserved of all ancient cities, retrieving its furniture and libraries and statuary, but in the long run, as Lord Keynes remarked, we will all be dead, as much part of the past as hapless Herculaneum.

In the meantime, inadequate care is taken to protect the excavated areas of Ostia, Pompeii, and Herculaneum. Every year sun, rain, and tourism nibble away at each with dolorous persistence. The three dead cities are dying again, and one is despairingly moved to ask, *Quis custodiet custodes?*

V

GREEK FIRE

> . . . *Paestum, the last vision I shall take with me on my way north, and perhaps the greatest.*
>
> GOETHE, Italian Journey

PAESTUM IS A PENDANT to the archaeology of mainland Italy, the most southerly and isolated of the great sites. Its three noble temples rise on a desolate plateau, between the sea and the mountain, some twenty-five miles southeast of Salerno. The amber columns are in uncompromising Doric and have an inner radiance, like pale Greek fire, in this brambled solitude in the loins of Italy.

Temples of Paestum Though the present view is less pastoral than this engraving (c. 1810), the landscape is still relatively uncontaminated by development. This is essentially the view Goethe saw of the three great temples which survived chiefly because they were in the middle of a malarial swamp.

Once Paestum was a Greek colony known as Poseidonia, founded by settlers from Sybaris in the seventh century B.C. In the next century the temples were built and a walled city took form. After its absorption by Rome, the city was famous for its gardens—Virgil speaks admiringly of its roses which flowered twice—and lamented for its tendency to malaria. Because of the disease Paestum was finally abandoned in the ninth century, and its intact temples were not rediscovered, incredibly, until 1740.*

An early visitor was Goethe, who visited the temples in 1787. "At first sight they excited nothing but stupefaction," he wrote. ". . . Our eyes and, through them, our whole sensibility have become so conditioned to a more slender style of architecture that these crowded masses of stumpy conical columns appear offensive and even terrifying. But I pulled myself together, remembered the history of art, thought of the ages with which this architecture was in harmony, and in less than an hour I found myself reconciled to them and even thanking my guardian angel for having allowed me to see these well-preserved remains with my own eyes."

* A new and exciting find at Paestum has been the discovery of the vast burial ground of the Lucanians, the little-known people who took over the city from its Greek founders and changed its name from Poseidonia to Paestum. Though the Lucanians had been scorned as culturally underdeveloped, their painted tombs showed an unexpected sophistication and vivacity. A new museum may be built to preserve the finds from the necropolis.

Goethe's reaction suggests how much taste had been cheapened by Roman ruins, but in the end the stumpy columns of Paestum imposed their majesty on him. Each temple has an eloquence of its own. The temple attributed to Poseidon is the best preserved, its fifty limestone columns all in place, each tapering only slightly as it rises to massive architrave beams. The "Temple of Ceres" is the smallest, and it is feminine Doric, with columns that narrow more delicately to circular capitals rooted in the pediments. In the so-called "Basilica," the earliest of the temples, there is a leaf decoration in the necking of the capitals. The three together live in harmony with each other, and with the sea and mountains that frame them in a canvas awash with light.

Not far from Paestum, just north of Naples, is the ruin of Cumae, where the famous Sibyl informed Aeneas of his destiny. Virgil, who knew the Greek cities well, was conscious of what Rome lacked and gave the Sibyl words that express precisely what one feels in confronting the superb originality of Paestum:

> Let others better mould the running mass
> Of metals, and inform the breathing brass,
> And soften flesh into a marble face;
> Plead better at the bar; describe the skies,
> And when the stars descend, and when they rise.
> But, Rome, 'tis thine alone, with awful sway,
> To rule mankind, and make the world obey. . . .
>
> [*Aeneid, VI*, TRANSLATION BY DRYDEN]

Chapter Seven

MISS HAVISHAM'S HOUSE

ENGLAND

Ancient sites in England

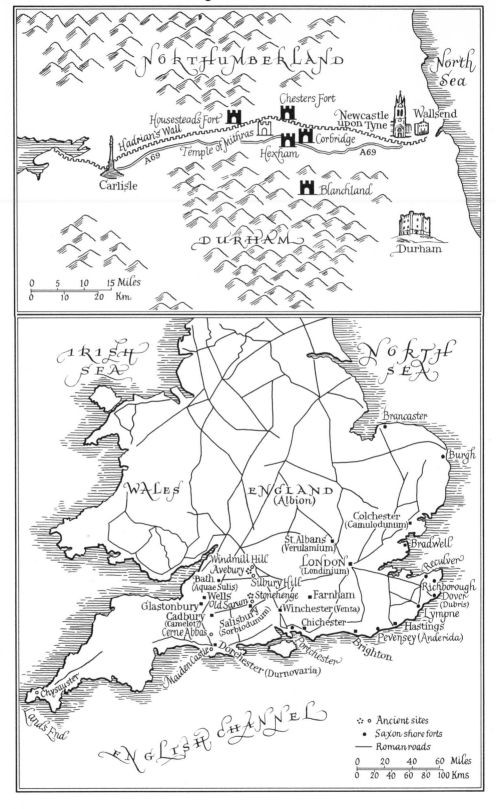

I

THE GREAT LEAP BACKWARD

Oh, call back yesterday; bid time return.
SHAKESPEARE, Richard III

THERE IS AN APPEALING BALMINESS about England's preoccupation with the past. Only the other day, while walking around Covent Garden market, I came upon this entirely typical inscription on the portal of St. Paul's Church, facing a street thick with squashed fruit and loud Cockney oaths:

NEAR THIS SPOT
PUNCH'S PUPPET SHOW
WAS PERFORMED IN ENGLAND
AND WITNESSED BY SAMUEL PEPYS
1692

In smaller letters below was this addendum: "This Notice was Caused to be Inscribed by The Society for Theatre Research and Model Theatre Guild." England expects every profession to do its historical duty.

As a generality, the word "old" has the siren charm for an Englishman that "new" has for an American. Though Her Majesty's Government is avowedly intent on modernizing archaic institutions, every effort to do so meets robust opposition. England was the last major Western country to adopt the new-fangled Gregorian Calendar, and her people today view with glum misgiving the advent of decimal currency, a reform first urged more than a century ago. "Every Englishman," Emerson remarked, "is an embryonic chancellor: his instinct is to search for precedent."

If none exists, one can be concocted. An example was the Investiture of the Prince of Wales at Caernarvon Castle in July 1969, an event contemplated with awe and curiosity by millions who saw it on a world-wide telecast. Here was the handsome Prince kneeling before the Queen, swearing to be her liege and man, before an assemblage of courtiers whose knightly swords, great scarlet capes and splendid tunics conjured up visions of the Round Table and the Age of Kings. Sitting in the stands and hearing trumpets throb from Caernarvon's battlements, I could hardly bring myself to believe that the ceremony actually dates to the less than remote year of 1911, when Mr. Lloyd George invented the ritual to help secure the Welsh vote. The sole previous royal heir to be so Invested was the Prince's uncle, Edward VIII.

Much in England is not as old as it seems. Take the Houses of Parliament, a Gothic fantasy rising on the banks of the Thames, enclosing a bell that peals like the stroke of doom. The building's interminable corridors, in which I always manage to get lost though I have trod through them hundreds of times, virtually reek of History. Yet the edifice is a comparative stripling, a Victorian juvenile that passed straight from youth to the Middle Ages.

The history of the Palace of Westminster (the building's more august name) is instructive. Long centuries ago the Court of Exchequer kept its accounts not with paper and pen but with notched sticks, much as Robinson Crusoe kept his calendar while marooned on his island. As Dickens, once a Parliamentary reporter himself, tells the rest of the story:

> In the reign of George III an inquiry was made by some revolutionary spirit whether, pens, ink and paper, slates and pencils being in existence, this obstinate adherence to an obsolete custom ought to be continued, and whether a change ought not to be effected. All of the red tape in the country grew redder at the bare mention of this bold and original conception, and it took until 1826 to get those sticks abolished.
>
> In 1834, it was found that there was a considerable accumulation of them; and the question then arose, what was to be done with such worn-out, worm-eaten, rotten bits of wood? The sticks were housed in Westminster . . . and so the order went out that they were to be privately and confidentially burned. It came to pass that they were burned in a stove in the House of Lords. The stove, over-gorged with these preposterous sticks, set fire to the panelling; the panelling set fire to the House of Commons; the two houses were reduced to ashes; architects were called in to build others; and we are now in the second million of the cost thereof.

The cause for surprise in this tale is that Parliament did not ship those ridiculous sticks in silver caskets to the British Museum. The magpie instinct is pandemic in England. Everything is stuck away in cases, labeled, classified, and squirted with preservative. What isn't publicly collected is privately hoarded. In London one finds shops that cater to the specialized appetites of cartophilists, philumenists, fromologists, and tegestologists—collectors, respectively, of cigarette cards, matchbox covers, cheesebox labels, and beer coasters. Living in England is at times like being a guest in Miss Havisham's House, the wedding cake forever kept on the bridal table in tender memory of things past. An item in *The Times* captures the spirit: "It is recorded that there are only 72 Great Auk's eggs in existence. Great Britain owns 44, the United States 14, France 7, Germany 5, and Holland 2, while Denmark, Portugal and Switzerland own one each. It is gratifying to note that the six eggs sold yesterday were all acquired by British collectors."

The English collect the past, consult the past, and invent the past. In the case of people, this is sometimes done with the least promising of materials, a notorious illustration being St. George, the national patron. The slayer of dragons is an integral part of the English tapestry, the very image of intrepid chivalry. Yet, what is the truth about St. George? In the words of Emerson, certainly no Anglophobe:

> George of Cappadocia, born at Epiphania in Cilicia, was a low parasite, who got a lucrative contract to supply the army with bacon. A rogue and informer, he got rich and was forced to run from justice. He saved his money, embraced Arianism, collected a library, and got promoted by a faction to the episcopal throne in Alexandria. When Julian came, A.D. 361, George was dragged to prison; the prison was burst open by a mob, and George was lynched, as he deserved. And this precious knave became, in good time, Saint George of England, patron of chivalry, emblem of victory and virility, and the pride of the best blood in the modern world.

No doubt some of these awkward facts contributed to the recent decision of the Vatican to demote St. George from the calendar of saints, to the distress of some of the same Englishmen who otherwise complain that Rome is too given to superstitious veneration of relics.

But of all the feats of posthumous reclamation, none excels in interest King Arthur and the knights of Camelot.

Camelot was invented to fill a void. The void was acutely embarrassing for a people so devoted to the past; too many chapters of British history were simply blank. During the 600 years in which classical civilization evolved, the British Isles were peopled by fierce, preliterate tribes whose level of culture, while clearly not contemptible, was below that of the Mediterranean. The

Arthur's Camelot? The question cannot yet be answered, but South Cadbury Hill has a regal setting and a traditional identification with Arthur. (PHOTO H. J. P. ARNOLD)

four ensuing centuries of Roman occupation, though they saw the advent of literacy, better roads, new towns, and Christianity, did not add pages of excessive glory to the British record. The Dark Ages which followed the collapse of Rome were darker in Britain than elsewhere; there was no British equivalent of Charlemagne to illuminate them.

In this murk a few historical figures can be dimly ascertained, one being a Celtic general named Artorius, who is mentioned by name in the ninth-century annals of the Welsh chronicler Nennius as the victor of an important battle at Mount Badon some time around A.D. 518. The period was a deeply troubled one in England. Rome had fallen, Hadrian's Wall had been overrun, and the Romanized Britons had long before been told to fend for themselves. And somehow many Britons did manage to retain the rudiments of Roman civilization despite the onslaughts of Picts and Scots and of barbarous new-comers from Europe, the Anglo-Saxons. The Romanized Celtic population was forced to retreat by the invaders, Wales and the English West Country becoming the last redoubt against the pagans. At this point Artorius, or Arthur, appears and he seems to have rallied the Celts, winning a series of twelve battles, culminating in Mount Badon (present whereabouts un-known), which secured for his people an interlude of tranquility. All of this can be pieced together from tantalizing fragments in a variety of sources:

ecclesiastical annals, bardic songs, and Welsh legends, some of them containing such familiar names as Mordred, Mark, Tristan, Iseult, Kay, and Bede-
vere.

Geoffrey Ashe, in his excellent compendium *The Quest for Arthur's
Britain*, supplies this convincing portrait of an Arthur who is not a king but
rather a Celtic military hero:

> We may picture him as a rustic noble, born in the 470s or there-
> abouts, of still dimly-Romanized stock. Hence his name, Artorius.
> His youth was spent in raiding and feuding. By an unusual flair for
> leadership he attracted a following. His personal corps—the
> "knights," if we care to use the word—aided British kings against
> Anglo-Saxon encroachments. He made himself indispensable over
> the whole zone of his operation, becoming, in a crude way, a
> statesman. But, despite victory, his standing was never quite secure.
> Quarrels with the monks, probably over levies in kind, deprived him
> of proper recognition in the writings of the only people who wrote.
> He met his end fighting an enemy to whom there is no reason not to
> give the name Mordred.

Thus the historical Arthur. The Arthur of romance emerges around
1136, when a churchman named Geoffrey of Monmouth endowed a Dark
Age warlord with new-found glamour. Geoffrey was apparently half Welsh,
and his father was named Arthur; he claimed that he drew on ancient
documents "in the British language" (presumably Welsh) for his wonderfully fertile *History of the Kings of Britain*. A border chieftain no more,
Arthur here becomes one of the great kings of Europe, the scion of a royal
British line founded by Brutus, the grandson of Aeneas. Born in Tintagel in
Cornwall in circumstances made mysterious by the sorcery of Merlin (who
also makes his debut here), Arthur succeeds to the throne as a youth and,
after defeating the Saxons, goes on to conquer France and Scandinavia. Of
his capital, Caerleon-upon-Usk, and his fellowship of knights, Geoffrey cannot offer praise enough. Did anyone suggest that Dark Age Britain was lack-
ing in civilized polish? Geoffrey rebuts the canard: "Indeed, by this time
Britain had reached such a standard of sophistication that it excelled all other
kingdoms in its general affluence, the richness of its decorations, and the
courteous behavior of its inhabitants." In the end, while Arthur is embarking
on the conquest of Rome, a rebellion led by his nephew Mordred breaks out
in Britain and the King returns to quell it. In the final battle Arthur receives
a deadly wound and then vanishes to Avalon.

So the void was filled, and Geoffrey's narrative became so swiftly accepted that within a generation a commentator on the *History* was able to
write, "What place is there within the bounds of the empire of Christendom

to which the winged praise of Arthur of Britain has not extended?" There was a good reason why bards everywhere seized gratefully on the Arthurian tales—they offered a secular counterweight to the more austere New Testament, enabling poets to combine piety with rousing battles, hunts, and courtly love. The story was also politically helpful to the Plantagenets, who could now claim, as heirs to the redoubtable Arthur, to be equal in pedigree to the heirs of Charlemagne. Thus King Henry II saw to it that his grandson was named Arthur; the boy was to rule as Arthur II, and save for his untimely death (he had ambitious uncles) would have done so.

Equally, Arthur proved a useful ally to England in coping with the pretensions of the Welsh, whose bards insisted that Arthur would somehow return from Avalon once more to help his people. Henry II was delighted when he learned that Avalon was actually Glastonbury, a place safely in English control; he ordered the monks of Glastonbury Abbey to search for Arthur's body, and lo, in 1190, the remains conveniently came to light under a great stone slab inscribed in Latin: "Here lies buried the renowned King Arthur in the Isle of Avalon." Within the tomb the bones of a huge warrior and of his wife (her blond tresses still intact) were found. Arthur was reburied in the Abbey proper, where he remained until the Reformation.

The centuries passed, and the saga grew like a medieval tapestry. British, French, and Teutonic minstrels wove in new stories—Parsifal and the Grail, Tristan and Iseult, Lancelot and Guinevere—and supplied the magical name Camelot. By the time Malory sat down to compose *Morte d'Arthur*, the Round Table was as much an English asset as the crown jewels. In 1485 Caxton published Malory's brilliant synthesis, and, providentially, this happened to be the year that the War of the Roses finally came to a close. Henry Tudor succeeded to the throne as Henry VII, uniting the blood lines of England and Wales. The first Tudor exploited to the full his Welsh descent —the Welsh Red Dragon was on his battle standard—and saw in Arthur a healing hero symbol. The King's first son was named Arthur and was baptized in Winchester, then thought to be the original site of Camelot. It is intriguing to think that Arthur II might have been the monarch of Reformation England, but this was not to be; the heir died as a boy, and the crown passed to Henry VIII.

At about this time, what purported to be the original Round Table suddenly turned up. It was a big slab of oak, fifteen feet across, boldly inscribed: "Thys is the rownde Table of Kyng Arthur wt. xxiiii of hys namyd Knyghts." When Charles V visited England in 1552, his boastful host, Henry VIII, took the Emperor to Winchester to see the great disk, which had been unsubtly repainted in green and white, the Tudor colors. The Round Table still hangs today in Winchester Castle, the unlikely backdrop to the courtroom in which the Bloody Assizes took place.

Arthur, champion of the faith and embodiment of destiny, was permitted a few centuries of rest in Avalon before being pressed into national service again in the Victorian Era, when Tennyson, the Poet Laureate, found in him the poetic image of Imperial Britain. *The Idylls of the King* present a Camelot more seemly than Malory's. Guinevere's fateful adultery is deftly played down and manliness played up, a change in emphasis assisted by a hint from Queen Victoria that some allusion to Albert would be welcome in the Laureate's work. Even the Paris Commune of 1870 makes an offstage appearance in Tennyson's Dark Age epic. In "The Final Tournament" there is a Red Knight who accosts a swineherd and makes him convey this message to King Arthur:

> Tell thou the King and all his liars, that I
> Have founded my Round Table in the North,
> And whatsoever his own knights have sworn
> My knights have sworn to counter it—and say
> My tower is full of harlots, like his court,
> But mine are worthier, seeing they profess
> To be none others but themselves—and say
> My knights are all adulterers like his own,
> But mine are truer, seeing they profess
> To be none other. . . .

But propriety triumphs, and the Red Knight is overwhelmed: the border warlord was now a Victorian gentleman.

Still more surprising is the last incarnation of King Arthur, in the pages of T. H. White's *Once and Future King*, a fable confected of whimsy and hemlock. Here conventional heroics are gently deflated, and the dying Arthur soliloquizes moodily about the insane root of violence:

> Man must be ready to say: Yes, since Cain there has been injustice, but we can only set the misery right if we accept a *status quo.* Lands have been robbed, men slain, nations humiliated. Let us now start fresh without remembrance, rather than live forward and backward at the same time. We cannot build the future by avenging the past. Let us sit down as brothers, and accept the Peace of God.

It is a Round Table seen through post-Imperial eyes, through the lethal mist of nuclear fall-out. Yet, whatever White's intentions, his book became an Anglo-American phenomenon, inspiring a Disney film, a musical comedy, and a movie epic. In the United States, Camelot has come to connote the Kennedy years which ended in the Avalon of Dallas; the rose of illusion has taken root across the Atlantic.

In the midst of this Arthurian revival—and possibly as a consequence of it—came exciting news: in 1967 archaeologists launched a campaign to unearth Arthur's Camelot.

II

LOOKING FOR CAMELOT

ON A FINE FALL DAY IN 1968 I took a train to Camelot. It was a charming and tranquil experience. The Dark Ages could not have seemed more innocently remote from Cadbury Hill, near the Dorset-Somerset border in the West Country, where the Camelot Research Committee was winding up a season's dig. The scenery was absurdly peaceful: a collage of Trollopean villages and of grassy fields brushed by a soft wind. The most menacing things visible were the gray and pregnant clouds. As I ascended the steep dirt road to Camelot, it began raining, and I scrambled to the top feeling Arthurian in my valor, only to see that I had been preceded by a mother pushing a pram and an elderly gentleman with a walking-stock.

We gathered in the tent, having tea and biscuits while waiting for the guide, who turned out to be a pleasant schoolteacher volunteer. As we waited for the rain to pause, she explained to us that the archaeologists did not expect to find a shaving mug with Arthur's name inscribed on it. The hope rather was to find traces of the sixth-century military camp appropriate to a Celtic warlord—the historical Arthur.

Cadbury Hill was chosen for the dig because John Leland, the royal antiquarian to Henry VIII, had written of it: "At South Cadbryi standith Camallate, sumtyme a famous toun or castelle. The people can tell nothing thar but what they have hard say that Arture much resorted to Camalat." The credibility of this traditional identification was supported when a trial trench uncovered pottery of the right vintage. But, in truth, in several seasons the Quest for Camelot had not yet unearthed anything sensational. A military wall 1,200 yards long, of the desired period, was found, and so was a mysterious cruciform pattern—mistakenly thought on its discovery to have been the foundation of a church that was never built. No large buildings had yet come to sight, the major disappointment.

Nobody seemed particularly discouraged. The volunteer workers were getting exercise, and the professional staff was professionally serene. The hilltop itself was a maze of roped areas in which deep or shallow pits had been dug. The dress was varied; some volunteers had white helmets, others wore bathing suits. A sign on a wooden hut, written partly in Gothic letters,

Digging for Camelot Volunteer workers scavenge under the supervision of professionals at the hilltop site. The fence is to keep visitors away. The spirit of the dig is conveyed by the hut, with its excavation scoreboard. (PHOTOS KARL E. MEYER)

conveyed the spirit of the place: "you are now entering Site K—ye first Tintagel 'D' discovered here!" Tintagel D is a Mediterranean pottery of the kind that would turn up in the camp of a Dark Age chieftain with the inclination and means to maintain some Roman standards. Other bits of this ware have been found at Tintagel in Cornwall and nearby Glastonbury, both places with strong Arthurian associations.

Professor Leslie Alcock of University College, Cardiff, the director of the campaign, was moving from pit to trench, wearing a floppy hat and carrying a notebook. I asked him how he decided where to dig on the fourteen-acre hilltop, and he explained that air and contour surveys had been made, and also a survey using a soil-conductivity meter that was being given its first test at Camelot. Nicknamed "The Banjo," the device uses a radar technique to detect underground irregularities. With this data, archaeologists could aim their spades at promising targets.

I also learned that South Cadbury Hill was one of seventy Iron Age fortresses in the West Country, of which the most formidable is Maiden Castle. Many of these forts came into use again after Rome, in the year 411, told the British to defend themselves against the encroaching Picts and Scots and the Anglo-Saxon invaders. The area around South Cadbury was a contested frontier, and its great mound is like a whale-shaped island rising in a green sea. From it other islands are visible, including Glastonbury Tor, which by tradition is the Isle of Avalon.

Once beacons would flash from peak to peak, and war horns would emit a terrifying blast, summoning the cavalry of Artorius, the *dux bellorum* of the Celts, to meet the heathen Saxon infantry (one theory is that Arthur owed his victories to his skillful use of cavalry, a tactic bequeathed by the Romans, but some authorities—including Mr. Alcock—dispute this). Yet around South Cadbury today the blast of war has given way to the click of the croquet ball, and Camelot is suffused with T. H. White's Peace of God in the gentlest country on earth. Not a bad ending for the story, and perhaps the handful of sherds unearthed have a wider significance than is immediately apparent. Or so I reflected as I said goodbye to the guide and descended the hill with a wary eye on Somerset's scapegrace sun.

What is the importance of the Camelot dig? Is it worth spending so much for so little? And have scholars succumbed to the worldy temptation of exploiting Arthurian associations to attract popular support for what is at best a marginally interesting project? These questions became a matter of polemical interest not long after I visited the hilltop site when they were sharply asked, in an article in *Antiquity*, by Charles Thomas, Professor of Archaeology at the University of Leicester.

Mr. Thomas was perturbed by the participation of Camelot scholars in

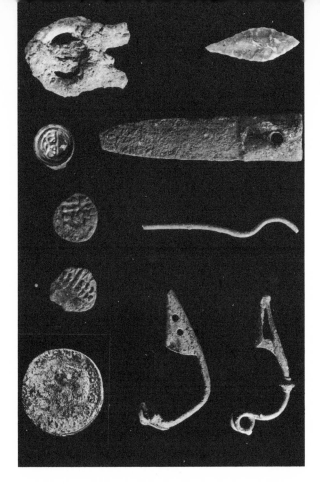

Finds at South Cadbury
The pottery unearthed in the first season's dig was of the right style for the Arthurian period, and the coins suggest that King Canute had a mint at Cadbury, attesting to the site's ancient importance. (COURTESY PROFESSOR LESLIE ALCOCK)

what are known as "Arthurian fringe" activities. He confessed to a sense of "slight distaste" at the sale of spurious "knighthoods" at Tintagel and to the televised caperings in Merlin's cave in which a prominent Arthurian scholar "was seen to participate." He further objected to the presence, on the committee sponsoring the excavation, of persons whose interest was non-archaeological and whose view could hardly be objective since they were committed to a belief in the historicity of Arthur. In sum, the trappings of the campaign left him with "a feeling, perhaps, that there lurks a danger that the project might be brought into a shadow of disrepute—because results can be journalistically misrepresented, or *a priori* theories allowed to colour the interpretations given in popular media, in order to satisfy a publicity machine which now seems indispensable to keep so costly a campaign rolling along."

Thus challenged, the Camelot Research Committee vigorously rejoined that (1) the expenditure of $12,000 per annum for three years was not an excessive cost; (2) reports of the South Cadbury dig were subject to rigorous control of professional archaeologists; (3) the site was interesting for its own sake, all Arthurian considerations aside; and (4) the danger of bringing archaeology into journalistic disrepute was not confined to the quest for Camelot but posed a recurrent problem at every major campaign. As to the finds at South Cadbury, they have been sufficient for Sir Mortimer Wheeler, *doyen* of British archaeologists and president of the Camelot Committee, to declare that they opened "an impressive vista of British history, ranging from the Stone Age ramparts of 3000 B.C. or earlier to a final refortification in the 11th century A.D., when kings Aethelred the Unready and Canute minted coins there."

Underlying the dispute is a matter of fundamental importance. The Arthur of romance is an example of the universal tendency to endow the past with a purpose, to take the miscellany of human events and form it into a mosaic with a grand design. Sometimes this purposeful past is deliberately contrived, using elements of obvious myth, as one suspects was the case with Geoffrey of Monmouth. On other occasions the conception of a moralizing past is formed by historians who believe in good faith that they are using documented evidence with scrupulous precision.

In England historians of genius took what they thought to be the facts of the past to construct an edifice as noble in its way as the Houses of Parliament—yet later English historians, in a brilliant exercise of iconoclasm, have shown that the building was no less spurious an antique. According to the traditional theory, the immensely influential Whig view identified with Macaulay, English history is a story of a slow, sometimes faltering procession of triumph, leading ever upward to the present. As a zealous acolyte, Dean Farrar, once headmaster of Marlborough College, saw it:

> Through the confusions of nations, the great idea of humanity lives and grows: from the soil of deciduous peoples and decaying races springs up the mightier bole of the great people of England, greater, better, more perfect than the peoples out of which it grew—The Briton bequeathed us his faith and awe; the Roman his laws and order; the Saxon his freedom and manliness; the Dane his strength and intrepidity; the Norman his cultivation and enterprise. They died and passed away; and we, the children of all of them, are nobler than any. "We are the heirs of all ages in the foremost files of Time."

For two generations English historians have chipped away at this conventional edifice, scrutinizing the very molecules from which it was made. Their conclusion is that the past offers no such comforting architecture, that, in the words of one skilled demolitionist, J. H. Plumb of Cambridge University, "The future of history and historians is to cleanse the story of mankind from those deceiving visions of a purposeful past."

Yet if the design of history is swept away as a wishful manmade artifact, what is left to provide mankind with confidence and optimism in facing a scary future? For most of us the problem is central (though less so, in the

British Museum: Elgin Marbles Beyond the pedimental figures are the friezes as they are now displayed in the new gallery built with funds provided by the late Lord Duveen. The effect is as gray as a British February morning. (COURTESY BRITISH MUSEUM)

West, for believing Christians and Marxist-Leninists). Plumb's answer is that the historian, armed with the evidence of archaeology no less than with written documents, must stress the success as well as point out the failure in human endeavor: "Here is a message of the past which is as clear, but far more true, than the message wrung from it by our ancestors."

The peaceful testimony of Cadbury Hill is but one of many bits of evidence suggesting that mankind has had its success no less than its failures. The objects dug from its soil provide the ingredients of a new vision of the past, grounded in verifiable truths about our ancestors, enabling us to look back with clarity. "Historians can use history to fulfil many of the social purposes which the old mythical pasts did so well," writes Plumb in *The Death of the Past*, "It can no longer provide sanctions for authority, nor for aristocratic or oligarchical elites, nor for inherent destinies clothed in national guise, but it can still teach wisdom, and it can teach it in a far deeper sense than was possible when wisdom had to be taught through the example of heroes."

This, surely, provides the vindication for the Camelot dig, and it is appropriate that it should involve the person of Arthur himself. The mythical king was at the capstone of the traditional English edifice of history, a figure who, even if he did not exist, seemed to express the purposes of the island's destiny. As Churchill, a wholehearted believer in the Whig view of history, said after critically examining the historicity of Camelot: "It is all true, or it ought to be, and more and better besides. And wherever men are fighting barbarism, tyranny and massacre, for freedom, law and order, let them remember that the fame of their deeds, even though they themselves be exterminated, may perhaps be celebrated as long as the world rolls round."

It is this view of history as a sermon built around an easily grasped moral that archaeology continually undermines. If not a single object with a clear Arthurian association is found at Camelot, the excavation will have succeeded nonetheless, by furnishing a fresh brick of truth to a history freer of illusion. In this respect, the English obsession with the past has justified itself. It is no accident that England, beginning with Gibbon, has led the way in developing an analytic view of history. Nor is it an accident that British archaeologists have opened so many new windows in the rambling mansion of the past.

III

THE IMPORTANCE OF BEING INSULAR

> *Not only England, but every Englishman is an island.* FRIEDRICH VON HARDENBERG (1799)

THE ARCHAEOLOGIST HAS a unique and enviable status in Britain. A decade ago a survey of London schoolchildren showed that one in three wanted to be an archaeologist when he grew up. This was partly due to the BBC's extensive patronage of archaeology, which at one point made household names of Sir Mortimer Wheeler and Professor Glyn Daniel of Cambridge. But it is also traceable to a proud awareness of the manifold achievements of British archaeologists. The Tomb of Tutankhamen, the Palace of Knossos, the Death-Pit of Ur, the Winged Lions of Nimrud, the Neolithic town of Çatal Huyuk, and the Babylonian Flood tablets are among the trophies unearthed by British diggers. Modern excavation techniques were pioneered by Pitt-Rivers, the rigorous classification of potsherds systemized by Flinders Petrie, and Captain O. G. S. Crawford first saw the archaeological potential of aerial photography. British cryptologists were the first to decipher cuneiform and the Mycenaean Linear B script—the latter challenge described as "the Everest of modern archaeology." Fittingly, the most audacious of all prehistoric leg-pulls was also executed in England: the Piltdown man, "discovered" in 1912 and declared a humbug in 1949.

In a period of decline for Britain as a world power, archaeology is still an

British Museum: The Dying Lioness This superb hunting scene is on one of the friezes brought from Nimrud by Sir Henry Layard. (COURTESY BRITISH MUSEUM)

empire on which the sun never sets. At a modest cost to the taxpayer, the British government helps to maintain archaeological outposts in Jerusalem and Iraq, in Ankara and East Africa, in Egypt and Persia, and of course in Athens and Rome, all of them coordinated through the Council for British Archaeology. At home the impulse to dig has encouraged the formation of societies in every county and has given steady employment to the government's Inspectorate of Ancient Monuments and the Society of Antiquaries. Yet, in candor, the British Isles do not offer riches of Mediterranean magnitude to the spade. As Sir Mortimer Wheeler has said, "If Britain is not and never can be a major battlefield in the study of ancient civilizations, it is at least the ideal training-ground for our field armies."

Still, the field armies have come up with a number of finds that suggest interesting insights about Britain. One is that the width of the English Channel is of crucial importance—it is sufficiently narrow to permit continual Continental influence, and yet wide enough to insularize the various invaders who have poured across it. V. Gordon Childe is writing not about the present but about the prehistoric epoch when he observes, in his influential *Dawn of European Civilization:* "But islands they already were. Would-be colonists embarking on frail craft must discard unessential equipment and relax the rigid bonds of tribal custom. Any culture brought to Britain must be insularized by the very conditions of transportation."

Let us examine the process at work.

The first farming began around the Mediterranean, about 3000 B.C., and spread westward to Europe, reaching Britain some 500 years later. It was exceedingly primitive agriculture. The earliest known farm was excavated in 1925 at Windmill Hill, on a chalky promontory in Wiltshire overlooking Avebury. No traces of dwellings were found. The farm consisted of ditched corrals or causeways, which probably served as centers for the seasonal round-up of livestock. These were not permanent village sites, according to Stuart Piggott, the farm's leading interpreter, but are best understood "as a permanent rallying point for several small scattered communities at a certain time of year."

Soon the Windmill Hill people encountered other newcomers who were ardent bearers of a religious idea that originated in the Mediterranean area and spread through Europe to Scandinavia. These were the megalith builders, who had already reached the Scottish islands before sending missionary parties to the south of England. This people buried its dead collectively in long mounds or cairns, of which there are approximately 200 in Britain alone. The biggest in England is the West Kennet Long Barrow, not far from Windmill Hill. The colonists intermarried with the first agriculturalists, producing a hybrid community which scholars call Secondary Neolithic. It was this community that around 1800 B.C. built Stonehenge I, clearing the circular site for the more imposing sanctuary that was to follow.

The next arrivals were the aggressive Beaker Folk, so-called because of the bell-shaped pots they produced. They came from Holland and the Rhineland around 2000 B.C., bringing with them, apparently for the first time in Britain, the art of making metal—and of brewing beer. With their superior technology, they overpowered the Secondary Neolithic peoples and, becoming dissatisfied with Stonehenge I, improved it by hauling eighty bluestone rocks, some weighing five tons, from Wales to the Salisbury Plain. The distance overland and by water is some 150 miles, and their feat was entertainingly duplicated for a BBC program by a team of schoolboys who in 1954 took a single rock by raft and sledge from the Prescelly Mountains to Stonehenge, thus convincing scoffers that it could be done.

By 1500 B.C. the Beaker Folk ceased being Good Europeans and had become Ancient Britons, acquiring a new identity as the Wessex People. Britain was now part of a flourishing Bronze Age Common Market as the Wessex chieftains developed a metal trade with Europe. Prosperity enabled the Britons to rebuild Stonehenge once again, this time by dragging eighty enormous sarsen stones from the Marlborough Downs, twenty miles away, and hoisting them into the linteled circle and horseshoe of trilithons still visible today. One can infer from this a Wessex military mastery over southern England, since the work gangs plainly labored for years in an unprotected open plain.

British Museum: An Assyrian Tank   The battles depicted on the Assyrian friezes are an invaluable primary source for ancient military history. A battering ram, not unlike a tank, can be seen on this bronze door. (COURTESY BRITISH MUSEUM)

Trade routes continued to expand, extending to astonishingly distant places. Egyptian beads have been found in Wessex graves. An even more exhilarating discovery was made in June 1953 at Stonehenge when Professor R. J. C. Atkinson was preparing to take a photograph of sarsen stone 53. For the first time he noticed two carvings on the great slab—the outlines of an ax and a dagger. The ax was of a familiar Bronze Age type, but the dagger resembled those found in Mycenae in Greece. Atkinson believes that the architect of Stonehenge III "must certainly have been a man who was familiar with the buildings of contemporary urban civilizations of the Mediterranean world." Britain at that time, he goes on to remark, was more truly part of Europe than at any other time until the Roman conquest.

The next thousand years were a retrograde period, the first Dark Age, as waves of European warrior peoples, beginning with the Battle-Ax folk, swept across the Channel. Crafts were of a high level during much of this millennium, but Britain was riven by wars between tribes like the ferocious Belgae and the earliest Celts, who both worshipped and hunted heads. Such was the Britain Caesar found, and he speaks respectfully of the crafts and the fighting ability of the tribes he encountered. But to these Britons, Stonehenge was already a riddle.

Caesar's two invasions failed, but pointed the way to the successful conquest of Britain in 43 A.D. by General Aulus Plautius, who led an army of 50,000 men across the Channel. For four centuries Rome ruled Britannia, yet the Channel helped to defeat attempts to Romanize the inhabitants with the same thoroughness experienced in Gaul. In the end, according to G. M. Trevelyan, Rome left behind three things of value: Welsh Christianity, a network of roads, and the traditional importance of cities like London.

Reminders of the Roman era litter the English landscape: country villas, temples, baths, theaters, city walls, milestones, Channel fortresses, and even a lighthouse. Seven thousand miles of Roman roads have been mapped. One can assume, in driving through England, that if a road is straight, its original engineer probably spoke Latin. Yet, despite this enterprise, the Romans left little mark on the popular memory—the one name of the period that remains a household byword is Queen Boudicca, and she was a native rebel against the imperial intruders. Regrettably, not even central heating—a feature of every villa—commended itself to the British.

Why did Rome make so light an impression? One answer is that the Romans did not seriously attempt to colonize Britain; though veterans of the Legions were settled in Colchester, Gloucester, Lincoln and York. Another provocative answer is ventured by David Divine, military correspondent of the London *Sunday Times*, who blames Hadrian's Wall. Using modern cost-analysis techniques, he argues, in his *Northwest Frontier of Rome*, that the seventy-three-mile-long Wall required a garrison of 30,000 men, roughly double the usual estimate of scholars. The result, if his calculations are correct, is that Britain was quartered by an overlarge force, susceptible to constant involvement in emperor-making intrigues, much like the French Army in Algeria. The Wall, he finds, was a military success but a political

British Museum: An Israelite King   The only known portrait of an Old Testament Hebrew king is found on the obelisk of Shalamanaser, in which King Jehu is shown prostrate before the Assyrian warlord. (COURTESY BRITISH MUSEUM)

failure, draining away the energy and money that could have been better invested in civil administration.

Mr. Divine's ingenious case has not carried the field among scholarly guardians of the Wall, and it can be objected that he is too sweeping in his verdict, since the Roman occupation did give Britain a long period of relative peace and at least the infrastructure of a more advanced civilization. If the Romans had attempted a more intensive settlement, would it have made a decisive difference? Would the colonists have Romanized Britain or have become British Romans, acquiring the insular imprint of the natives? Even within the Empire, Britain was an offshore island, and her comparative self-sufficiency found an enduring image in the figure of Britannia, first stamped on her coins during the reign of Hadrian, and still on coins today, though somewhat shrunken on the new decimalized issue.

"Our Frontiers, bounded by the merciful sea, have, in His Goodness, been laid down by Almighty God, and they will remain fixed, immutable and inviolate, please the Lord!! until the end of Time," exulted an editorial in *The Sunday Pictorial*. Behind these ramparts of water, Britain has been able to look with irritating superiority upon the Continent. "The Government wants to change our money system," the *Daily Express* recently snapped, "but half the world's trade is done in pounds, shillings and pence. Instead of Britain switching to decimal coinage, why don't the foreigners change to sterling?" Or, as the woman said when asked her religion at Tower Bridge Court in London, "British!"

The outlook is retroactive, extending to the Druids (whose cannibalism is dismissed as Roman propaganda) and to Ancient Britons of every breed. Recently *The Times* published a photograph which was rashly captioned "Barbaric British Chieftain of about 1600 years ago." This was too much for Major F. B. Topham (Retd.), who rushed to his writing table to admonish *The Times:* "Barbaric Britain indeed! Tacitus in his *Vita Agricolae* tell us: 'To robbery, slaughter and plunder the Romans give the lying name of Empire; they make a solitude and call it peace.' Who, I wonder, were the barbarians?" *

* As another letter to *The Times* explained, "The truth is that no country in Europe but our own can conceive it is possible that action can be dictated by purely moral motives, entirely regardless of self-interest . . . we must recognize that our moral standpoint is beyond the comprehension of other European countries." This, and some of my other quotations, were taken from the "This England" feature of the *New Statesman*, a unique source for social archaeologists.

IV

THE SHAPE OF THINGS PAST

And see you the marks that show and fade,
Like shadows on the Downs?
O they are the lines the Flint Men made,
To guard their wondrous towns.
KIPLING, "Puck's Song"

THAT WAREHOUSE OF THE PAST sitting in Bloomsbury, the British Museum,
illustrates the best and the worst in the way the English display their choicest
artifacts. Much of the museum has the congested mustiness that once impelled
Walter Pater to lament that museums induce "the feeling that nothing could
ever have been young." The great Egyptian statues seem to melt into an
incorporeal gloom in the gallery that encloses the Rosetta Stone, and even the
new wing provided for the Elgin Marbles has an icehouse chill, giving the
sculpture the appearance of luminous cadavers in a morgue. But reform is
gradually taking place, and some galleries have been renovated (notably the
Greek rooms) while others are grudgingly yielding their clutter to improved
display techniques.

A gallery I particularly like is the Babylonian Room on the upper floor,
which houses the Sumerian treasures found by Sir Leonard Woolley in Ur of
the Chaldees. In 1922 Sir Leonard came upon a grisly death-pit containing
seventy-four skeletons, mainly of women who were presumably killed to
accompany their lord and master. Yet the same grave incongruously yielded
objects of cheerful delight: a he-goat rearing on its legs to sniff golden petals,
a bull-headed lyre (the oldest yet found), and gaming-boards with seven
numbered counters for each player. It is like overhearing laughter in the
charnelhouse, the frivolous souvenirs of a slaughter occurring some 4,500
years ago, more than a thousand years before the Fall of Troy.

Tucked away in an obscure crevice in the upper floor is a collection of
Aztec objects which were most probably part of the trove sent by Cortés to
impress his Most Christian King at the time of the Mexican Conquest. The
jade-encrusted skull and sacrificial dagger, both so instantly evocative of the
Aztec world, would hold a place of honor in any lesser museum. Not so far
away is the Mildenhall Treasure, found in Suffolk and acquired in 1946, the
family silver of a fourth-century Roman or Romanized Briton. The great

British Museum: A Sumerian Goat One of the prizes unearthed by Sir Leonard Woolley at Ur of the Chaldees. (COURTESY BRITISH MUSEUM)

dish, about two feet wide, and the silver service, all adorned with a pagan frolic, are straight from Petronius, a *Satyricon* in plate.

On the lower floor, in the King Edward Gallery, one unexpectedly encounters the treasure found in the Sutton Hoo ship burial, discovered in Suffolk in 1938 and meticulously exhumed. The excavators were able to establish the outline of an eighty-foot ship in which a Viking-style burial was made; no body was found, and the craft was probably a cenotaph of a seventh-century Saxon chief whose remains were lost at sea. Four thousand cut garnets adorn the belt found in the ship, and the baldric or outer harness in the royal wardrobe contains more gold than has been unearthed in any other Saxon grave. If the Mildenhall dish recalls *The Satyricon*, Sutton Hoo is Beowulf: hard-hewn, ruthless, the golden pillage of war.

Another prize exhibit has been perambulating for some time because of the remodeling program, but somewhere one should be able to find the portrait statues of Queen Artemisa and King Mausolus, which once crowned the Mausoleum of Halicarnassus, one of the Seven Wonders. These two proud bodies once reigned over the most magnificent of mortal tombs; they were obtained for Britain by her Ambassador in Constantinople, who stripped the friezes from the Mausoleum as Lord Elgin did at the Parthenon. Everywhere in the museum one finds similar evidence that the antiquarian, no less than trade, follows the flag. The Rosetta Stone was seized from the French in Alexandria as a prize of war. Sir Henry Layard, while a diplomat, uprooted the Winged Lions of Nimrud and the Assyrian friezes

British Museum: The Mildenhall Treasure   This richest of Roman hoards of plate included a superb platter adorned with satyrs. (COURTESY BRITISH MUSEUM)

British Museum: The Sutton Hoo Treasure A grim mask of a Saxon chieftain was among the finds buried in a ship on the Suffolk coast. (COURTESY BRITISH MUSEUM)

with their encyclopedic depiction of warfare—and he also managed to carry off the Black Obelisk of the Assyrian warlord Shalamanaser III, which contains the only known portrait of a Hebrew king (Jehu, shown prostrate before his conqueror).

This suggests the deeper conundrum in the continuing debate over whether Britain should return the Elgin Marbles to Greece, a demand based on the argument that the Turks, who then ruled in Athens, had no moral right to hand over another people's property to a Scottish nobleman. But if the museum acceded to the demand, where could it logically stop? The great museums of the world are filled with booty whose provenance will not survive scrutiny. Does anyone expect the British Museum to preside over the liquidation of its own empire? For generations to come the museum will probably remain what it is—a collection of Himalayan scope and grandeur, or, as the old Baedeker guidebook judged it to be, "the greatest in the world." And perhaps that is no bad thing.

To obtain some grasp of prehistoric England, to retrace "the lines the Flint Men made," one must travel from London to the West Country. Fortunately, the area in England that was first settled is still among the least settled, meaning that the ancient sites exist in a landscape still mercifully unspoiled. I know of few pleasanter trips in the itinerary of archaeology than the circuit one can make from Winchester to Dorset, via Salisbury and Bath, preferably in a car.

I begin with Winchester simply as a deceleration chamber for the fugitive from London. It is a town with ancient roots, serving as a tribal center for the Belgae before Vespasian's Second Legion overwhelmed it, when it became Venta Belgarum. Once King Alfred's capital, its past importance is reflected in the size of its cathedral, the longest in Europe, extending 556 feet and containing the tombs of Jane Austen and Izaak Walton, both excellent decelerators. In the castle hangs King Arthur's Round Table, with every knight named, an irresistible fake.

Winchester offers a springboard for the trip through the chalk hills of Wiltshire to Salisbury, whose cathedral spire soon thrusts into view, turning the windshield into a landscape print. Salisbury is Trollope's Barchester, and on its periphery is Wilton House, my own favorite of the English stately homes, and Old Sarum, where tufted ramparts and a conical mound mark the original city site, abandoned during the Middle Ages.

Just over nine miles from Salisbury is Stonehenge, about which I have already said much. Not long ago I visited these famous stones on June 21, Midsummer Day, when the British Druid Order congregated at 4:49 a.m. to greet the rays of the new season's sun. Before this great event the Order was found in the chartered buses that had brought them on their annual pilgrimage; they affably gave me brochures describing their cult (they claim Wil-

Stonehenge from the Air The bluestones were carried from Wales, and the great sarsens from a quarry twenty miles away. (PHOTO AEROFILMS LTD.)

Avebury: Aerial View This great stone circle encloses an entire Wiltshire village. Like many major British sites, Avebury is in unpolluted countryside, though only a few hours by train from London—a manifest pleasure of English archaeology. (PHOTO AEROFILMS LTD.)

liam Blake as a past disciple), but I cannot pretend I understood much of what I read. Druids believe, I gathered, that the elements are Wine, Bread, Salt, Fire, and Water, each with its mystic attributes which form part of a Druidic Succession reaching back to the ancient Celts, but just how was not made clear.

As sunrise approached, the robed Companions of the Order advanced to the stone circle, led by a Chief Druid who bore aloft a colorful banner and whose sandaled feet had a jaunty tread. When the first rays appeared—thankfully, they were not obliterated by the usual drizzle—four chirps of a great horn welcomed them. A blood-red rose, a silver vessel, and a wooden dish with wafers on it were laid on a white cloth, and were then sprinkled with sacramental water. The Chief Druid then cried "Arise, O Sun," and a ritual was chanted in English, with passages like this: "From whence has come the mystic word?" "From the Most High, in the Golden Age, when the mysteries were revealed to the Son of Man," etc., etc.

While the rite proceeded, police patrolled a barbed-wire barricade erected to protect the Druids from an exuberant audience composed mainly of teen-agers. In 1969 the crowd burst through the barrier, disrupting the rite with shouts such as "Bring on the lions! We want a human sacrifice!" Others of the youngsters were hippies, attracted by a cult that exalts Flower Power; some were dressed in what they regarded as ancient Egyptian style, with silver stars pasted on their forehead. None of this pleased Chief Druid Thomas L. Maughan, a retired Glasgow oil man, who said in disgust, "Never has an audience sunk to so low a level." Those who can demonstrate a serious interest in Druidism can receive a pass to get inside the enclosure by writing directly to the Druid Order, 77 Calton Avenue, Dulwich, London S.E. 21.*

___

* Druidism and pseudo-archaeology have become a fad among English hippies, who have seized on Alexander Thom's *Megalithic Sites in Britain* (Oxford, 1967), an austerely serious

Druids at Stonehenge Each vernal dawn on June 21 brings modern Druids to the sanctuary for a mystic ritual that is resolutely performed amid teen-age catcalls. (PHOTO KARL E. MEYER)

View of Avebury   A nineteenth-century engraving shows Avebury as it appeared before archaeologists had partially restored the stone circle which had been vandalized by villagers.

A short drive from Stonehenge is Avebury, the largest megalithic stone circle in Europe. It once contained about a hundred upright stones, the heaviest weighing some forty tons, which formed a ring within a moat and a bank enclosing no less than 28.5 acres and extending 1,100 feet across—so big that a village has been built within it. The villagers once turned with wrath on the stones, tipping them into pits filled with burning straw and smashing them apart with sledgehammers. But a scrupulous restoration has righted some of the fallen stones and marked the sites of others, so that the circle is visible as one traces it through pastures populated with tranquil cows (nearby is the Red Lion pub, reputedly on the site of the sanctuary's sacrificial altar).

Avebury did not come to scholarly notice until it was rediscovered by the indefatigible John Aubrey, biographer and student of Stonehenge, while he was fox-hunting in 1648. Twenty years later Pepys stopped in the village, and he was taken by a countryman (his diary records) to "a place trenched in like Old Sarum almost, with great stones pitched in it, some bigger than those at Stonag in figure, to my great admiration: and he told me that most of learning coming by do come and view them, and that the King did so: and that the Mount cast hard by is called Selbury, from one king Seall buried there, so tradition says."

---

book, and linked Thom's "megalithic yard" with mystic lore about the Egyptian pyramids. This is done in a book with an underground vogue, *The View over Atlantis* (London: Sago Press, 1969) by John Michel, who stirs together in an effervescent cocktail most of the crank theories of the past century, including the thesis that ancient English churches are mysteriously aligned on a Druidic grid. His previous work is *The Flying Saucer Vision*.

The Mount "cast hard by" is Silbury Hill, the largest manmade mound in Europe, rising 130 feet above the surrounding meadows, with a volume of 12.5 million cubic feet. Its purpose remains a mystery. Recently the BBC provided the funds for the first full-scale assault on the hill, an ambitious campaign directed by Professor R. J. C. Atkinson, the most recent excavator of Stonehenge. The project has prompted the usual tempest among archaeologists, and Atkinson has had to dismiss the "brash and ill-informed criticisms" of certain colleagues. He has also had to shrug off the complaint of television critics that as a production the dig was anti-climactic because no spectacular finds have been shown on the cameras that have followed the Professor into the very innards of the mound.

The persistent tradition that Silbury is a tomb has encouraged treasure hunters over the centuries to bore within it, without any known results. Archaeologists have speculated hopefully that the hill might enclose the tomb of the master builder of Stonehenge, but so far the grave—if it exists—has defied all attempts to find it. What Atkinson has discovered is unburned vegetable matter which at long last has provided a reliable date for the mound. The carbon date of the roots and stems turned out to be 2145 B.C. plus or minus 95 years, a date that makes Silbury Hill a contemporary of the megalithic tomb builders, and not of the Bronze Age Wessex peoples who gave Stonehenge III its final monumental form.

This makes Silbury Hill a neighbor in time as well as place of the nearby West Kennet Long Barrow, the largest chambered tomb in England, measur-

Silbury Hill The largest manmade mound in Europe, Silbury Hill persists as an enigma despite recent excavations sponsored by the BBC. No tomb or treasure has been found in this great hummock outside Avebury. (PHOTO AEROFILMS LTD.)

ing 350 feet in length and reached through a pleasant meadow. Two pairs of burial chambers have been found in the barrow, one of them containing some thirty skeletons, ten of them children, which had been buried at intervals over period of centuries. Around it is a pastoral landscape with nothing to offend the eye.

From Avebury the highway leads to Bath, the Aquae Sulis of the Romans and the outstanding Georgian city of Britain. Bath's crescents and squares, its arcades and greenery, are arranged with harmonious felicity on the banks of the Avon—one likes to think that it owes some of its orderly gridwork and exemplary town-planning to the Romans, who came here to heal their rheumatic limbs, building a magnificent bath and temple to Sul or Sulis, the deity of the local springs. Evidence of the Roman city came to light in 1755, and successive excavations have peeled back layers of the ancient settlement. The ruins are reached through Beau Nash's Pump Room, which frames an open-air pool, now extensively restored with a reassembled colonnade of busts. Below are two circular baths and adjoining suites of hot and cold rooms; thermal vapors form a veil of gauze as one penetrates the depths. During the annual music festival, held in June–July, the Roman swimming pool is opened to visitors, briefly recalling Sulis to life.

South of Bath, as one continues the circular route, lie Wells Cathedral and the honey-toned town of Bradford-on-Avon, with its tiny Saxon church, all within the vicinity of Glastonbury and South Cadbury Hill, the realm of

West Kennet Long Barrow   The longest barrow in England was a mortuary for descendants of the Windmill Hill settlers, the earliest English farmers. (PHOTO AEROFILMS LTD.)

Maiden Castle Behind the turfed ramparts of this great hill fort, the warlike Belgae sought to resist Vespasian's legions. It is the most formidable of Iron Age forts that dot the English countryside. (PHOTO AEROFILMS LTD.)

Arthur. Pressing farther south, the trip culminates in Thomas Hardy's Dorchester, a city dating to the Iron Age, later serving as a Roman stronghold against the warlike Belgae. A few miles south is Maiden Castle, the largest Iron Age fortress in Britain, a serpentine coil of massive ditches and moats. In a notable series of campaigns during 1934–1938 Sir Mortimer Wheeler excavated the castle, tracing its growth from its earliest phase in 250 B.C. as a dwelling site to its expansion into a military earthwork in which an entire hilltop, spreading over forty-five acres, was enclosed. Before the Romans, the castle repeatedly changed hands and was at one time held by King Cunobelin, or Cymbeline, whose story was told by Geoffrey of Monmouth and dramatized by Shakespeare. Cymbeline was a ruler of the Belgae, and these were the fighters who defended the fortress when it was besieged in 44 A.D. by Vespasian, then still a general. Sir Mortimer found in the ramparts the skeleton of a British defender whose spine was pierced by a Roman ballistic bolt: a cry of defiance and agony which vivifies a silent page of history. The skeleton is in the local museum in Dorchester.

Of the innumerable other prehistoric English sites, I mention only one, an Iron Age village that lies a good way farther to the west, near Land's End at the tip of Cornwall. This is the village of Chysauster, which has been skillfully restored so that one can easily picture what it was like. There are nine houses, each with a central courtyard, fireplace, and drain—and each with its private garden in the back, an English touch. As Jacquetta Hawkes writes of the site, here one can perceive, in an Iron Age summer, "the sun glaring in the courtyard where the dogs lie on the paving, the rooms dark as caves, a woman sweating as she pounds away with the heavy grindstone, small children kept safely in sight by the closed door of the passageway. All a little smelly and untidy, but not too uncomfortable and wonderfully companionable." One's imagination is quickened by the Cornish desolation, the abandoned tin mines, the hills ribbed with rocks, the gulls, the raw wind.

Roman Britain, to take a leap forward in time, has more bulk but less style than prehistoric Britain; it is the difference between engineering and folk art. There is an unvarying uniformity in Roman remains, and not only in Britain. Across a great arc of Europe, from Cologne on the Rhine to Budapest on the Danube, and down to North Africa and Asia Minor, one finds everywhere the familiar mosaics and amphitheaters, villas and walled towns, all struck from a single mold. Surely no other empire extending over so large an area and embracing such diverse peoples has been able to impose its norms of planning and architecture so pervasively, and permanently.

Because so many English towns owe their foundation or enlargement to the Legions, pavements everywhere cover the work of the Caesars. Periodically in London new Roman remains come to light, sometimes to the consternation of developers who must then cope with a National Monument; in 1954 a Temple of Mithras was uncovered in the City of London, complete with a treasure (now exhibited in the Guildhall Museum). In walking around the City one comes unexpectedly upon great globs of stone—surviving segments of the seven-gated wall that encircled the city, its path partly marked by a street suitably called London Wall.

The most impressive Roman remains near London are to be found at St. Albans, less than an hour's bus ride away, the city once known in Latin as Verulamium. Here successive excavations have unearthed the remains of shops and dwellings, of a notable mosaic showing a lion killing a stag, and of the finest Roman theater found in Britain. The great abbey nearby was built with masonry ransacked from the ruins, and the resident Barons of Verulam (Francis Bacon among them) have borrowed the old name for their title, a measure of how the Roman occupation has been absorbed and its memory domesticated. It is this that distinguishes St. Albans: the past has been turned into a picnic ground, its relics organically interwoven into the English Sunday.

Farther afield is a more spectacular Roman remain, a palace built as a reward for a Quisling. It is found near Chichester (reachable by train in two hours), the sister city of Chartres, where a proud cathedral rises over a country town still partly enclosed by Roman walls. During the summer there is a local theater festival, which can be worked into the itinerary (as can

Roman Theater, St. Albans   The best preserved of Roman theaters is an hour's drive from London. Like the city of Verulamium around it, it was pillaged for masonry to build the great abbey nearby. (PHOTO AEROFILMS LTD.)

the Bath Music Festival in the trip to Stonehenge and the West Country). On the outskirts of Chichester is Fishbourne Roman Palace, discovered in 1960 when workmen were cutting a water-main trench across a field.

The palace was apparently built as a payoff to a petty local ruler who collaborated with the Romans, becoming "King Cogidubnus, Legate in Britain of the Empire." He was well compensated; his court included spacious audience chambers and opulent baths, giving him the appearance if not the substance of power. After the Legate's death in around 100 A.D. his palace was cut up into smaller apartments by humbler inhabitants before it finally burned to the ground about 270 A.D. In walking through the vast shed housing this expertly excavated and intelligently arranged site, one catches a glimpse of the problems the conquerors had with British workmen. A large tile floor, built by imported specialists, was later overlaid by clumsy locals who were unable to recreate its geometric pattern, muddling the design. The excavation of the palace, it might be noted, was partly underwritten by the London *Sunday Times*—a rivalry in archaeological patronage exists on Fleet Street, and the paper's chief competitor, *The Observer,* has been one of the sponsors of the digs at Camelot and at Masada in Israel.

But the outstanding monument left by Rome can only be seen in at least a weekend's foray, Hadrian's Wall. I would recommend an approach by way of Durham, dominated by a gloomily impressive cathedral, with an overnight stop at Blanchland, where a hotel has been built in the well-preserved remains

Hadrian's Wall It once stretched for 73.5 miles across the Northumberland countryside, but intact stretches—such as this one, near Housesteads Fort—are now rare. (PHOTO AERO-FILMS LTD.)

Hadrian's Wall: Housesteads Fort The fort was one of fourteen built at intervals along the wall manned with garrisons ready to repel any assault reported from the network of watchtowers. (PHOTO AEROFILMS LTD.)

of a border-country monastery. From Blanchland one can reach the Wall by way of Hexham, where the Abbey is made of Roman masonry (including inscribed fragments of Imperial decrees). A sensible procedure is to pass from Hexham to Corbridge, a Roman station less than a mile from the town. This characteristic compound has repair shops, storehouses, granaries, and other amenities necessary for the morale of troops guarding the northern frontier of the Empire.

A good walk along the Wall is possible near Housesteads Fort, a great rectangular enclave that was one of fourteen on the 73.5-mile barricade which crosses the narrow neck of England from Tyne to Solway Firth. On the Wall's parapet, one gets an idea of its military utility. The Wall was not intended to seal in Picts and Scots, since it was low enough to be easily stormed. But it had a network of guards who could immediately signal for assistance, and the Wall was paralleled by a highway along which troops could be rushed from garrisons. It possessed eighty mile-castles and 160 wall turrets, which were like a chain of alarm bells for summoning the cohorts that manned it.

The construction of this continuous watchtower was ordered in 122 A.D. by Hadrian, whose express purpose, a biographer states, was "to separate Rome from the barbarians." A generation later a further barrier was built across the Forth-Clyde isthmus in Scotland, the tufted Antonine Wall, fronted by a forty-foot fighting ditch; this acted for a period as a forward line of defense against the Caledonians. These impressive fortifications were unlike the Maginot Line in that they worked; though Hadrian's Wall was overrun on at least three occasions—in A.D. 197, 296, and 367—it did provide an effective shield, enduring almost until the Legions were withdrawn at the end of the fourth century. Whether the Wall was worth the effort, whether the resources committed to it could have been better spent on the subjugation rather than containment of the barbarians, whether the restive foreign troops quartered here provided the tinder for constant intrigues—these are questions one can think about in tramping the damp Northumberland moors alongside the most astonishing military monument left by Rome and the most extensive ruin in Great Britain. Hadrian's Wall is a parable of power with an ambiguous moral, and, as such, belongs as much to the modern as the ancient world.

Chapter Eight

THE MOON'S
DARK SIDE

MEXICO

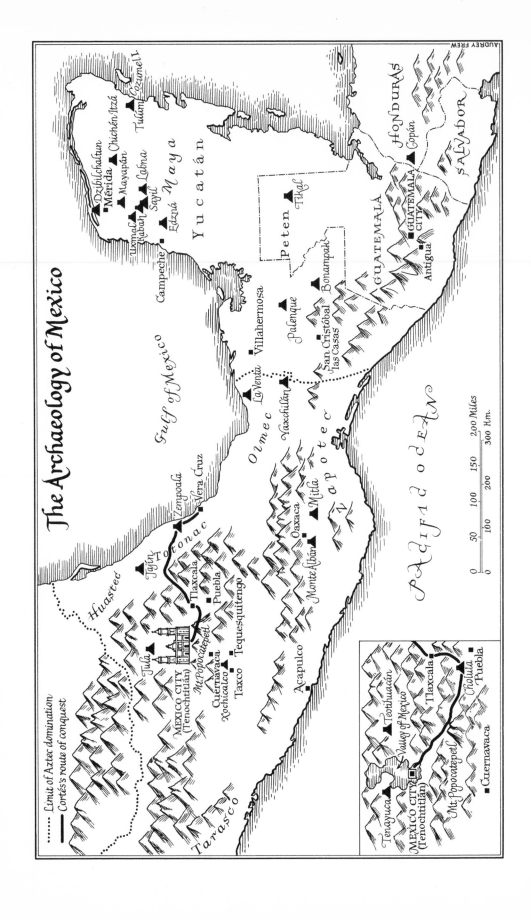

The Archaeology of Mexico

······ Limit of Aztec domination
——— Cortés's route of conquest

AUDREY FREW

I

THE GREAT GAME

Can it still be asked from whence came the men who people America? VOLTAIRE (1765)

I N A GUST OF PRESIDENTIAL HYPERBOLE, Mr. Nixon called the lunar landing in 1969 the greatest event since Creation. Distressed Christians protested that the President had overlooked a more recent Event of some passing significance to their faith. But Mr. Nixon's secular memory was no less fallible, since he also failed to mention the discovery of the New World, an event whose importance an American President should be the last to minimize.

Indeed, to its first Western explorers the New World constituted a moon filled with marvels more dazzling than anything yet brought back by the astronauts. On its dark side were the Indian civilizations, whose very existence had never been guessed and whose discovery posed a delicate and vexatious theological problem. The Italian historian Francesco Guicciardini, writing in the 1530s, noted that the Columbian voyages had "given some cause for alarm to interpreters of the Holy Scriptures" because the Americas seemed to confute verses of the Psalms which declared that the sound of the songs had spread to the very edges of the world. This was taken to mean that faith in Christ had spread over the entire earth through the mouths of the Apostles—an interpretation contrary to truth, Guicciardini coolly observed, "because no knowledge of these lands had hitherto been brought to light, nor have any signs of relics of our faith been found there." So sensitive was this point that these words were deleted from all editions of *Storia d'Italia* which appeared before 1774.*

* This detail was shrewdly noted by Sidney Alexander in his superb translation of *The History of Italy* (New York: Macmillan, 1969).

Thus, what can be called the Great Game of American archaeology, the dispute over who discovered the New World, owes much of its origin to a fine Scriptural question. When the Spanish friars came to Mexico after the Conquest, they rejoiced to hear tales of fair-faced and bearded gods who had come to the Americas long ago from far away. Clearly, these must be the Holy Apostles. And the Indians? Manifestly, they were the Lost Tribes of Israel. As one Dominican, Fray Diego Duran, reasoned, the Aztecs were Hebrews, "considering their way of life, their ceremonies, their rites and superstitions, their omens, and false dealings, so related to and characteristic of those of the Jews."

Still, the matter could not be disposed of so simply; one hears a doubting friar saying peevishly, "But, Brother Diego, they don't *look* Jewish." More ingenious explanations were proffered. In Peru an early chronicler, Agustín de Zarate, decreed that the Incas were survivors of the drowned continent of Atlantis. As early as 1607 a book was published entitled *The Origin of the Indians of the New World;* the author, Fray Gregorio García, almost in despair, gave this composite answer to the worrisome riddle: "The Indians proceed neither from one nation or people, nor have they come from one part alone of the Old World, or by the same road, or at the same time; some have probably descended from the Carthaginians, others from the Ten Lost Tribes and other Israelites, others from the lost Atlantis, from the Greeks, from the Phoenicians, and still others from the Chinese, Tartars and other groups."

Over the centuries the list has steadily lengthened. Among those soberly nominated as the discoverers of America are:

Egyptians	Trojans	French
Babylonians	Romans	English
Hittites	Moors	Welsh
Canaanites	Frisians	Irish
Ethiopians	Huns	Danes
Scythians	Basques	Norsemen
Madagascans	Polynesians	Canary Islanders
Portuguese	Koreans	Mandingoes
Old Spanish	Assyrians	Men of Ophir
Etruscans	Japanese	Men of Tarsus

—not to speak of the lost continents of Mu and Lemuria, or the claim pressed by Peking that a Chinese monk named Fa Hsein landed in Mexico in 412 A.D. So earnestly is the Great Game taken that it has prompted attempts to sail the Atlantic in a papyrus boat, has caused an Anglo-Irish viscount to die in debtors' prison because of the expense of publishing nine costly volumes intended to confirm the Lost Tribe thesis, and has inspired the Mormon church to finance extensive excavations in Mexico (the *Book of Mormon* holds that the New World was settled by various Semitic tribes, including the Jaredites, refugees from the Tower of Babel).*

All of which impelled an anonymous parodist on the London *Daily Telegraph* to announce a sly new hypothesis—that the Aztecs discovered Europe, using stone boats and the Aztec stone compass. The paper related that the idea was supported by the discovery in the English midlands of a fragment of a step pyramid and a piece of obsidian thought to be part of a tear-off stone calendar. Moreover, a local authority, the Reverend J. S. Instep, "states in his book, *Our Aztec Heritage*, that there is a recognizable Aztec strain in the Stretchford population even today, and that Aztec customs, such as large-scale human sacrifices, have never completely died out."

But another discovery was not a joke. Working quietly, with hardly a nod to the great publicity wind machines, three unsung archaeologists have found persuasive evidence that two groups of pre-Columbian voyagers did cross the Pacific and land on the coast of Ecuador. This one hard nugget in the vast fog of surmise has deep and unsettling implications for a question that has troubled archaeologists no less than Spanish friars: Did the Indians invent their own civilization?

The story begins in the cluttered offices of the Department of Archaeology in a lofty warren of the Smithsonian Institution in Washington, D.C. In 1953 a tall Ecuadoran named Emilio Estrada marched into the office, introduced himself to Clifford Evans and his wife, Betty J. Meggers, both staff archaeologists, and announced that he wanted to excavate in Ecuador. Estrada was a successful businessman in Guayaquil and an expert sailor—he had helped Thor Heyerdahl obtain the wood in Ecuador used to build *Kon-Tiki*. He was also restless with merely selling automobiles and appliances.

As it happened, the Evanses were planning an ambitious campaign in Latin America, with the aim of digging coastal sites—long passed over by archaeologists in favor of the flashier inland ceremonial centers—to determine how much maritime contact took place among the ancient Indian civilizations. Clifford Evans has a salient jaw, a stubborn eye, and a pithy tongue. "A problem in American archaeology," he once told me, "is that so many of the best ones are landlubbers—they don't know anything about sailing. If Heyerdahl proved anything in the *Kon-Tiki* trip, it was that it is possible to go more than four thousand miles in an open boat and survive. Until somebody did it,

* Thor Heyerdahl attempted the Atlantic crossing in 1969 and again in 1970 in order to demonstrate that the ancient Egyptians could have made the same trip. The viscount was Lord Kingsborough, whose *Antiquities of Mexico* (1830–48) remains a valuable source, however dotty its motive. The Mormons finance the New World Archaeological Foundation, whose work is considered reputable. The list ought properly to include a French abbé, Brasseur de Bourbourg, who in 1855 bravely announced that the Maya language had affinities with Scandinavian; in the course of five trips to the Americas he came upon an incalculably valuable treatise on the Maya language compiled by a forgotten cleric, Bishop de Landa. The balminess of the Great Game has been oddly fruitful for scholarship.

Digging at Valdivia Businessman-archaeologist Emilio Estrada discusses a find with Betty Meggers on the site which yielded the first convincing evidence of a pre-Columbian trans-Pacific contact. (PHOTO CLIFFORD EVANS)

the possibility was only hypothetical. It took a stunt to show to the landlubbers that ancient mariners might have been better seamen than some of us liked to admit."

Thus, Estrada's visit was propitious. Ecuador was high on the list of target sites because so little digging had been done there and because winds and currents made its coast a likely point of maritime contact. Soon the Evanses went to Guayaquil and began training Estrada; he was a responsive pupil, learning not only how to excavate but how to publish results in monographs of first-class quality and how to manage the museum which he founded. In their first season the trio found evidence of an unsuspected two-way trade between Indians of coastal Ecuador and Guatemala. But in a site near the fishing village of Valdivia, on the southern coast of Ecuador, something more curious emerged from the wet soil.

Abruptly, around 3200 B.C., incised pottery appeared at Valdivia, pottery without any known archaeological pedigree and of an established date earlier than sherds found elsewhere in the New World. As Betty Meggers remarks in her report of the find, the appearance of pottery "can only be interpreted as the result of introduction of a well-established tradition from elsewhere." Estrada himself began a search for pottery styles that might show a kinship with the Valdivia ware. He found that strikingly similar work had been produced in the same period on the Japanese island of Kyusha, at the

Valdivia: The Pottery Link Characteristic potsherds found in the Ecuador site (left) are pictured next to similar incised fragments discovered in the Kyusha island of Japan. Designs shown here are only a few of the many which had comparable similarities. (PHOTO CLIFFORD EVANS)

opposite edge of the Pacific, a place from which favorable winds and tides could plausibly send a stray fishing craft across the sea.

In another dig near the town of Bahia in North Manabi Province other puzzling finds came to light—house models, pottery figures seated in a Buddha position, headrests and pan-pipes with tubes graduated to the center instead of from one side to another in the usual New World fashion. None of the work fitted known American styles; carbon-dating placed the first appearance of the artifacts at around 500 B.C. As Miss Meggers judiciously comments, a second trans-Pacific contact was indicated, probably the result of a trading vessel drifting to Ecuador from Southeast Asia, where comparable pottery styles flourished at the time. "We can guess little more than the fact that a trans-Pacific contact took place," she reports, "but the secretive smile on the La Plata seated figurine suggests that he could tell a fascinating story, if only he could speak." *

In 1960 I happened to meet Emilio Estrada. He had come to Washington chiefly on a political mission, to administer some healing private diplomacy in behalf of an erratic and irascible Ecuadoran who had then been elected President—later I learned that Estrada had long been his rival in national politics. We talked about sailing, about the baroque complexities of Ecua-

* Betty J. Meggers, *Ecuador* (London: Thames and Hudson, 1966), p. 94.

Two Bahia Pieces The seated figurine and pottery headrest are among many pieces found in Ecuador which fit no known New World style, resembling instead Southeast Asian work and suggesting a second trans-Pacific contact centuries after Valdivia. (PHOTO CLIFFORD EVANS)

2 CM.
1 IN.

doran politics, and about archaeology. "Nothing," Estrada said, his enormous shoulders leaning forward, his hands as eloquent as his eyes, "nothing has given me more satisfaction than digging up pots." But, sadly, a year later he was dead, felled by a heart disease.

His death came shortly after a final season of field work; his name later appeared as co-author with the Evanses of the bulky report published by the Smithsonian on the early formative period of coastal Ecuador. Recalling that he had been the first to suggest the link between Valdivia and Japan, his colleagues observed in the preface, "His co-authorship of this report is not simply a tribute—it is a position fully earned."

The report itself is a fascinating artifact: dynamite padded in scholarly cotton. The Evanses begin with an essay on the theoretical significance of pots, and then in chapter upon chapter the evidence is arrayed with soldierly precision, recording the most subtle variations of coastal pottery styles and comparing Valdivia ware with that of the Joman period on the island of Kyusha. It is spare, meticulous, and unsensational.

This cautious approach reflects an awareness that the Ecuadoran finds are a potential bombshell in a pitched battle in American archaeology, the combat between the diffusionists and the independent-inventionists, to use the clumsy but accepted terms. Something large hinges on the outcome of this scholarly struggle.

At this point it is necessary to sum up a few of the agreed-upon facts about the settlement of the New World. Two generations of research have fairly clearly established that the aboriginal stock of the Americas derives from Asiatic peoples who migrated across the Bering Strait beginning around 15,000 B.C. and possibly earlier. As waves of invaders dispersed through the Americas, different communities evolved distinctive cultures. On this outline there is general agreement. But when the Indian cultures flowered into rich variations, culminating in the high civilizations of the Andes and Mesoamerica, a more difficult question was posed: to what extent were these civilizations autochthonous and to what extent the hybrid products of Old World contacts?

An older generation of Americanists, exasperated with fables about the Lost Tribes and mysterious Muvians, came doggedly down on the side of independent invention. As Earnest A. Hooton, a Harvard anthropologist, was moved to complain: "We have set up for Aboriginal America a sort of *ex post facto* Monroe Doctrine and are inclined to regard suggestions of alien influence as acts of aggression."

A characteristic expression of the orthodox consensus is this passage from *The Ancient Maya* (1947) by the late Sylvanus Morley, long the dean of Mayanists: "The whole Maya story was unfolded within the confines of the Yucatan peninsula. . . . Its origins, rise and first florescence in Old Empire times were exclusively due to the genius of the Maya people. . . . The Maya developed their unique civilization practically without influences from the outside."

But a younger generation of scholars approached the question with a more open mind. Hostilities can be said to have commenced in 1949, when, on the occasion of a Congress of Americanists in New York, the American Museum of Natural History—once a stronghold of independent-inventionists —prepared a special exhibit showing parallelisms between Old and New World cultural traits. The case for diffusion was forcefully put by Gordon F. Ekholm, the museum's associate curator of archaeology:

> The large number of highly specific correspondences in so many fields precludes any possibility of mere accidental coincidence. There is no psychological law which could have caused people on both sides of the Pacific to stylize the lotus plant in the same manner . . . to invent the parasol and use it as a sign of rank and to invent the same complicated game. There is no other explanation than the assumption of cultural relationships. We must bow to the evidence of facts, even though this may mean a completely new start in our appraisal of the origin and development of the American Indian higher civilizations.

The diffusionist view is not without its awkward difficulties—for example, what about the wheel? If contacts did exist between Old and New World civilizations, why is it that the pilgrims from the sophisticated Old World failed to confide the secret of the wheel to the New, where the true wheel has been found only on children's toys in Mexico? A rebuttal is that Indian civilizations had little use for the wheel, since there were no horses or oxen in pre-Columbian America, and since human labor was cheap and abundant. But the answer is not wholly satisfactory, because the wheel can also be used in making pottery.

On the other hand, independent-inventionists must cope not only with striking correspondences in styles but also with bothersome gaps in the archaeological record. For example (writes Michael D. Coe of Yale, not a diffusionist himself), "It is embarrassingly plain that we have not the slightest indication of how pottery came to Mexico, or even whether it was independently invented there. Hints we have, yes, but hardly anything in the way of sound proof." * If the Mexican Indians devised their own civilizations, why is so crucial a link in the chain of evidence so elusive?

As with other debates, the argument could end in a compromise between the extreme claims of diffusionists and independent-inventionists. The distinctive character of pre-Columbian civilizations may be entirely due to the

---

* Michael D. Coe, *Mexico* (London: Thames and Hudson, 1962), p. 67.

Indian genius, while important details could have been influenced by chance contacts with the Old World—a Japanese fishing vessel, thrown upon the shores of Ecuador, could conceivably have trigged a mutation in cultural forms among the indigenous inhabitants. The finds made by the Evanses and Emilio Estrada have moved this fascinating possibility from the fog of surmise to the firmer terrain of arguable fact.

What is unarguable is that the pre-Columbian world evolved in relative if not absolute isolation. Here—on the moon's dark side—there was proof, at once exhilarating and frightening, of the range of human possibilities. Nowhere was this more true than in Mexico.

II

DEATH AND FLOWERS

> *There is nothing like death in war,*
> *nothing like the flowery death*
> *so precious to him who gives life:*
> *far off I see it: my heart yearns for it!*
> Aztec song, translation by
> ANGEL MARÍA GARIBAY

THE AZTECS CAME LATE into the Valley of Mexico—the date has been fixed at 1168 A.D.—descending from the north in the wake of the fall of Tula, capital of the more advanced Toltec peoples. There was a power vacuum, and the newcomers quickly filled it, imposing in the process a way of life whose idealism was more apparent to the Aztecs than to their unfortunate neighbors. The Aztecs believed in the divine duty of war because the sun had to be kept alive with blood.

The Aztec world was a tapestry of death and flowers, a mingling of the downright macabre and of exalted mysticism. Floral beauty meant much to the tribe. Its nobles carried elaborate bouquets, and in Tenochtitlán, the capital built on a lake, countless small boats plied among the piers and canals, bringing fresh blooms from nearby gardens. (Even today, in a market in a lake fourteen miles southeast of Mexico City, Indians speaking the Aztec tongue sell flowers from dugout canoes—the market is called Xochimilco, "the place where the flowers grow.")

Yet in this floral paradise all male children were dedicated at birth to violence. The attending midwife would say: "My very loved and tender son, here is the doctrine that was given to us by the gods. The place where you were born is not your true house because you are a soldier and servant of the

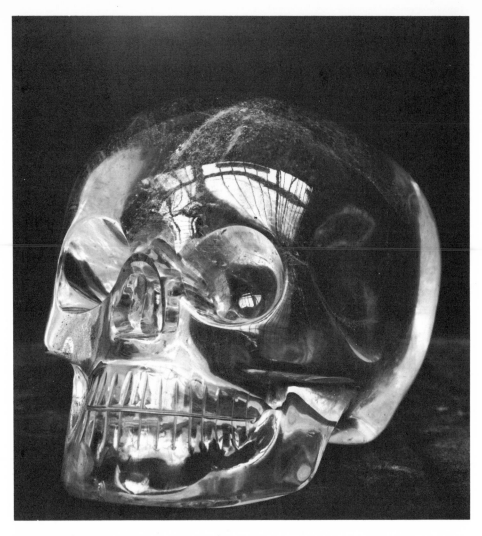

Aztec Skull The Aztec aesthetic of death is conveyed in this striking piece now in the British Museum. (COURTESY BRITISH MUSEUM)

gods. . . . Your obligation is to give the sun the blood of your enemies to drink, and to feed the earth with the corpses of your opponents."

Not content with normal wars, the Aztecs devised a curious custom to assure that there would always be battles to fight—the Wars of the Flowers. When a famine scourged central Mexico in 1450, the Aztec priests concluded that not enough hearts had been offered to the gods. So the tribe reached a solemn agreement with five neighboring peoples to fight ritual wars whose primary purpose would be to capture live prisoners for the hungry altars. In a Flowery War, or *xochiyaoyotl*, an equal number of combatants would meet at an appointed time and place, and every care was taken to avoid wasteful slaughter. Once, in a fight between the Aztecs and Cholula, the two sides contended furiously for a day and many prisoners were captured. The next morning an Aztec messenger asked the Cholulans if they wished to continue. No, was the polite reply, enough captives had been taken to satisfy the gods. Both armies marched peaceably home again.

In this violence there was a dignity, even a redeeming tenderness. When an Aztec took a prisoner, he said, "Here is my well-beloved son," and the captive replied, "Here is my revered father." There was a mystical kinship between the victim and the victor: the one was not degraded, and the other rarely showed a lust for blood. The annals of the early Spanish friars relate a number of instances in which brave enemies were offered their freedom by their Aztec captors; they voluntarily chose the altar instead.

Some rituals were irredeemably barbaric, such as the sacrifice of children to Tlaloc, the rain god, or the grisly fire ceremony in which captives were broiled on embers, their hearts torn from their blistered body while they were still agonizingly alive. But there was also the poignant ceremony honoring the sky god Tezcatlipoca (Lord of the Smoking Mirror). For this sacrifice the best-looking and bravest prisoner was chosen a year in advance, and during that time he became the incarnation of the god himself. He was attended by devoted priests, who accompanied him as he strolled about playing lovely melodies on a flute. Shortly before his execution four girls were chosen to be his companions; they would weep copiously on his last day, when he would lead a joyous procession to the temple. In mounting it, he would pause and break a flute at each step, a melancholy token of the end of his reign. After his heart was ripped from his breast, his body was carried down the stairs, not flung to the bottom in the usual manner. His skull, however, was strung on a rack with all the rest.

Jacques Soustelle, who saw something of modern cruelty during his years in Algeria, says in mitigation of the Aztecs: "At the height of their career the Romans shed more blood in their circuses and for their amusement than ever the Aztecs did before their idols. The Spaniards, so sincerely moved by the cruelty of native priests, nevertheless massacred, burnt, mutilated and tortured with a perfectly clear conscience." Or, as Prescott remarks in *The Conquest of Mexico*, death at the Aztec altar opened a clear path to paradise for the victim, whereas the Inquisition "branded its victims with infamy in this world and consigned them to everlasting perdition in the next." *

Still, the Aztec cosmos was highly unstable and dominated by gods whose nature was irreconcilable, and the tribe seemed anxiously aware of it. From the more civilized Toltecs the Aztecs learned to revere Quetzalcóatl (the Plumed Serpent), who in his guise as a god-king was a lover of science, a preceptor of the arts, and a teacher of humane morality. Quetzalcóatl was said to have opposed human sacrifice, asserting that the gods would be content with the killing of butterflies and birds instead. His influence can be discerned in the strain of humanism mixed with Aztec ferocity. Aztec literature reflects the contrary tendencies of the Aztec spirit. Consider, for example, this appealing prayer of an Aztec chieftain upon his election:

> Grant me, Lord, a little light,
> Be it no more than a glowworm giveth
> Which goeth about by night,
> To guide me through this life,
> This dream which lasteth but a day,
> Wherein are many things on which to stumble,
> And many things at which to laugh,
> And others like unto a stony path
> Along which one goes leaping.
> [*Translation by Lesley Bird Simpson,
> after Bernardino de Sahagun*]

Or take this harsh paean, which so clearly reflects the influence of the rival influence on the Aztecs, that of their tribal deity, Huitzilopochtli (Hummingbird-on-the-Left), the war god:

> The battlefield is the place:
> where one toasts the divine liquor in war,
> where are stained red the divine eagles,
> where the jaguars howl,
> where all kinds of precious stones rain from ornaments,
> where wave headdresses rich with fine plumes,
> where princes are smashed to bits.
> [*Translation by Angel María Garibay*]

---

* In a tangential vein, there is the anecdote told about the late Morris Raphael Cohen. He once asked his class at City College in New York to imagine that a superhuman being appeared on earth and offered to teach mankind a trick that would make life incomparably more pleasant. "In return," the philosopher went on, "the god demanded only the blood sacrifice of 50,000 lives a year. With what indignation would this proposal be rejected! Then came the automobile."

Aztec Dagger The sacrificial knife is also part of the small but select British Museum collection, some of which may have been part of the Aztec treasures sent to the King of Spain by Cortés. (COURTESY BRITISH MUSEUM)

Living in a precarious and menacing universe filled with a confusion of voices, the Aztecs were susceptible to panic when the unexpected occurred —such as the arrival of the Spaniards. It is true that the invaders had the advantage of horses and guns, neither of which the Mexicans had seen, and they also imported the deadly secret weapon of smallpox. Equally important, they were led by a Castilian of formidable courage and political guile. But when all is said (observes Octavio Paz), "The conquest of Mexico would be inexplicable without the treachery of the gods, who denied their own people."

In the years immediately before the Conquest, the Aztecs were distressed by a concatenation of omens that defied priestly explanation: comets were seen by day, temples were damaged by lightning, monstrous people appeared in the streets of the capital, some with two heads. When Moctezuma ordered that a large stone be brought for the sacrifice and skinning of men, the stone upbraided the Emperor's servants, saying: "Poor wretches! Why do you labor in vain? Have I not told you that I will never arrive in Mexico? Go, tell Moctezuma that it is too late. He should have thought of this before. Now he no longer needs me; a terrible event, brought on by fate, is about to happen!"

More upsetting still, a strange bird, resembling a crane, was brought before Moctezuma. It had a mirror on the crown of its head, and when the Emperor peered into the glass, he saw men running across a plain, mounted on animals that looked like deer. The ruler cried to his magicians, "Can you explain what I have seen? Creatures like human beings, running and fighting!" When the seers looked into the mirror, they saw nothing.

By an astonishing coincidence, Cortés arrived in 1519, or one-reed in the Aztec reckoning, a year in which it had been foretold that the bearded god-king Quetzalcóatl would return after four centuries in exile. The combination was simply too much for the Aztecs. A self-paralysis set in among them; their own religion proved to be their fatal weakness, especially since they were led by a brooding forty-year-old emperor who felt the gods were against him.

The practice of human sacrifice, in particular, proved a major military liability. The incessant wars with neighboring tribute states had made the Aztecs understandably unpopular, enabling Cortés to win Indian allies. Moreover, the need to feed the insatiable altars did much to nullify Aztec prowess in battle. Instead of trying to kill, the Aztecs sought to capture the Spaniards alive. At one critical point Cortés himself actually fell into Aztec hands, and he managed to escape because his opponents were so intent on taking him prisoner.

Moctezuma was beaten before the war began. He and his people were immobilized by a suicidal fatalism until it was too late. The Emperor moved like a victim to the altar, all but inviting the final Aztec sacrifice. Cortés simply obliged.

When it was over, a survivor wrote these sad lines:

> Broken spears lie in the roads;
> We have torn our hair in grief.
> The houses are roofless now, and their walls
> are red with blood.
>
> Worms are swarming in the streets and plazas,
> and the walls are spattered with gore.
> The water has turned red, as if it were dyed,
> and when we drink it,
> it has the taste of brine.
>
> We have pounded our heads in despair
> against the adobe walls,
> for our inheritance, our city, is lost and dead.
> The shields of our warriors were its defense,
> but they could not save it.
>   [*Translation by Miguel León-Portilla*]

This grief is still felt in Mexico. If you travel the length and breadth of Mexico, you will not find a street or village named after Hernán Cortés, or even a statue of him in a public square. He is reviled and officially invisible in the state whose modern form he created. Yet, by the standards of his age, the Conqueror was not an excessively ruthless figure. When he landed near what is now Veracruz, leading a tiny force of 553 men and sixteen horses, he was greeted as a deliverer. He was able to overthrow the Aztecs only because they were so universally detested.

Yet Cortés is invisible today, and the hero of the Conquest to most Mexicans is Cuauhtemoc, the last Aztec Emperor and nephew of Moctezuma. The cruelties of the Aztecs are passed over by the same Mexicans who sternly reproach Cortés for the torture and murder of Cuauhtemoc, an act of policy with some hard logic to it. Every educated Mexican knows the words shouted by the Aztec chieftain to a less manly companion as both were having their feet scorched by the Spaniards: "And am I on a bed of roses?" (*"Estoy yo acaso an algun deleite o bano?"*) Hardly anyone quotes the statements of Cortés deploring needless brutality except to disparage him as a hypocrite.

The truth is that the Aztec obsession with war and sacrifice does not trouble most Mexicans as much as the fact that Cortés was a foreigner whose arrival opened a period of imperialist exploitation. Moreover, death itself does not repel; it fascinates. "Death is present in our fiestas, in our games, our thoughts," writes Octavio Paz in *The Labyrinth of Silence*. "To die and kill are ideas that rarely leave us. We are seduced by death." This attitude is ritually reflected each November 2, the Day of the Dead, during which families picnic in cemeteries and children munch sweetmeat skulls or bread baked in the shape of bones. A noble death can redeem a mean life: on this both Aztec and Spaniard were in agreement. As Paz observes, most of Mexico's national heroes were failures whose end was disastrous and magnificent: Cuauhtemoc, Hidalgo, Morelos, Madero and Zapata.*

Almost unavoidably, archaeology has been dragged into the graveyard, as in the notorious Battle of the Bones. It began in 1946, when the remains of Cortés were rediscovered in the chapel walls of the Hospital of Jesus in Mexico City, where they had been hidden a century before during the War of Independence against Spain. The find provoked a confrontation between the dominant anti-Spanish Left and the pro-Spanish Right. "The remains of Cortés ought to be buried along with the bones of Franco!" spat the left-wing labor leader Lombardo Toledano. The skeleton was in fact reburied in the hospital, but not before it had been minutely examined by the National

---

* The list might also include Santa Ana, a foxy if bumbling general whose incompetence helped the United States win the Mexican War. But Santa Ana was lucky enough to lose a leg in a battle at Veracruz. He used the leg as a holy relic, having it buried at one point in a magnificent cenotaph. Thus he benefited from the national fixation with death while still alive—because (as one commentator notes) part of him was already buried. Later, in a new turn of Mexican politics, his famous leg was exhumed and vengefully destroyed.

A Flowery War Drawn after the Spanish Conquest, the illustration depicts a battle between Tenochtitlán and Tlatelolco. The purpose was to seize live prisoners for the altars.

Institute of Anthropology and History. Cortés-haters were gratified when a report suggested that the Conqueror was pint-sized, bandy-legged, and had an atrophied lower jaw.

A bizarre sequel occurred in 1949 when it was announced that the remains of Cuauhtemoc had been fortuitously found in a church at Ixcateopan, a remote village near the Pacific Coast. A dying parishioner had purportedly communicated the secret to the village priest, who at once proclaimed from his pulpit: "This church is for me a venerated crypt, holding the remains of our last Aztec emperor. And I say to you and let my words be carried by the four winds to all the world, that, in truth, our last emperor is here interred."

Within weeks Dr. Eulalia Guzmán, Mexico's most learned Cortés-hater, hurried to the village and soon a crypt was unearthed that contained some charred human bones and an oval plaque inscribed "1525–1529 Rey e. S. Coatemo." Were these truly the bones of the last Aztec ruler? Dr. Guzmán affirmed that they were. She was supported, in what became a political as well as a scientific battle, by the entire Left, ranging from nationalists to Communists, while the Right scoffed that the bones were fake. A Cuauhtemoc Week was proclaimed by the ruling Party of the Revolution, and there were parades all over Mexico. There was even the curious spectacle of a pro-Communist candidate for the presidency going to the village to swear over the supposed bones of an Aztec emperor eternal fealty to the anti-imperialist cause.

Caught unhappily in the middle were the archaeologists. Two successive commissions were appointed by the government to appraise the bones, and their verdict was less than patriotic. "When our report was made public," wrote the scholarly president of the second commission, "the hostility of certain journalists was vociferous. They described us as a gang of traitors, and in several periodicals they went to the extreme of demanding that we be shot."

Despite the findings of science, popular opinion has decreed that the bones are genuine. Every year there is a pilgrimage to the shrine in the tiny village where they have been interred. And at the opening of a new National Museum of Anthropology in Mexico City in 1964, the Minister of Public Education felt it prudent to declare: "The ceremony that brings us together confirms most admirably that Cuauhtemoc did not die in vain."

III

MORNINGS IN MEXICO

"MEXICO CITY has no intention of resting satisfied with a great yesterday, but is determined upon making a future for herself. Between visit and visit, certain spots in the city grow almost out of recognition. Hitherto dirty squares are found changed into flower-decked plazas; squat buildings of colonial days are demolished and rise as skyscrapers, and an enlightened government is found spending vast sums on beautifying the old capital."

Though it sounds like a modern travel brochure, the passage is from the first edition of T. Philip Terry's *Guide to Mexico*, published in 1909. The mutability of Mexico City is its most immutable law. From the rooftop restaurant at the Majestic Hotel you presently look down on the Zócalo, once the geographical center of the Aztec capital, and upward at a skyline dominated by the Torre Latino-Americana, the tallest building south of the Rio Grande, a forty-four-story skyscraper resting on floating piers. (There is no stone stratum beneath the city; everything lies on a bed of viscous clay.)

But in 1909 Mexico was ruled by Porfirio Díaz, a right-wing dictator. A year later the Mexican Revolution began, the first great upheaval of its kind in this century, as you are frequently reminded. One result of the Revolution is that the Indian legacy has become a visible part of the cityscape and an integral part of official doctrine. This is spectacularly true of University City, home of the University of Mexico, on the periphery of the capital. In its spacious layout, its monumental vistas, and its vast murals, it consciously recalls the atmosphere of Tenochtitlán, the Aztec capital which the Spaniards destroyed to build Mexico City. Not far from it, built of tough gray-black volcanic rock, is an array of ballcourts that look like dimunitive copies of pre-Columbian courts found everywhere in Mesoamerica. They are used for playing jai alai, a national sport.

Another manifestation of the cult of the Indian is the generous support given archaeology. When I was in Mexico, I chatted with an eminent beneficiary of this support, the late Dr. Eusebio Dávalos Hurtado, director of the National Institute of Anthropology and History. Dr. Dávalos presided over the empire of the past, no less than 11,000 archaeological sites, of which eighty-one are enclosed in state-protected zones. The Institute also maintains churches and other buildings deemed of historic importance, conducts extensive research and excavation programs, operates twenty-one museums, and publishes a bewildering array of guides. Under Dr. Dávalos, the Institute's budget increased from about $1 million in 1960 to roughly four times that amount at the time of his death in 1967.

"For us," he told me, "the great breakthrough came when we persuaded the government that archaeology was not only important in developing national pride, but was also important for tourism, a major source of hard currency." The benign sacrifice of greenbacks constitutes a token of the modern potency of the ancient gods. Two of the outstanding achievements of Mexican archaeology owe their origins to an enlightened amalgam of self-interest and the quest for knowledge—the new National Museum of Anthropology and the excavations of the pyramids of Teotihuacán.

The museum is the most magnificent of its kind in the world. Incredibly, it sprang from the drawing boards to completion in only twenty months, just in time for President López Mateos to dedicate it before leaving office—a deadline as politically important as pre-Columbian calendrical cycles.* Its site is in Chapultepec Park, where Moctezuma had his summer palace, his aviary and zoo, and his collection of human dwarfs. At its entrance is the 200-ton statue of Tlaloc, the rain god, whose arrival at this site provoked a cloudburst. In the central patio there is a single pillar of bronze supporting an immense canopy measuring 4,000 square feet, a monumental umbrella from which a circular waterfall spills down.

In its galleries the museum pairs past and present, so that the archaeology of a given region is accompanied by displays of contemporary arts and crafts. Major attractions, like the famous Aztec Calendar Stone, are given an almost theatrical display with the clever use of spotlights. A brilliant reconstruction

* Chief architect Pedro Ramírez Vásquez received the commission on condition that the work would be finished within the President's term of office. He was assisted by a team of forty specialists who collaborated in designing the twenty-three principal rooms. In all, the site occupies 100,000 square yards, and total cost of the museum was $11.6 million.

Mexico City: The Anthropological Museum A huge metal umbrella rises over the entrance patio, a curtain of water falling around the pylon that supports the canopy. Opened in 1964, the museum is credibly described as the greatest of its kind. (COURTESY MEXICAN TOURIST OFFICE)

of the Pyramid of Quetzalcóatl at Teotihuacán reflects its flamboyant colors on a black floor that is like a polished obsidian mirror. After visiting the museum, Sir Philip Hendy, then director of the National Gallery in London, reported to *The Times:* "In museography Mexico is now ahead of the United States perhaps by a generation, of the United Kingdom perhaps by a century."

Altogether, the museum possesses 100,000 items, about seventy percent of the known archaeological items still in Mexico. In looking at the choicest objects from a thousand sites, one shares the awe of Bernal Díaz, a soldier in the Conquest, who wrote years later, recalling his first glimpse of Tenochtitlán: "When we saw so many cities and villages built in the water and other great towns on dry land and that straight and level causeway going toward Mexico, we were amazed and said it was like the enchantments they tell of in the legends of Amadis, on account of the great towers and quays and buildings rising from the water, and all built of masonry. And some of our soldiers asked whether the things we saw were not a dream."

In the museum's admirably arranged introductory halls, the ascent of Mesoamerican civilization is charted, beginning with man's arrival in Mexico, perhaps as early as 25,000 B.C., proceeding through the more firmly dated food-gathering cultures of 7000–5000 B.C. to the earliest agriculturalists of 5000–2500 B.C. In these millennia, men in Mexico evolved from hunters of mammoth to growers of maize. Then, around 1200 B.C., there is a quantum leap forward with the appearance on the Gulf Coast of the Olmecs, the

Teotihuacán: Pyramid of the Sun Bigger in volume, though lower in height, than the Great Pyramid in Egypt, this mountain of adobe encased with stone dominates a city that perished around 700 A.D., leaving not even its name behind. (COURTESY AMERICAN MUSEUM OF NATURAL HISTORY)

mysterious Sumerians of Mesoamerica.

No one knows what the Olmecs called themselves or what language they spoke, and until a little over a generation ago their very existence was doubted. During 1939–1947 excavations in the humid state of Tabasco confirmed their existence as diggers found temples, calendrical inscriptions, superb jade figurines, and sculptured idols of the jaguar, which the Olmecs worshipped. The most striking discoveries were the colossal Olmec heads, with their queer helmets and ovoid grimaces: several of the heads can be seen in the museum.

The formative Olmecs opened the way for the Classic Period. In the first nine centuries of the Christian era Mesoamerica had its golden age. Three great civilizations rose, flourished and decayed, leaving behind spectacular monuments. In central Mexico the Teotihuacanos—their true name is unknown—built a ceremonial city with pyramids rivaling those of Egypt. To the south, in Oaxaca, the Zapotecs created a temple complex almost as imposing on the crest of Monte Albán, while in Yucatán and in Central America, the Maya filled jungles and plains with towering structures. Having achieved unexampled heights, all three classic civilizations then inexplicably fell.

Teotihuacán was the first to perish, apparently in a violent cataclysm; in the Maya region whole cities were abandoned without any evidence of a struggle, and the same was true at Monte Albán. What caused the Time of Troubles? There is still no satisfactory answer. Wars, revolutions, plagues, famines, earthquakes, breakdowns in the agricultural system: all have been adduced as causes for the collective suicide of three civilizations. But the riddle has not been solved.

After the Time of Troubles a third major era unfolds: the post-Classic. In this period Mexico comes to resemble a patchwork-quilt of nations, some old and some young, all broadly similar but as individually distinct as the countries of Europe. Among the newcomers were the Tarascans in the west, the Totonacs and Huastecs on the Gulf Coast, and the Mixtecs in Oaxaca. In the central highlands two aggressive warrior peoples emerge, first the Toltecs and then the Aztecs, and each briefly extends a militarist empire over a vast terrain. But this was an epilogue, not a preface: the book was soon over. What we see in the museum are its surviving pages, filled with a profusion of brilliant pictures with still largely unreadable captions.

The landscape, too, was to me a picture book with frustrating silences. The great pyramids of San Juan Teotihuacán lie some twenty-five miles northeast of Mexico City; thanks to the lobbying of Dr. Dávalos and the National Institute, they can now be reached by a modern highway that runs ruler-straight through a drab plain bounded by brown mountains. Trees known as *perules*—false pepper trees—provide a willow foliage mottled with

Tula: Atlantean Figure One of a row of warriors that gazes from the top of the main temple in the ancient Toltec capital. (PHOTO KARL E. MEYER)

Monte Albán The main plaza of the Zapotec ceremonial city looks out upon violet-hued mountains in the great Valley of Oaxaca. (COURTESY AMERICAN MUSEUM OF NATURAL HISTORY)

red berries that relieves the severity of the stark plateau, the clumps of cactus, and the succession of dun-colored villages through which I passed.

Once there was a metropolis on this barren tableland. Occupied for perhaps as long as a thousand years, it had a population of anywhere from 10,000 to 300,000 people. Its known area was six square miles, but it was probably far bigger. Yet the identity of its builders was a mystery even to the Aztecs, who arrived in the Valley of Mexico five centuries after Teotihuacán was abandoned in around 850 A.D. In 1843 Prescott wrote: "A nation has passed away—powerful, populous and well advanced in refinement, as attested by their monuments—but it perished without a name. It has died and left no sign." The description still stands.

The name Teotihuacán means "Abode of the Gods" in Nahuatl, the language of the Toltecs and Aztecs. The city's religion centered around deities that came to be worshipped by successor peoples, such as Quetzalcóatl, whose name was later borrowed by a Toltec god-king, always a source of confusion. But Teotihuacán was not simply a ceremonial center like those built elsewhere in Mesoamerica at the same period: it was also a city with a resident population. In the early 1920s the Swedish archaeologist Sigvald Linne found several residential complexes, including one in the eastern part of Teotihuacán with no less than 175 rooms arrayed around courtyards in which rainwater was collected in basins. Drains emptied the basins, which were supplied with finely polished stone plugs—some were found *in situ!*

In 1963 Mexico budgeted more than a million dollars for an extensive exhumation of the oldest city in North America. The long Avenue of the Dead was finally cleared of debris, and the many ceremonial platforms adjoining it were restored to their ancient shape. The city was divided into seven zones, and in each the soil was meticulously sifted for evidence about its builders. Finds included a quantity of decorated pottery, typically shaped like a flower vase standing on three slab-like legs, and a number of brightly colored murals. Further evidence of the fire that once swept the city was unearthed. But there were no sensational revelations: the page remains largely blank. Only a few inscriptions were found, and no major burials (the Teotihuacanos cremated their dead, a practice always irritating to archaeologists).

Like the scholars, I was only able to deduce and speculate. The lack of walls suggested that Teotihuacán was militarily secure, and the cunning placement of the huge structures implied a mastery of geometry and a certain theatrical instinct. Two mountains of adobe faced with stone dominate the skyline: the Pyramid of the Sun and the Pyramid of the Moon (the names go back to pre-Columbian times). The first is the bigger, towering 216 feet over a base measuring 720 by 260 feet, making it two-thirds the height of Egypt's Great Pyramid but bulkier in volume. The smaller pyramid, with a base 511 by 426 feet, is sited at a right angle to the giant and faces the head of the

Avenue of the Dead. Once the pyramids were coated with stucco and painted; once the streets were paved and filled with plumed nobles. Seen with the pyramids cleanly profiled against the uncluttered plain, the vista was surely contrived to elicit a gasp of awe from the astonished pilgrim. It still does.

Yet, for all its impressiveness, I found Teotihuacán a ghostly place, like a deserted stage set. Its nameless builders have left no identifiable descendants, and it broods in a meridian of solitude. In this respect it is less memorable than Monte Albán and Mitla, two magnificent sites created by the Zapotecs, whose heirs still vivify the state and city of Oaxaca.

The city of Oaxaca is some 350 miles south of the capital and about 2,300 feet lower, with an altitude of 5,068 feet. Its climate is semi-tropical and its setting cinematic: the mauve and purple peaks of the Sierre Madre del Sur form a jagged backcloth to a city built of stone with the color of pale lime ice. Unprepossessing at first glimpse, Oaxaca ingratiates itself quickly to anyone who is not in a hurry, or so I found.

In the evening the main square became a pageant. Families perambulated, a military band played with a *brio* to match the performers' epaulets, and Indian vendors swarmed around the sidewalk cafés, particularly that of the Hotel Marques del Valle. On successive evenings I was recognized by Zapotec traders, who target a victim with kamikaze determination. I remember especially a tiny Indian who would hold up a *serape* of such vast dimensions that only his nose peeped above it, like an improbable clothespin. As much as a nod, and the body materialized: "Chip, *amigo*, a boggan!"

Over a history covering two thousand years, the Zapotec has been a broker and trader between the Indians of the highlands and those of Yucatán and Central America. Elsewhere in Mexico the Indians tend to regard the foreigner with impenetrable eyes and stoic muteness. The Zapotec is different. He is gregarious, a xenophile, a consummate trader. His markets are celebrated, and his offspring trained from childhood in the arts of selling. Youngsters proffer Chiclets, women vend skirts and beautifully sewn shawls or *rebozos*, and men specialize in *serapes* and knives of a distinctive style—the carved handle is surmounted by an eagle and the blade inscribed with the maker's name and a Spanish proverb.

At Monte Albán, which I reached by a winding road that climbed a hilltop five miles southwest of the city, the specialty was *idolitos*, tiny clay figurines of dubious provenance hawked by youngsters of enormous charm. In the years of its splendor Monte Albán must have been a market as well as a ceremonial center—how could the Zapotec have resisted that spacious plaza set among terraces of living rock? All the other amenities were close at hand: pyramids, temples, a ballcourt, an observatory, burial vaults, and the staircases that are the trademark of Mesoamerican builders.

Around 900 A.D. all fell silent as Monte Albán was abandoned by its builders. Some five centuries later, newcomers from the north, the Mixtecs, burst into the Valley of Oaxaca and made the Zapotec shrine their own, to the extent of re-using the ancient tombs. In 1932 Dr. Alfonso Caso, the dean of Mexican archaeology, was engaged in clearing the great site. He was examining these Mixtec graves when in Tomb No. 7 he came upon an intact burial of a noble of high rank and his slaughtered servants. No richer find has been made in the New World; it established that although the Mixtecs were poor builders, they were expert goldsmiths and jewelers. For the first time sculptured gold was found which substantiated the description of the incredible treasures found by the Conquistador. Here were masks and ornaments of beaten gold and quantities of carved jade, turquoise mosaics, a rock-crystal goblet, objects of amber, jet and coral—and a pearl the size of a pigeon's egg. The trove of more than 300 pieces (now handsomely displayed in the fine local museum in Oaxaca) also contained a collection of jaguar bones on which mythological and historical scenes were carved.

The find encouraged Dr. Caso to learn more about the Mixtecs. In studying ancient codices he was able to recover almost a thousand years of history, establishing the names and deeds of great Mixtec chieftains, notably the fierce ruler Eight-Dear Ocelot-Claw, born in 1011 A.D. and buried with barbaric splendor fifty-two years later. The reconstitution of the Mixtec annals is perhaps the *tour de force* of Mexican archaeology.

As to the Zapotecs, after their departure from Monte Albán the tribe founded a new ceremonial capital at Mitla, forty-two miles east of Oaxaca.

Mitla: The Great Palace   Aldous Huxley called the mosaics of Mitla "petrified weaving." The engraving is from the pioneer work by Denis Charnay, *The Ancient Cities of America.*

The style was a surprise. At Monte Albán an exhilarating spaciousness characterizes the site; at Mitla there is a deliberate compactness, as if the retreating Zapotecs were looking inward even in their architecture. Of the five palace-like buildings, the so-called Hall of the Columns contains the most introspective decorative detail—its walls are brocaded with the patterned motifs still seen today on Zapotec textiles. Some 100,000 shaped stones were used to create these complicated mosaics, which Aldous Huxley likened to "petrified weaving." (Adjoining the Hall of the Columns is a colonial church, recalling the notoriety Mitla achieved in early Spanish chronicles, which alleged that abominable sacrifices took place here when the palace was the residence of the Zapotec High Priest.)

A side effect of a trip to Oaxaca, I found, was to quicken my interest in the Indians of Mexico. To begin with, how many of them are there? When I returned to Mexico City, I put the question to Dr. Miguel León-Portilla, the director of the Inter-American Indian Institute. Articulate, learned, and enthusiastic, Dr. León-Portilla has won an international reputation with his fine translations of Aztec poetry. But, like Dr. Caso, who has been head of the National Indigenous Institute as well as a leading archaeologist, Dr. León-Portilla combines a compassionate concern with the live Indians and a scholarly interest in their dead past.

He calculated that Mexico is about thirty percent Indian, meaning that about a third of the country's 28 million inhabitants live in communities in which Indian traits predominate. At the time of the Conquest there were 700 tribes speaking fourteen distinct languages and innumerable dialects; today some 55 tribes survive. The aim of Mexican policy is to give the Indian full citizenship in a country where he often feels a stranger. Dr. León-Portilla spoke realistically about the difficulties of assimilating Indians into what we are pleased to call civilization. In its hemisphere-wide activities the Institute has found that the Indian traits which disappear first, when a community is brought into contact with modern ways, are language, dress, and household furnishings. The trait most resistant to change is belief in a witch-doctor; field workers have found it wiser to collaborate with the tribal sorcerer rather than attempt to undermine his authority. (In Mexico the Church, too, has long ago come to terms with pagan survivals. Priests tolerate a certain confusion, in Indian parishes, between St. Michael and Huitzilopochtli, and between St. John and Tlaloc.)

As our talk concluded, I asked Dr. León-Portilla what the Institute regarded as its single most useful venture. He beamed, and motioned to a secretary, who brought me a compact booklet. "We publish it in Spanish, Portuguese, and English," he said. "It is by far our best-seller." The title was: *Pregnancy, Childbirth and the Newborn: A Manual for Rural Midwives.*

* * *

Oaxaca involves a voyage, but two archaeological sites of major interest I found within easy reach of Mexico City: Xochicalco, a sacred city and fortress, and Tula, the ancient capital of the Toltecs.

Xochicalco is about thirty miles south of Cuernavaca, and a three-hour drive from Mexico City. The trip can provide two bonuses. In leaving the capital on Avenida Insurgentes, one can stop en route at Cuicuilco, just beyond University City. This is the site of a circular temple of the formative period; it was dramatically engulfed by ash and lava when the nearby volcano, Xitli, erupted around 300 A.D. Its coiling ramparts take on an additional grimness from the pitch-black volcanic debris that blankets the surrounding landscape.

The other bonus is a unique resort hotel I discovered on the way. Hacienda Vista Hermosa, near Lake Tequesquitengo, was once a sugar mill dating back to early colonial times—it is said to have been originally built by Cortés—and it has been cleverly modernized, retaining a grandiose atmosphere as a modern hotel. Door keys are a yard long, the balconied rooms are like regal suites, and the restaurant has a ceiling with a hole blasted into it during a battle in the Mexico Revolution—this is in Morelos, the state of Zapata.

In a short drive I arrived at Xochicalco, an array of ruins—temples, plazas, ballcourts, and fortifications—located on an eyrie high above the Morelos countryside. The site has a politico-cultural significance. Apparently built during the uneasy transition between the Classic and post-Classic periods, Xochicalco shows a mingling of Toltec, Maya, and Zapotec influences. On the principal pyramid there is a bold bas-relief of the Plumed Serpent in the Toltec style, but chiefs wearing Maya headdresses also make an unexpected appearance on the frieze. In 1961 three stelae, or memorial tablets, were discovered, each covered with glyphs and numerals of the Maya-Zapotec system.

What does this intermingling signify? In my visit to Xochicalco I met Dr. César Saenz of the National Institute, who was then supervising new excavations. His theory was that the ceremonial center was a neutral meeting place for intertribal elites, and that at one point Toltec, Maya, and Zapotec astronomers held an important conference here. The frieze on the temple, in his view, commemorates this summit seminar of what were then the most learned astronomers in the world. It is tempting to see Xochicalco as a kind of pre-Columbian Delphi, a place removed from strife where the learned could safely confer about the stars.

I was further struck by the mobility of the Indians in visiting Tula, about fifty miles north of Mexico City in the green landscape of Hidalgo State. For years the ancient Toltec capital eluded scholarly search because of the prevalent misconception that Teotihuacán was actually the capital of this warrior people. Incredibly, serious excavations did not begin until 1938 at the small town of Tula, which bore the same name used to describe the sumptuous capital in early chronicles. The remains of an enormous ceremonial city were promptly found under a thin blanket of earth.

The most impressive remain is Pyramid B, which had a colonnaded hall at its base and a roof supported by giant atlantean figures of Toltec warriors. Known as the Temple of Quetzalcóatl, the pyramid shows the absorption by the Toltecs of the ideals of Teotihuacán; it is also associated with the most famous of all rulers in pre-Columbian annals. After their descent into the Valley of Mexico, the Toltecs came to be led by a king named Topiltzin, who took for himself the name of Quetzalcóatl. This was the god-king for whom Cortés was mistaken, and Tula was his capital.

There are two versions of his fate. Some say that his enemies, who worshipped the sky god Tezcatlipoca, tricked the king into drinking *pulque*, and that Quetzalcóatl became drunk, committing a carnal offense that impelled him to immolate himself. His heart then rose to the heavens and became the planet Venus. But others say that the pious king sailed to the east, prophesying that he would someday return.

In fact, the Toltecs did go east, and Maya legends speak of the arrival in 987 A.D. of a Mexican known as Kukulcan, which means Plumed Serpent in the Maya tongue. After the god-king's departure, Tula continued as the center of the Toltec Empire for two centuries until a combination of famines and wars forced the dispersal of the entire tribe—some following in the path of Quetzalcóatl to Maya lands. Tula became a desolation and was mourned as a lost Jerusalem. An Aztec poem says of Tula:

> Everywhere there meets the eye,
> everywhere can be seen the remains of clay vessels,
> of their cups, their figures,
> of their dolls, of their figurines,
> of their bracelets,
> everywhere there are ruins,
> truly the Toltecs once lived here.
> [Translation by Miguel León-Portilla]

Chichén Itzá: El Castillo The great pyramid was redesigned by the Toltecs and restored by the Carnegie Institution in the 1920's. Some would say it was over-restored. (PHOTO RENE BURRI, MAGNUM)

IV

SOME MAYA SITES

THE TOLTECS CAME SOUTH, and settled in Chichén Itzá; of that there can be no doubt. The architectural features alone of this spectacular Maya city attest to the presence of the invaders. Sylvanus Morley counts thirteen Toltec touches in the sprawling ruins: extensive colonnades, the Plumed Serpent motif, grisly skull-racks, atlantean warriors with Toltec costumes, and figures of the rain god Tlaloc among them. Chichén Itzá is a fraternal twin of Tula, some 800 miles overland to the north, with mountains, jungles, and swamps in between.

Thus the most visited of Maya cities is to some measure deceptive: it has a Maya core but Toltec stucco. I found it deceptive in another way. It has been somewhat over-restored by the Carnegie Institution, giving a movie-set quality to El Castillo, its most imposing monument. This pyramid can be mounted by climbing its 365 steps—one for each day of the solar year—and on its top, within a square temple, one descends an interior stairway to a hidden shrine found by the Carnegie archaeologists. In the inner sanctuary there is a jaguar throne, painted red with jade encrustations, and a figure known as a Chac-Mool. He looks almost stupidly sinister: a wide-eyed creature lying with his knees raised and his hands holding a sacrificial saucer above his navel. Chac-Mool is another Toltec souvenir; others like him, with the same expression of blank brutality, have been found at Tula.*

Chichén Itzá is set in a landscape that is monotonously flat, an immense plain of *milpas*, or cornfields, enlivened with a sparkling profusion of wildflowers and polychromatic birds. An unusual feature of the terrain is that it has few lakes or surface streams. Water is provided by *cenotes*, or wells, which puncture the peninsula's limestone crust. These wells are formed when a portion of the crust collapses, creating craters fed by underground streams. The most famous *cenote* is the Well of Sacrifice at Chichén Itzá. Reached by a dramatic 900-foot-long causeway leading from the Great Plaza, the Well is a fearsome abscess about 180 feet across, with sheer sides dropping some eighty feet to a vast disk of water covered by green algae—Richard Halliburton, the professional adventurer, once gamely dived into it.

Early Spanish chroniclers claimed that the Maya threw live victims (especially virgins) and precious ornaments into the Well of Sacrifice during periods of drought. In the 1890s a North American named Edward H. Thomson came to Yucatán chiefly to satisfy himself that Altantis was not a myth. He then heard the legends about the *cenote*, and from 1904 to 1907 he laboriously plumbed the Well, retrieving an impressive amount of pottery, jade and gold jewelry, and human bones from it. He covertly shipped his finds to Harvard's Peabody Museum, using the diplomatic pouch (he was a United States consul at the time), a stratagem that provoked an angry but unsuccessful Mexican lawsuit. Years later, in 1959, Harvard quietly returned some of the gold objects to Mexico, but most of the collection remained in Cambridge. To provide Mexico with a better collection, a second campaign at the Well was organized by Dr. Eusebio Dávalos Hurtado in 1961. Hundreds of further offerings were sucked up by an air-lift whose nozzle was trained on the muddy well-bottom by skin divers. Besides well-preserved rubber and wooden idols, and innumerable bells with their clappers removed —they had been "killed" prior to their sacrifice—the archaeologists found the

---

* Chac-Mool's name combines that of the rain god Chac with the Maya word for the paw of an animal. This genus of idol was discovered and baptized by a typically quirky figure in Maya pseudo-scholarship—Augustus le Plongeon, a French-American who argued in the last century that the Maya and the Egyptians were both survivors of Atlantis, and that the Sphinx was built by Queen Moo, a Maya princess who had fled to Egypt.

Chichén Itzá: A Panorama A reconstruction by the widely esteemed Tatiana Proskouriakoff shows the processional way that led from the Great Plaza to the Well of Sacrifices. (COURTESY TATIANA PROSKOURIAKOFF)

skull of a girl who might have been eighteen years old at the time of her death.

Was this one of the celebrated virgins? Most of the fifty or so skeletons dredged up by Thompson a half-century ago turned out to be those of adult men. Harvard's Dr. Earnest Hooton examined the few feminine remains and his comment seems definitive: "All of the individuals involved (or rather immersed) may have been virgins, but the osteological evidence does not permit a determination of this nice point." According to the Spanish chroniclers, victims at the Well were assured before their plunge that they would come out alive on the third day. They were also instructed to ask the gods for favors while they were underwater. But one visitor to Chichén Itzá in 1552 heard this reassuring story: "Holding a virgin for sacrifice in the said way and the priest telling her . . . to ask their gods . . . to send them good times, she replied that she would not say any such thing, since they were going to kill her. And the boldness and assurance of that virgin in her speech had so great an effect that they left her and sacrificed another in her place."

From Chichén Itzá I made the seventy-mile drive west to Mérida, the somnolent capital of Yucatán. The road takes one through pleasant villages with evocative Maya names—Pisté, Yokdzonot, Holcá, Kantunil, Xocchel, Hoctun, and Thamek—each with its gleaming white church and cubical houses. It takes another hour's drive north of Mérida to reach Uxmal, aesthetically the most satisfying of the Maya cities in Mexico.

Unlike Chichén Itzá, Uxmal shows little Toltec influence and is instead a Maya ceremonial center of predominantly Classic style. One contrast is the absence of human figures dressed in Toltec plumes on the friezes; another is the general lack of skull motifs and other mementoes of human sacrifice. Uxmal leaves the impression, as Sacheverell Sitwell remarked, of "orderliness without suffering and bloodshed." It is a fugue and not a dirge.

There are three memorable buildings. The House of the Magician is the loftiest in Uxmal, a pyramid about ninety feet high, the lower part of which is a stairway steeply angled like a monumental ladder. With some relish, guides tell how the House of the Magician got its name. It appears that an old witch-woman succeeded in hatching a child from an egg. In a year the child was full-grown, though, unhappily, in the shape of a dwarf. He was sent to challenge the King of Uxmal, who confronted the dwarf with a series of seemingly impossible tasks. The King was vexed when the challenger accomplished them all, and the dwarf was commanded to build a great palace overnight. The House of the Magician duly sprang up. Now truly angry, the King proposed to the dwarf that rock-hard *cocoyol* nuts were to be broken on the head of each of them—beginning with the dwarf. The witch provided her son with a magic skull-plate, enabling him to survive, but the King's head cracked open. The dwarf was acclaimed as the new King of Uxmal, while the witch retired to a cave, where she still lives, snatching children, from time to time, to feed her pet serpent.

At the base of the pryamid is the Nunnery Quadrangle (a name supplied by the Spaniards). The first discerning report about this splendid compound was made by John Lloyd Stephens, a North American traveler who came to Yucatán in the 1840s along with a talented English artist, Frederick Catherwood. As Stephens described the Nunnery, "We enter a noble courtyard with four great façades looking down upon it, each ornamented from one end to the other with the richest and most intricate carvings known in the building of Uxmal; presenting a scene of strange magnificence, surpassing any that is now to be seen among its ruins." On the friezes, symbolic likenesses of the gods are boldly woven into a lattice-work pattern; a homely touch is provided by miniature replicas of the thatched huts used then (and now) by the Maya farmer.

Not far away is one of the glories of the New World, the Palace of the Governors, which Sylvanus Morley called the most wonderful building of pre-Columbian times. It resembles a lozenge of ivory. Placed on a terrace 600 feet long and 40 feet high, the palace has a carved façade with hook-nosed

Uxmal: Palace of the Governors Called the most beautiful building of pre-Columbian America, the palace is shown as it appeared to Frederick Catherwood in 1840. Below, a reconstruction by Tatiana Proskouriakoff (COURTESY OF THE ARTIST)

gods at the corners and interlocking gridworks filling its panels; the design comes perilously close to dissolving in its own detail, but from a distance it turned into lace as I looked at it.

Once the palace was reputedly the seat of the Xiu dynasty, which ruled Uxmal at the time of the Conquest. The Spaniards, always conscious of pedigree, made the Xiu heirs into hidalgos, providing them with a residence suitable to their rank. There are genealogical charts for the Xiu (pronounced shoo) compiled fifteen years after the Conquest and kept up to date until 1821, when Mexico won its independence and the Xius lost their noble residence. Morley was able to use these documents to locate the present head of the family; in his book he includes a photograph of Don Nemesio Xiu, a successor to kings, standing in front of his current home, a thatched house. Don Nemesio is a corn farmer in Ticul, a town near Uxmal.

It should be said that rural life, in all its manifestations, exorcises the ghostly emptiness of Uxmal. Everywhere around the ruins I saw cornfields and well-tended plots of mangoes, avocados, and bananas. Along the roadside there was a permanent and gregarious rural population of chickens, mules, dogs, and pigs, often accompanied by quail whose whirring flights disturbed the silence, agitating a flock of perpetually indignant turkeys.*

The turkey, in fact, was one of Mexico's gifts to the West. In French the fowl is called *dindon*, a contraction of *coq-d'Inde*, signifying "the Indian bird." Another benison was the tomato, whose name derives from the Nahuatl word *tomatl*, just as the Aztec term *ahuacatl* was Latinized as "avocado." In southern Mexico the Indians learned to make a drink of the cacao bean which they termed *xocalatl*, whence comes "chocolate." Smoking, too, was a New World innovation, and the plausible claim is made that "cigar" and "cigarette" derive from the Maya *xigar*, which means to suck. (The Maya word for smoking could not export so easily—it is *tzootz*, and it also means kissing.) In language as in other things, the Indian presence is as subtle as it is ubiquitous, seen only when examined in the light, like a watermark.

Uxmal and Chichén Itzá do not involve difficult travel, since resort hotels flourish at each site. The prevalence of tourists can extinguish the joy of seeing the ruins: turn to gaze at the rain god carved on a façade and a hand vigorously waves you from camera range as a North American visitor, girdled with a vast gadget bag and sixteen sorts of light meter, aims a telephoto at a protruding stone snout—two strange and goggled creatures confronting

---

* The bird life of Yucatán is marvelous in its variety and plumage. I shared a room at Uxmal with an English bird-watcher, Mr. Stephen Harrison, a retired BBC producer, who went everywhere with a vast bird directory under his arm and a beatific glow on his face. "Think of it," he said to me, "two thirds of all known bird species are in Mexico and Central America!" Each day he would gleefully check off a dozen varieties in his directory.

Palace of the Governors, Details
The intricacy of the mosaic in this singular building is conveyed in drawings by Catherwood, who, along with John Lloyd Stephens, was the modern rediscoverer of **Uxmal**.

each other across a chasm of time.

Palenque, the most dramatic of the Maya cities, requires an elaborate expedition beyond the usual range of Thomas Cook. As yet there is no luxury hostelry at Palenque, located deep in the jungle State of Chiapas. One vainly hopes there never will be; Palenque should be preserved in its remoteness as a National Park of Archaeology, forever outside the bounds of organized tourism.

My trip began in Villahermosa, capital of the sweltering state of Tabasco, a city with lethal mosquitoes, a fine local museum, and a park containing colossal Olmec heads from La Venta. From Villahermosa you then reached Palenque by an interminable train running on an eccentric schedule, or you flew. The plane was a single-engined Cessna with room (barely) for three passengers, baggage, and a gum-chewing pilot. Aloft, we fluttered at an altitude that made possible an intimate examination of the terrain below as it thickened into matted verdure cut by a meandering river and the brown ribbon of a highway being built to Palenque.

Before take-off, a radio call was put through to Don Domingo Lacroix González, proprietor of Hotel Lacroix in Palenque, to alert him for my arrival. The message was conveyed by shouts into a complaining, static-ridden transmitter. When the pilot landed, deftly avoiding both potholes and pigs in the small airfield carved from the jungle, Señor Lacroix, properly forewarned, was there in his jeep.

Palenque: The Great Pyramid Here the Mexican archaeologist Alberto Ruz discovered, in 1949, the first tomb burial in a New World pyramid, confounding the long-held certitude that American pyramids were never used as tombs. (PHOTO INGE MORATH, MAGNUM)

Palenque: The Palace The sole tower in Maya ceremonial cities is this almost Italianate campanile which rises over the ruins of Palenque in the jungles of Chiapas. (PHOTO INGE MORATH, MAGNUM)

The village of Palenque was so remote that not even the sales force of Coca-Cola had penetrated to it. Only Mexican beer and soft drinks were served in the main square, where four dusty roads converged. The main street was democratically shared by livestock, pedestrians, and the jeeps belonging to Hotel Lacroix. When I was there, Sunday brought a festival. At the *paseo* in the main square, *mestizo* girls wheeled in endless slow circles. On a rise nearby, candles were lit in a half-destroyed church. The fiesta had as its climax a dance in the casino. Curiously, there was less salacity than in a New England village—even when the tempo of the dance quickened, the steps were slow and precise. The expressions were solemn, and partners paired for an evening; though the glances were molten, manners were chaste.

Hotel Lacroix had only recently been electrified, and a generator rumbled noisily each evening, providing enough power to illuminate bare bulbs for a few hours. Otherwise, flashlights were essential equipment; they were needed to reach the makeshift restaurant a few dirt blocks from the hotel. The four tables were made of mahogany, and a jaguar skin (shot at the ruins) was nailed to the unbuffed mahogany walls. A pet spider monkey and

Palenque: Inscribed Tablet Catherwood's meticulous drawing is notable for the accuracy with which glyphs totally alien to the artist's eye were copied.

its two tame offspring pattered on the floor, and there were wild orchids in table vases. Only a single menu was offered: beefsteak, with a choice of soups and beers.

The church across from the hotel was a roofless shell, a memorial to the power of a priest-hating local dictator in Tabasco who had briefly extended his power into Chiapas. When Graham Greene visited Palenque in 1938, he heard of a local priest who had been a friend of the dictator Garrido Cannabal and who had been given a safe-conduct invitation to go to Tabasco on the pretext that the priest, a skilled bricklayer, was needed for a building job. When the work was finished, the priest was murdered. Garrido subsequently instigated an auto-da-fé in Palenque. As Greene describes it in *Lawless Roads*, "The evil work was not done by the villagers themselves. Garrido ordered every man with a horse in Tabascan Montecristo to ride over the fifty-six kilometers and superintend—on pain of a fine of twenty-five pesos. . . . The statues were carried out of the church while the inhabitants watched, sheepishly, and saw their own children encouraged to chop up the images in return for little presents of candy."

The crowding jungle, human and natural, constitutes the drama of existence in Palenque, where inhabitants cannot count on God's help, or even polite attention. Only five miles away lie the bones of a great city, with its own roofless churches and shattered images. Yet a kind of greediness colored my own response, the next day, to the incomparable ruins of Palenque because there were only three *estranjeros* in total possession for the weekend —myself, a French Canadian student and a young architect from Kalamazoo, Michigan. Our jeep bumped down the road into a sea of thickening foliage. When the city came into view, it was like a toy ruin used to decorate a child's aquarium. It almost sprang out of the jungle, its bleached stones mounted on green velvet. The first glimpse of the palace, the main edifice, was almost the same view that presented itself to John Lloyd Stephens in 1840: "Through openings in the trees we saw the front of a large building richly ornamented with stuccoed figures on the pilasters, curious and elegant, with trees growing close against it, their branches entering the doors; in style and effect it was unique, extraordinary and mournfully beautiful."

Though the bigger trees had been sawed away, the panorama remained the same. The palace was a labyrinth coated with lichen, swarming with bats, and encrusted with carvings. It had an almost Italianate tower, like a campanile. Its stucco sculpture showed Maya nobles, their noses hooked and their skulls flattened, surrounded by courtiers sitting cross-legged. Around the palace there were smaller temples, each on a hummock of earth. Aside from the caretaker, there are no human inhabitants. The population consisted of hummingbirds, parrots, lizards, and howler monkeys: it was a spectacular natural zoo amid buildings of weird beauty, especially when visited at dawn, when the macaws cry and the jungle quivers with life.

No one knows what the original name of this sacred city was. First settled before the birth of Christ, Palenque reached its florescence between the seventh and tenth centuries. Excavations have yielded tantalizing suggestions of its former prosperity, most spectacularly in 1949–1952, when the Mexican archaeologist Dr. Alberto Ruz was working in the sixty-five-foot Temple of the Inscriptions, a pyramid facing the palace. In a room on its peak there are panels inscribed with 620 hieroglyphs with dates covering a 200-year period—the date believed to be contemporary with the temple is 692 A.D. Ruz noticed that the floor of the chamber was covered by two large slabs, one of which had a double row of holes provided with removable stoppers. When the perforated slab was raised, a vault and staircase were found beneath it. This was in 1949, and it took four field seasons to clear away the rubble that clogged the passage. Eventually a large crypt was found, some eighty feet below the top of the temple. Within the funerary chamber was a monolithic sarcophagus richly decorated with carvings. When the stone lid was raised, the coffin disclosed the skeleton of a tall man between forty and fifty years of age, with a life-size mosaic mask on his face. The burial furnishings included a glittering multitude of jade figures and two finely modeled stucco heads.

With this discovery, textbooks had to be rewritten. Scholars had insisted,

Palenque: Small Temple Set against an emerald *selva*, this temple has the jewel-like quality that is Palenque's signature. Once thousands crowded the plazas of this city; it is populated now by parrots, monkeys, hummingbirds, and occasional tourists. (PHOTO KARL E. MEYER)

with uniform certitude, that New World pyramids were different from those in Egypt because they contained no burials. Yet as one looks at this amazing crypt, reached in a downward plunge through a winding passage adorned with stalactites, one reflects that the annoying riddle remains unanswered: why did Classic Maya civilization die? As Michael Coe writes, "Almost the only fact surely known about the downfall of Classic Maya is that it really happened. All the rest is pure conjecture."

Palenque is one of many sites in the Central Area of Maya Classic civilization—a belt of some 800 square miles that runs through the base of the Yucatán thumb, reaching as far south as Honduras and north to Chiapas. Much of this terrain is dense jungle, yet it was here that the Maya first developed impressive ceremonial centers, hit upon the concept of the mathematical zero at least half a millennium before Europeans awakened to the same useful discovery, developed a multiplicity of calendars, and not only calculated solar-eclipse cycles but also figured the average lengths of the synodical revolutions of Venus. In Toynbee's terms, seldom has so oppressive a challenge met so vigorous a response.

Then, in the tenth century, all the sacred cities of the Central Area were abandoned, great centers like Palenque, Tikal, and Copán among them. The

Maya virtually disappeared from the jungles they had briefly vanquished, dispersing to northern Yucatán, where such cities as Uxmal and Chichén Itzá enjoyed a post-Classic revival that perpetuated Maya civilization until the arrival of the Spaniards. Such are the broad outlines of the problem. Perhaps the solution may yet be found in the decipherment of the Maya glyphs, of which only a third can be read. In what may be a fascinating breakthrough, references to actual historic figures have been found in the stelae of Piedras Negras, a Classic site in the Guatemala rain forest. The discovery was made by Tatiana Proskouriakoff, a Carnegie Institution scholar known for her vivid sketches showing Maya monuments in their ancient splendor. In 1960 she noticed that within a single group of glyphs on some stelae the dates never covered a period longer than an average lifetime, indicating that the inscriptions might have recorded history and given the names and reigns of Maya lords. Further research has supported her insight, and she has been able to identify the names and titles of prominent Maya women as well as men. By degrees an entire tract of history may be recovered from oblivion and the vexing puzzle approached in a fresh light.

"I cannot help believing that the tablets of hieroglyphics will yet be read," wrote John Lloyd Stephens, who more than anyone else is the modern rediscoverer of the Maya. But an accepted decipherment has not yet been offered, nor has a century of research altered the essential judgment of the Maya cities reached by Stephens in 1841: "They are different from the works of any other known people, of a new order, and entirely and absolutely anomalous: they stand alone."

Uxmal: The House of the Dwarf Dominating a flat milpas field in Yucatán, this Maya pyramid is typical of the engineering skill and monumental imagination in the Sun Kingdom of the Americas. (PHOTO MARILYN SILVERSTONE, MAGNUM)

Chapter Nine

UTOPIA LOST?

P E R U

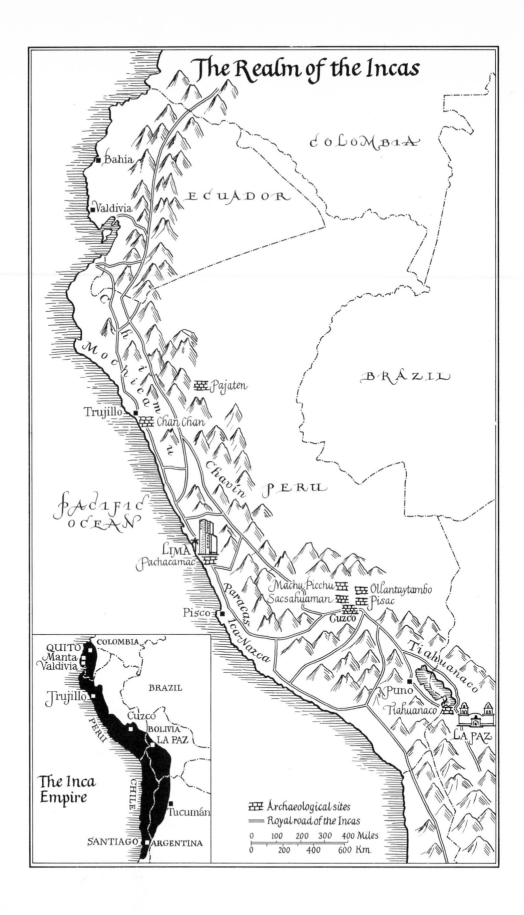

The Realm of the Incas

COLOMBIA

ECUADOR

Bahia

Valdivia

PACIFIC
OCEAN

Mochica

Cajabamba

Pajaten

Trujillo

Chan chan

Chavin

PERU

BRAZIL

LIMA
Pachacamac

Machu Picchu
Sacsahuaman

Ollantaytambo
Pisac

Paracas

Pisco

Cuzco

Ica-Nazca

Tiahuanaco

Puno
Tiahuanaco

LA PAZ

The Inca Empire

QUITO COLOMBIA
Manta
Valdivia

Trujillo

BRAZIL

Cuzco

BOLIVIA
LA PAZ

PERU

CHILE

Tucumán

SANTIAGO ARGENTINA

Archaeological sites
Royal road of the Incas

0   100   200   300   400 Miles
0   200   400   600 Km.

I

THE PLANNED PARADISE

I was born like a lily in the garden,
And so I was brought up.
As my age came, I have grown up.
And, as I had to die, so I dried up.
And I died.

SONG BY THE INCA PACHACUTI, C. 1470

IN 1959 THE TRADE WINDS OF MY CALLING carried me to Peru, which was then, from a professional viewpoint, distressingly calm. Someone suggested a side trip to Machu Picchu, and without quite knowing what I was going to see I found myself aboard an airliner that rose, like a silver condor, into the white fastness of the Andes, soaring from sea level at Lima to the ancient Inca capital of Cuzco, 11,007 feet higher. Attached to each seat within the aircraft there were rubber tubes from which I sipped oxygen while ascending; otherwise, if the cabin were pressurized, one would risk collapse on leaving the plane.

A day or so later, having become somewhat acclimated to the altitude, I went by train—a curious bug-shaped vehicle powered by gasoline—to Machu Picchu, which turned out to be an intact Inca city poised on a mountain peak overlooking the roaring Urubamba River 2,000 sheer feet below. In the morning mist the city seemed like a Chinese painting suspended weightlessly in mid-air; through the mist I could see the humid jungles of the upper Amazon. Machu Picchu was one of a chain of fortified cities along the Urubamba River, but, unlike the rest, it eluded the Spanish conquerors and was not rediscovered until 1911. Only those whose imagination has entirely atrophied could find Machu Picchu unimpressive, in the grandeur of its setting and in its testimony to the vanished genius of the Peruvian kingdom.

Machu Picchu Undiscovered by the Spaniards, this Inca city was inhabited for a hundred years after the Conquest, and then it was inexplicably abandoned and forgotten. (PHOTO JEAN-CHRISTIAN SPAHNI)

Machu Picchu: Three-Windowed Temple These windows mistakenly led the modern rediscoverer of the Inca city, Hiram Bingham, to conclude that he had found the earliest capital of the Peruvian people. Most scholars now date the city to a late period. (PHOTO JEAN-CHRISTIAN SPAHNI)

As a political writer, I was struck by what the site said about the past and present of the Andean Indian. Inca artisans possessed no metal tools, had no knowledge of the wheel, and lacked draft animals capable of hauling heavy loads. Yet from a quarry which I visited they managed to wrest apart immense blocks of stone, assembling them in the city with such precision that a knife blade still cannot enter the seams. It was visible testimony to the advanced social organization of an Indian empire which, inexplicably, or so it seemed, was subdued by a relative handful of Spaniards.

In the area around Cuzco much remains unchanged. The Indians speak the same language as their Inca forebears, wear the same clothes, and use the same tools. But their life today is so debased that for many it is made bearable only by chewing the leaves of the plant from which cocaine is derived. It was as if they lived on a different planet from their ancestors, and I wondered why. In asking the question, I had taken the first step in what was to become an avocational obsession with archaeology.

Andean history is as rich and various as that of Mesoamerica, and there is an odd parallelism between the two regions. In Mexico advanced cultures trace their origin to the enigmatic Olmecs on the Gulf Coast; in Peru there was a contemporaneous formative culture, likewise mysterious, which flourished on eastern slopes of the Andes, the Chavín. As in Middle America, there was then a succession of classical civilizations—the Nazca and Mochica on the coast, and the dimly known Tiahuanacans, who created a cultural empire in the Andes not unlike that of the Teotihuacanos in the Valley of Mexico. Next came an aggressive warrior nation, the Chimu, which played a role comparable to that of the Toltecs in Mexico in preparing the way for the culminating civilization which the Spaniards encountered, the Incas. As in Mesoamerica, the religion of Peru was based on sun worship, and, astonishingly, there was also a myth in South America about a fair-faced, bearded god-king, Tici Viracocha, whom the early friars identified with a Holy Apostle, just as they had done with Quetzalcóatl in the north.

Even the Spanish Conquest in the two regions followed a roughly similar course. Francisco Pizarro sailed from Panama in 1531 with 180 men and twenty-seven horses, and this derisory force sufficed to overwhelm the greatest Sun Kingdom of the pre-Columbian era, an empire extending 2,500 miles from what is now Ecuador through Peru and Bolivia south to Chile. A less prepossessing figure than Cortés, Pizarro was illiterate, illegitimate, and a onetime swineherd. He was sixty at the time of his Conquest. It is true that he had the fortifying example of Cortés, who had subdued Mexico a decade earlier. It is also true that, like Cortés, he was helped by the timing of his arrival in Peru—he happened to come when there was a dynastic war between two claimants to the Inca throne. Yet Pizarro's feat was the equal of his

Machu Picchu: Dwellings Only a roof is needed to make these buildings habitable again. (PHOTO JEAN-CHRISTIAN SPAHNI)

predecessor's, and in some respects surpassed it in audacity. He conquered a Rome at the apogee of its power.

The Aztecs were detested by their neighbors because of their constant war-making. But in the Andes an empire developed which was consecrated to that contemporary ideal, law and order. The Incas governed with an almost totalitarian rigor from one end of South America to the other. As Prescott writes, by degrees and without violence there arose "the great fabric of the Peruvian empire, composed of numerous independent and even hostile tribes, yet, under the influence of a common religion, common language, and common government, knit together as one nation, animated by a spirit of love for its institutions, and devoted loyalty to its sovereign."

In this great fabric each thread was made part of a pattern by a paternalistic state. Every detail of life, from the tilling of land to the arranging of marriages, was supervised by a watchful civil service whose recruits were drawn from the ablest of males. All was woven together by a superbly engineered and well-maintained road system which the chronicler Pedro Cieza de León described as "the greatest road there was in the world as well as the longest." Extending over as much as 10,000 miles, the network of highways was the bloodstream of the empire; through it flowed taxes, royal messengers, and marching armies. The Inca reigned as a god over a planned paradise which the French scholar Louis Baudin has likened to a socialist empire dedicated to "gloomy perfection." Some skeptics (like Sally Falk Moore, in her *Power and Property in Peru*) feel that the picture is often overdrawn, but even they acknowledge the impressive breadth and thoroughness of Inca planning.

And yet, ironically, the essential character of the state contributed decisively to its undoing. The splendid highways were used to lethal advantage by Pizarro's tiny force, and the hermetically authoritarian system enabled the Spaniards to immobilize the entire empire by seizing, and then murdering, the god-king, the Inca Atalhualpa. Once they possessed the reins of power, the Spaniards found they were ruling an Indian population conditioned to accept authority, no matter how cruel, and a social system as oppressive as that of the Incas without its benign virtues.

There are surely few more curious footnotes in Latin American history than the death of Ernesto (Che) Guevara, a zealous idealist who equated Utopia with socialist planning, as a direct result of the fatalistic servility among Bolivian Indians whose spirit was extinguished so long ago in the demi-paradise of the Inca Empire.

In visiting Peru, Lima and Cuzco are the polar points, the one the city of the victors and the other the capital of the vanquished, and in them one can imaginatively re-create the drama of the Conquest. It is fascinating to contrast Lima with Mexico City, both places in which the central historical event has been something that happened more than four centuries ago. In Mexico, as we have observed, since the Revolution a concerted effort has been made to erase the memory of Cortés and to exalt that of the Indian civilizations which he vanquished.

The priorities are precisely reversed in Lima, where the archaeological museum, though it has some fine exhibits, is a musty and neglected place, while an equestrian statue of Pizarro dominates the Plaza de Armas, whose spacious limits the hard-bitten Castilian himself measured out. (It has been noted that the sculptor was revealingly forgetful—Pizarro's sword is aggressively drawn, but there is no scabbard at his side.) Lima remains what it was —a colonial capital, an Hispanic bastion in an Indian sea.

The Indianism of Peru asserts itself immediately in Cuzco; at the airfield the porters speak Quechua, the language of the Incas, and women in big-brimmed hats hopefully proffer knitted sweaters in an Andean market atmosphere. James Morris has described Cuzco as "a little city of such supreme interest and historical symbolism, of such variety and punch, that in the South

The Inca World The sequence shows the principal officials of the Inca Empire as depicted by an artist not long after the Conquest.

The provincial administrator

The royal courier (Hatun Chasqui)

Those-who-mark-the-frontiers

The grand treasurer, keeper of accounts

The traveling inspector of the Empire

The Tahuantinsuyu supreme council

The Inca World   These drawings are reproduced from the admirably illustrated *The Incas: Royal Commentaries of the Inca Garcilaso de la Vega,* edited by Alain Gheerbant and translated by Maria Jolas (NEW YORK: ORION PRESS, 1961).

CONSEIO ALCALDE DECORTE
HANANCVSCOINGA
CAPACAPO-VATAC

The palace mayor in Hanan Cuzco

ALGVAZILMAIOR
CHACNAICAMAIOC
LVRINCVSCO

The grand alguazil in Hurin Cuzco

COREGIDORDEPROVINCIAS
TOCRICOCIVESMICHOC

The provincial corregidor

GOVERNADORDELOSCAMINOSREALES
CAPACNAИTOCRICOCANTA
INGA

The inspector of the roads

GOVERNADORDELOSPVENTESDESTE
CHACASVIOIOGACOSTINGA
GVAMBOCHACA

The inspector of the bridges

SECRETARIODELINGA ICOSEIO
INCAROVIPOCINILACAPAC
APOCOMARCAMA CHICVTNIINVIPOC

The secretary of the Inca

The first Inca, Manco Capac

The second Inca, Sinchi Roca

The third Inca, Lloque Yupanqui

The seventh Inca, Yahuar Huacac

The eighth Inca, Viracocha

The ninth Inca, Pachacutec Inca, Yupanqui

ELQVARTO INGA
MAITACAPAC

The fourth Inca, Maïta Capac

EL QVINTO INGA
CAPACIVPAQ

The fifth Inca, Capac Yupanqui

ELSESTO INGA
INGAROCA·CON

The sixth Inca, Roca, with his son

EL DECIMOINGA
TOPAINGA·IV

The tenth Inca, Tupac Inca Yupanqui

ELONZENOINGA
GVAINACAPAC

The eleventh Inca, Huaina Capac

EL DOZENOINGA
TOPACUCIGVAL

The twelfth Inca, Huascar

The Twelve Incas The same artist, Sebastian Poyamo, here depicts the royal house of the Sun Kingdom. Every schoolchild in Peru knows the names by heart.

American context she combines the compulsions of a Stonehenge, a small Seville, and a Katmandu." Once the heart of an empire encompassing 380,000 square miles, Cuzco was deemed to be the navel of the earth. Its approaches were guarded by Ollantaytambo, an enormous stone fortress composed of Cyclopean blocks all perfectly fitted together. The Inca city itself was dominated by the Temple of the Sun, within which the mummified remains of the Inca rulers were packed in pious bundles and tended by the Virgins of the Sun.

In November 1533 Pizarro entered Cuzco. The Inca Atalhualpa had already been slain, and the Temple of the Sun stripped of its gold in a vain attempt to ransom the Indian ruler. The Spaniards promptly renamed the main square the Plaza de Armas and almost as promptly began slaughtering one another—the twelve years of post-Conquest civil wars ended when Gonzalo Pizarro, brother of Francisco, was beheaded in Cuzco's plaza. When one of Gonzalo's lieutenants, Francisco de Caravajal, was led to the block (he was a vigorous eighty at the time), he said jauntily to the executioner, "Brother Juan, treat me the way one tailor treats another."

Even as a Spanish city, Cuzco retains its essential Inca identity. Its splendid churches adorned with Cuzcueño art are arrayed around streets in which the lower level of dwellings is formed of Inca stone so durable that the blocks have survived every earthquake, including the powerful tremor of May 21, 1959, in which a third of all the city's buildings were damaged. The rounded base of the Temple of the Sun remains, as does the foundation of the cloister of the Virgins, now the nunnery of Santa Catalina.

It was from Cuzco in 1911 that a young Yale instructor, Hiram Bingham, began a quest for the lost capital to which the Incas had reputedly retreated after the arrival of the Spaniards. Bingham used ancient chronicles as his guide in making his way on muleback through the jungles, plumed with wild orchids, that line the Urubamba River. A few weeks later, on July 24, he scaled Machu Picchu, having been told by a local farmer that there were strange ruins on its peak. On the saddle between two peaks, above a deep-winding gorge that cuts through vertical natural walls, Bingham came upon elaborate terraces, walls, a temple, and courtyards, the intact remains of a city in which some 2,000 people once lived. Machu Picchu (which means "Young Mountain") had been occupied for a century after the Conquest and then been mysteriously abandoned; Bingham enthusiastically claimed that it was the oldest of Inca cities, but in fact it dates from a far later epoch. Bingham had nevertheless found his lost city.*

* After the discovery, Bingham became involved in further adventures, first as a pilot in World War I and then as a Connecticut Republican who was elected Governor and Senator. In politics he is chiefly remembered for being censured by the Senate for allowing a lobbyist to attend a closed hearing—an action that created a precedent for the later Senate condemnation of Joseph R. McCarthy of Wisconsin.

Cuzco: The Temple of the Sun Once the residence of the royal virgins of the Sun, the walls of the temple now enclose a nunnery. This engraving is from E. Philip Squier's *Incidents of Travel in Peru*, a book which was to Andean archaeology what Stephens' works were to the Maya world.

The ruins were excavated by Bingham and have been made accessible by the Peruvian government through the construction of a single-track railroad that winds through the Urubamba Valley and brings visitors to the base of Machu Picchu. A steep road—called El Camino de Hiram Bingham and dedicated in 1948 by the explorer himself—enables a bus to ascend in low gear to the top, where a tourist hotel is located near the city.

It is in every way a superlative experience to climb above the city to the top of the loftier twin peak of Huayna Picchu (or "Old Mountain"), from which one can look down upon the Inca city, scarved in mist, its stones a testament to communal discipline and socialist planning. There is nothing like it in Greece or Palestine—and yet one should not overlook the admonition of Alexander von Humboldt, the great German scholar and traveler. "If we examine the mechanism of the Peruvian theocracy," he remarks in his *Essai politique sur la Nouvelle Espagne*, "generally so much overpraised in Europe, we observe that, whenever nations are divided into castes, and wherever men do not enjoy the right of private property and work solely for the profit of the community, we shall find canals, roads, aqueducts, pyramids, huge con-

Cuzco: The Fortress of Sacsahuaman This engraving, also from Squier's book, shows the fortress as it is seen from "The Seat of the Inca" in the foreground.

The Stones of Cuzco Inca masonry like this has withstood earthquakes that have tumbled later Spanish buildings. Yet the workmen who made these walls had no metal tools. (PHOTOS JEAN-CHRISTIAN SPAHNI)

struction of every kind. But we shall also find that these people, though for thousands of years they may preserve the air of external prosperity, will make practically no advance in moral culture, which is the result of individual liberty."

Still, the matter cannot be left here. To read Inca history simply as a right-wing morality play, discerning in it (as does Humboldt) a message about the sanctity of private property, is too facile. Looked at another way, the Peruvian Sun Kingdom seems a weird parody of the law-'n'-order ideal so earnestly commended by some political figures. In the Inca realm, law enforcement was swift and merciless; there was no coddling of criminals. Treason and disobedience were looked upon as the gravest of crimes, punishable by death, and the law itself was viewed as the embodiment of the ruler's will. Regarding anything approaching the concept of "law," writes Burr Cartwright Brundage, "there is an absolute blank for the obvious reason that in the Inca world law was still only *apup simi*, 'the word of the leader.' " *

From yet another vantage, the Inca cosmos has parallels with that of the modern corporation, with its stress on the virtues of discipline, hierarchy and efficiency. Interestingly, the Inca bookkeeper was a ubiquitous bureaucratic figure—he was the possessor of the *quipu*, the knotted string on which production records were kept. Most arable land was divided into thirds—a part for the gods and priests, a part for the king and a part for the people—much as a corporation shares its produce among stockholders, managers and workers. In contrast with the demonic spiritual intensity of the Aztecs, or the baroque calendrical observances of the Maya, the Inca was severely practical and had little time for idle speculation or aesthetic frippery (there is no ornamental carving on Machu Picchu). Truth, for the Inca, was not freedom or beauty or change; rather (remarks Brundage) it was "orderliness." The Incas were the consummate Organization Men.

However, for those ruthless or able enough to seize control of the throne (like modern corporations, the Incas never resolved the problem of assuring legitimate succession) there were rewards that went beyond vulgar stock options and retirement schemes. The body of the Inca was not only reverently mummified; it was attended by a permanent household, the *panaca*, as if it were a living being. The bundled mummy of the emperor was served food, had flies whisked from him, was entertained, taken to be relieved, put to sleep, received the finest leaves of coca from his plantations in the *montaña*, and received periodic tallies of the llamas in his herds. If he owned irrigating channels, the dead Inca's permission had to be sought for the

* Brundage, *Lords of Cuzco* (Norman: University of Oklahoma Press, 1967), p. 265. This volume and the same author's *Empire of the Incas* (1963) constitute an impressive modern synthesis of original sources by a scholar fluent in Quechua; I have consulted both with pleasure.

Machu Picchu In the background is Huayna Picchu, or "Old Mountain" in the Quechua tongue. Below is Machu Picchu, or "Young Mountain." (PHOTO AERO-FILMS LTD.)

employment of his waters. So loyal were the *panacas* to their deceased and
stuffed lords that men and women in the mummy's household resisted the
torturing racks and fires of the Spaniards who sought to locate the bodies to
strip them of gold.

It is in these bundled mummies, with their fiercely loyal attendants, that
one finds the absurd crowning emblem of the Inca state. The Spaniards were
well aware of the talismanic power of the mummies; the conquerors saw to
it that the last Inca rebel, Tupac Amaru, would leave no corporeal legacy.
In 1572, four decades after Pizarro's arrival, Tupac Amaru was captured,
baptized and brought to public execution in Cuzco. The Spaniards announced the sentence well in advance so that as many Indians as possible
would come to the old capital and see their last Lord perish. When Tupac
Amaru mounted the pillory, tens of thousands of his people broke into a
shriek of sorrow. The alarmed Spaniards untied the Inca's arms, so that he
could silence his people; with a regal gesture Tupac Amaru invoked a silence
as striking as the noise that preceded it. According to the reports of friars (and
their account is probably true in substance if inaccurate in detail), the
doomed Inca said:

> Incas and *curacas* [nobles], you who have come from the four
> quarters know that I am now a Christian. I must die and I die in the
> law of Christ. Formerly I and my ancestors told you that you
> should worship Inti [the sun god] and the *huacas* [mysterious
> divine powers]. All that was a lie, a trick. We also told you that
> whenever we entered Coricancha we used to speak to Inti and he
> would answer us, and therefore you, our subjects, had to obey
> those commands. That too was a lie; Inti could not speak, for he
> was only a lump of gold. My brother it was, Titu Cusi Yupanqui,
> who taught me to deceive you in this way, to pretend to speak to
> the sun and to thus ensure your obedience.

After speaking, Tupac Amaru (whom the Spaniards had baptized Don
Pablo) put his head on the block; with a single stroke the swordsman
severed it and held it aloft for the Indians to see. The head was put on a
pike, and later buried with the body in a secret place. The Spaniards seized
all property still owned by the Inca, and dispersed all the heirs, no matter
how young. There were no more rebellions; as the great Inca Pachacuti
prophesied, the time had come for great Sun Kingdom to die, and it died.

II

THE FUTURE OF YESTERDAY

> *Can man face the future with hope and*
> *with resolution without a sense of the past?*
> *And if not, can a new past, truer than the*
> *old, be manufactured to give him a like*
> *sense of confidence? These problems, I*
> *venture to suggest, lie at the very heart of*
> *our society.*
>
> J. H. PLUMB, The Death of the Past

WITH THIS ALL TOO BRIEF CONSPECTUS of the history of ancient Peru, we have concluded an all too brief pilgrimage through the world, or at least a small part of it, that archaeology has exposed to our incredulous view. At this point, assuredly, we should consider whether the trip has been worth making at all.

Some would say no. I found it disheartening to read *The Uncompleted Past*, a collection of essays by a brilliant young Princeton historian, Martin Duberman, who has come to feel that his field of study is a waste of time. In his own words, "For those among the young, historians and otherwise, who are chiefly interested in changing the present, I can only say, speaking from my own experience, that they doom themselves to disappointment if they seek their guides to action in a study of the past."

It is clearly a token of our own Time of Troubles that a professor of history should come so perilously close to agreeing with Henry Ford that the past is bunk. One can understand why it might seem like bunk to the young and impatient. What possible pertinence can a Mycenean potsherd have to the cruel and interminable war in Southeast Asia? How can anyone be sensibly concerned with the dicipherment of Maya glyphs when a third of the world lives in squalor? Who could seriously argue that a monograph on Paleolithic flint tools offers anything approaching a "guide to action" to those who want to reshape what passes for Western civilization? Can a world lurching into a gutter seeded with garbage and ghettoes, jukeboxes and the Bomb—can that world afford the luxury of looking backward?

The honest answer must be that archaeology, like history, cannot provide a "guide to action," and that in fact one of the achievements of both disciplines has been to undermine the notion that the past provides a neat blueprint for the future. It would be a deception to suggest that the spade is a weapon of ideology, though archaeological finds not infrequently have ideological significance. There is, surely, no greater disservice to the science of the past than to claim a glib "relevance" for it.

What archaeology offers instead is an antidote to hysteria. While a knowledge of the past may not enable one to paint a picture of the future, it can be of inestimable help in suggesting the size of the canvas. In a disordered time, when even Princeton historians talk in accents of fashionable despair, archaeology helps one to retain that most difficult of things to preserve—a saving sense of perspective.

It is useful to recall that, in other periods of change, despondent intellectuals have concluded that the past was irrelevant to pressing contemporary problems. The attitude was expressed during the Renaissance, the Enlightenment, the French Revolution and in the quarrels among nineteenth-century radicals. Indeed, a dispute over the supposed uselessness of antiquity inspired a satirical classic through which generations of students of English literature have been required to plod—Jonathan Swift's *Battle of the Books*.

In 1697, several prominent members of the Royal Society took up a polemical campaign that had begun in France; they confidently asserted—in an age still dazzled by Newton's great discoveries—that classical authors were inferior and had become irrelevant. Swift came to the support of Aesop and Aristotle; his *Battle of the Books* opens with a debate among the Olympians in which Momus, the goddess of Novelty, defends the Generation Gap in a burlesque that Vice President Agnew could approvingly quote:

> It is I [said she] who gave wisdom to infants and idiots; by me, children grow wiser than their parents; by me, beaux become politicians and schoolboys judges of philosophy; by me, sophisters debate, and conclude upon the depths of knowledge; and coffee-house wits, instinct by me, can correct an author's style, and display his minutest errors, without understanding a syllable of his matter, or his language; by me, striplings spend their judgment, as they do their estate, before it comes into their hands. It is I who have deposed wit and knowledge from the empire of poetry, and advanced myself in their stead. And shall a few upstart ancients dare oppose me?

The notion that everything is new is itself old, part of the past which is said to be disposable.

It further strikes me as odd that anyone who (like Martin Duberman) sympathizes with revolutionary movements should minimize the importance of the past in abetting the self-esteem of the oppressed. This impulse lies behind the widespread demand for Afro-American studies by black college students; the Negro, robbed of his history, is anxious to recover what some of his white teachers dismiss as a burden. "It is interesting that the last two years have witnessed a determination amongst the blacks to acquire a past of their own," remarked J. H. Plumb, the Cambridge historian, in 1969. "Like many a white past, it has little to do with history. . . . The same development occurred in Ghana, where the murals were painted to show how Ghana had invented both the alphabet and the steam-engine. There is no need for laughter and none to sneer; all the white pasts have made assumptions equally outrageous and for exactly the same purpose—to create both confidence and a sense of special virtue."

There is manifestly a deep need that is satisfied by a knowledge of our collective pedigree; without a past we are psychic orphans. An understanding of our origins may not provide a "guide for action," but it can give us the self-confidence we so desperately need to find a plan for our common survival. For this reason, I find grotesque the belief that the message of the past is essentially discouraging. After a century of demolition work on an illusion-ridden past steeped in chauvinism, it is ironic that a new generation of radicals should scorn the past because it might make less credible an illusion-ridden future.

As J. H. Plumb observes, "The past which mankind needs is no longer a simple one. Experience as well as science has made the majority of literate men aware of the vast complexity of human existence, its subtle interrelations. What, however, is becoming less and less stressed is the nature of the past, not only its successes, but also the shadow it casts across our lives. History, the dimension of Time, is ignored too frequently by sociologists, economists, politicians and philosophers; even theologians wish to escape from its clutches."

I believe that the evidence of archaeology supports neither an optimistic nor a pessimistic view of man—it supports both views, and its findings may yet, I hope, enable us to develop a maturer sense of the past, giving us a new identity not only as Americans or Chinese, rich or poor, old or young, white or brown, but as members of the same extended family. Archaeology can help us approach that transcendent goal; its discoveries will also vivify the dust it unsettles. The spade has done so already; may its power increase.

An Annotated Bibliography

I
Books in General *

One more pleasure of archaeology, if you have the luxury of space, is accumulating books and periodicals about the past. I particularly like browsing in second-hand bookstores in quest of original editions of the classic accounts of pioneer diggers and early explorers—fat, substantial volumes with steel engravings, written at a tempo that is *lento* and never *allegro*. Prices vary, but it is possible to find bargains on dusty shelves; there is a peculiar satisfaction in paying an absurd trifle for Dennis' *Cities and Cemeteries of Etruria* or anything by Schliemann (whose books are increasingly hard to find).

The best way to start is by getting *The World of the Past* (New York: Knopf, 1963), edited by Jacquetta Hawkes, a two-volume anthology of original accounts by discoverers and interpreters of antiquity. This collection is both a cornerstone of a library and a guide to purchases. Other useful introductory books include *The Meaning of Archaeology* (London: Thames and Hudson, 1968), a richly illustrated survey by Massimo Pallotino, the most eminent of Etruscologists; *Archaeology from the Earth* (London: Penguin, 1956) by Sir Mortimer Wheeler is a fluent and authoritative account of the techniques of the science; Glyn Daniel, *The Origins and Growth of Archaeology* (London: Penguin, 1967), weaves together a history with well-chosen excerpts from original sources; C. W. Ceram's two popularizations, *Gods, Graves and Scholars* (New York: Knopf, 1952) and the picture-book, *The March of Archaeology* (New York: Knopf, 1958), have had a deserved success, though both overemphasize the Mediterranean past; *The Testimony of the Spade* (New York: Knopf, 1956) by Geoffrey Bibby is a supplement to Ceram and a model of what a popular account should be—an accurate and readable survey extending from Paleolithic cultures to the Vikings and ancient Celts; Leo Deuel's *Testament of Time* (New York: Knopf, 1965) deals with the search for old manuscripts, and Ernst Dobholfer's *Voices in Stone* (New York: Viking, 1961) describes the decipherment of ancient scripts; *Digging into History* (New York: John Day, 1961) by

---

* There are usually American and English editions of the books I list; for reasons of convenience, I have simply cited the date and publisher of the volume in my own library, leaving it to the reader to use his own intelligence to find the citation for the appropriate side of the Atlantic.

Edward Bacon, editor of the distinguished archaeological section of the *Illustrated London News*, reports on the major discoveries in the productive years 1945–1959; Paul Johnstone's *Buried Treasure* (London: Phoenix, 1957) is an entertaining account of various BBC ventures into the past; finally, Rose Macaulay's *Pleasure of Ruins* (London: Thames and Hudson, 1966) is a deliberately unscientific corrective to the unromantic cataloguing of sherds.

Three vast volumes, each as big as a Mayan stela, are rewarding if physically unmanageable—*The Dawn of Civilization* (New York: McGraw-Hill, 1961), edited by Stuart Piggot; *Vanished Civilizations* (New York: McGraw-Hill, 1963), edited by Edward Bacon; and *The Birth of Civilization: Greece and Rome* (New York: McGraw-Hill, 1964), edited by Michael Grant; in these an authoritative synthesis of a century of digging is offered by experts in their respective fields. Another three-volume set is a diverting token of the interest in archaeology stimulated by the discovery of Tutankhamen's tomb—J. A. Hammerton, ed., *The Wonders of the Past* (London: Fleetway House, c. 1927), an illustrated survey written by contemporary specialists that turns up at bargain prices in second-hand bookshops on Charing Cross.

The general orientation of this book has been greatly influenced by J. H. Plumb's *The Death of the Past* (London: Macmillan, 1969) and by three admirable books by the humanist critic and historian, Herbert Muller: *Uses of the Past* (New York: Oxford, 1952), *The Loom of History* (New York: Harper, 1956), and *Freedom in the Ancient World* (New York: Harper, 1961). Additionally, I have found nutriment in two wide-ranging collections of essays: M. I. Finley, *Aspects of Antiquity* (London: Chatto and Windus, 1968); and Sir Mortimer Wheeler, *Alms for Oblivion: An Antiquary's Scrapbook* (London: Weidenfeld and Nicolson, 1966).

A special word should be said about periodicals. I subcribe to three: *Antiquity*, a British quarterly edited by Glyn Daniel (c/o W. Heffer & Sons, 104 Hills Road, Cambridge, England); *Archaeology*, published quarterly by the Archaeological Institute of America (100 Washington Square East, New York, N.Y. 10003); and *Expedition*, also a quarterly, the bulletin of the University Museum of the University of Pennsylvania (33d and Spruce Streets, Philadelphia 4, Pa.). There is an excellent French journal, published every other month, *Archeologia* (49 Avenue d'Iéna, Paris 16). Also to be commended are *Current Archaeology* (128 Barnsbury Road, London N.1), a British journal published by enthusiasts, and *Art and Archaeology Newsletter* (243 East 39th Street, New York, N.Y. 10016), an unassuming grab-bag collected by a layman. Both are published semimonthly. Finally, there are frequent and important articles in such standard publications as *Scientific American*, *Natural History*, *Horizon*, *National Geographic*, and *Illustrated London News*.

II
Into the Ice Age: France

For an overview of prehistory, an outstanding and up-to-date book is John E. Pfeiffer's *The Emergence of Man* (New York: Harper & Row, 1969), a popular account drawn from a hundred scholarly sources. Of the many books on cave art, one volume is outstanding for its illustrations, charts, provocative ideas and (alas) high cost: *The Art of Prehistoric Man* (London: Thames and Hudson, 1969) by André Leroi-Gourhan. For a critical supplement, see Peter J. Ucko and Andrée Rosenfeld, *Paleolithic Cave Art* (London: World University Library, 1967). Larger libraries have copies of Abbé Henri Breuil's many folio-sized monographs about specific caves, and I have examined them covetously; the closest thing to a synthesis is Breuil's *Four Hundred Centuries of Cave Art* (Montignac, France, 1952). I also enjoyed an introductory book, written with zest, by the German prehistorian Herbert Kühn, *On the Track of Prehistoric Man* (London: Hutchinson, 1955). A reflective treatise from which I have profited is *The Idea of Prehistory* (London: Penguin, 1962) by Glyn Daniel.

In visiting the caves, certain books are essential. A concise guide to all the caves is provided by Alan and Gale Sieveking in *The Caves of France and Northern Spain* (London: Vista, 1962). Geoffrey Grigson gives the impressions of a distinguished poet and critic in his luminous *Painted Caves* (London: Phoenix, 1952), while Glyn Daniel's *The Hungry Archaeologist in France* (London: Faber, 1963) combines culinary counsel with a tour of both the Dordogne caves and the megalithic alignments in Carnac, Brittany. An exemplary guide to the Dordogne is Freda White's *Three Rivers of France* (London: Faber, 1962). Books on individual caves include Annette Laming, *Lascaux* (London: Penguin, 1959) and Louis René Nougier and Romain Robert, *The Cave of Rouffignac* (London: Newnes, 1958), the latter a partisan volume about cave art of disputed authenticity. Finally, as an imaginative seasoning, one should read William Golding's impressive novel about ancient man, *The Inheritors* (London: Faber, 1961).

III
The Book of the Dead: Egypt

Books about Egyptology could fill a large *mastaba*. Of the many popular writers, one is pre-eminent: Dr. Barbara Mertz, a University of Chicago Egyptologist whose two fine volumes, *Temples, Tombs and Hieroglyphics* (New York: Coward-McCann, 1964) and *Red Land, Black Land* (London: Hodder and Stoughton, 1967), are enlivened by a sympathy for an ancient civilization whose unvarying uniformity I sometimes find exasperating. Another prolific popularizer is Leonard Cottrell, whose many books on Egypt are available in both hard- and soft-cover editions.

A volume that still stands in lofty isolation is James Breasted's *A History of Egypt* (New York: Scribner, 1910). The holder of the first American chair in Egyptology (endowed at Chicago in 1895), Breasted was a pioneer translator of original sources and the earliest celebrator of the heretic Pharaoh Ikhnaton; his *Development of Religion and Thought in Egypt* (New York: Harper and Row, 1959) remains a landmark. He has not been supplanted; the most ambitious modern rival to his *History* is *Egypt of the Pharaohs* (Oxford: University Press, 1961) by Sir Alan Gardiner, the leading English authority on hieroglyphics, whose book is dedicated to Breasted.

For anecdotes about the pillage of Egypt, I benefited from Leslie Greener's *The Discovery of Egypt* (London: Cassell, 1966) and John A. Wilson's *Signs and Wonders upon Pharaoh* (Chicago: University Press, 1964), an engaging account of Egyptology which stresses the American contribution. A good, solid synthesis of present knowledge of ancient Egypt is Cyril Aldred, *The Egyptians* (London: Thames and Hudson, 1961).

Among travel books, as Wilson remarks, "nothing has surpassed Baedeker's *Egypt and the Sudan* (8th edition, Leipzig, 1929)." Compiled by the German scholar George Steindorff, this guide is Teutonic in its thoroughness but is unfortunately rare and costly. The nearest equivalent is the Hachette guide to Egypt, available in French. For a commentary on the country today, see Simonne Lacouture, *Egypt* (New York: Vista, 1963). An older travel book of considerable charm is *A Thousand Miles up the Nile* (London: Geo. Routledge, 1889), by Amelia B. Edwards, who went to Egypt on a whim ("stress of weather," she explained to friends). The gossipy vivacity of her description of a trip up the Nile in a *dahabeeyah* restores to life the Egypt of Cromer and Thomas Cook.

On specific topics I benefited from Ahmed Fahkry, *The Pyramids* (Chicago: University Press, 1961); Christiane Desroches-Noblecourt, *Tutankhamen* (New York: Graphic Society, 1963); Charles F. Nims, *Thebes of the Pharaohs* (London: Elek, 1965); and Walter B. Emery, *Egypt in Nubia* (London: Hutchinson, 1965). I was entertained by W. M. Flinders Petrie's *Ten Years Digging in Egypt* (London: Religious Tract Society, 1893). Of the many novels, one is outstanding, *King of Two Lands* (London: Chatto and Windus, 1966) by Jacquetta Hawkes, a reconstruction of the times of Ikhnaton (but see also Dmitri Merezhkovsky's badly translated *Akhnaton: King of Egypt,* which anticipates Freud's thesis that the Jews acquired monotheism from the heretic Pharaoh). Finally, I have not mentioned Herodotus, who visited Egypt for three months in the fifth century B.C., because his account permeates everything that has been written since. The French archaeologist Mariette has said harshly of him:

> I detest this traveller who went to Egypt at a time when the Egyptian language was spoken, who with his eyes saw all the temples still standing; who had only to ask the first comer the name of the reigning king, the name of the king who preceded him, who only had to refer to the first temple for the history, religion—for everything of interest concerning the most fascinating country in the world. And who, instead of all that, tells us gravely that a daughter of Cheops built a pyramid with the fruits of prostitution. This is not what one should expect from Herodotus, and as for me I look upon him as a real criminal.

But Sir Alan Gardiner acquits the Father of History of intentional lying, and everyone, as Amelia Edwards remarks, "takes Herodotus up the Nile."

IV
Gods' Country: Israel and Jordan

Two solid introductions to Biblical archaeology are James B. Pritchard, *Archaeology and the Old Testament* (Princeton: University Press, 1958) and W. F. Albright, *The Archaeology of Palestine* (London: Penguin, 1960), each by a ranking American authority in the field. Jack Finegan's *Light from the Ancient Past* (Princeton: University Press, 1959) is a broader survey of the archaeological background to the Old and New Testaments. Books that the interested student will also want to examine and perhaps acquire include Joyce M. H. Reid and

H. H. Rowley, *Atlas of the Bible* (London: Nelson, 1963); D. Winton Thomas, *Documents from Old Testament Times* (New York: Harper & Row, 1961); and two fascinating volumes drawn from the outstanding scholarly journal in the field, G. Ernest Wright and David Noel Freedman, eds., *The Biblical Archaeological Reader* (New York: Doubleday Anchor Books, 1961), and David Noel Freedman and E. F. Campbell, eds., *The Biblical Archaeological Reader 2* (New York: Doubleday Anchor Books, 1964).

Travelers to the Holy Land will find it helpful to consult certain guides: Moshe Pearlman and Yaacov Yannai, *Historical Sites in Israel* (London: W. H. Allen, 1964); G. Lankester Harding, *The Antiquities of Jordan* (London: Lutterworth, 1963); Samuel Abramsky, *Ancient Towns in Israel* (Jerusalem: World Zionist Organization, 1963); and Christopher Hollis and Ronald Brownrigg, *Holy Places* (New York: Praeger, 1969), the last being typical of a number of glossily packaged guides. Of the many recent books on Jerusalem, Teddy Kollek and Moshe Perlman, *Jerusalem: A History of Forty Centuries* (New York: Random House, 1968) is a handsome coffee-table volume co-authored by the first Jewish Mayor of united Jerusalem in two millennia; Chaim Raphael, *The Walls of Jerusalem* (New York: Knopf, 1968) is an engaging compendium of legends and parables associated with the Holy City; Kathleen Kenyon, *Jerusalem: Excavating 3000 Years of History* (London: Thames and Hudson, 1967) is a scholarly account of recent excavations; and Norman Kotker, *The Earthly Jerusalem* (New York: Scribner, 1969) is a sensitively drawn historical portrait that I especially liked.

The controversy over the Dead Sea Scrolls can be traced by reading books by the protagonists, beginning with A. Dupont Sommers, *The Dead Sea Scrolls* (Oxford: Basil Blackwell, 1952), an early account which has survived later sieges surprisingly well. I also liked Yigal Yadin, *The Message of the Scrolls* (London: Weidenfeld and Nicolson, 1959); Frank Moore Cross, *The Ancient Library of Qumran* (New York: Doubleday, 1961); J. M. Allegro, *The Dead Sea Scrolls* (London: Penguin, 1961); and, above all, Edmund Wilson, *The Dead Sea Scrolls, 1947–1969* (Oxford: University Press, 1969), in which Wilson's 1953 articles that first carried the dispute to a lay audience are brought together with more recent (and more prickly) reportage.

Some superlative reports on specific sites include Yigal Yadin, *Masada* (London: Weidenfeld and Nicolson, 1966); Kathleen Kenyon, *Digging Up Jericho* (New York: Praeger, 1959); James Pritchard, *Gibeon: Where the Sun Stood Still* (Princeton: University Press, 1962); and G. Ernest Wright, *Shechem: The Biography of a Biblical City* (London: Duckworth, 1965). In a wholly different vein is Ronald Sanders, *The View from Masada* (New York: Doubleday, 1968), a penetrating essay about modern Israel as well as an account of the meaning of Masada.

One can find on dusty shelves of second-hand bookshops dozens of books about the Holy Land by nineteenth-century clergymen; sometimes entertaining and often boring, these pilgrims' accounts are now valuable chiefly for their illustrations. But one volume stands by itself (and it is not illustrated): George Adam Smith, *The Historical Geography of the Holy Land* (London: Hodder and Stoughton, 1890). Adam Smith appraises the sacred landscape with a Scottish theologian's erudition and a prophet's passion for truth; his prose irradiates all that it describes. No one seriously interested in Biblical archaeology will do without *The Historical Geography*, now available in a Galaxy paperback.

Of the hundreds of novels written about Biblical themes, I would single out one that hardly anybody reads: George Moore's *Brook Kerith* (London: Macmillan, 1916). In this forgotten novel Moore develops the thought that Jesus survived His crucifixion and sought refuge in an Essene monastery much like Qumran, where, years later, He was visited by Paul. To say more would be to spoil the astonishing *denouement* of a remarkable novel. Thomas Mann's *Joseph* tetralogy and Lion Feuchtwanger's *Josephus* trilogy are outstanding examples of archaeological fiction. A lesser-known title that might elude notice is Lionel Davidson's *A Long Way to Shiloh* (London: Penguin, 1968), about a British archaeologist who is pulled into a bizarre intrigue in Israel; the plot recalls Eric Ambler and Kingsley Amis, but the style is Davidson's alone. It is not to be missed.

V
Realm of Light: Greece

For anyone planning a trip to Greece, I would recommend a basic bookshelf of seven volumes. *The Greek Stones Speak* (New York: St. Martin, 1962) by Paul MacKendrick is the best one-volume survey of archaeology in Greek lands. The Hachette *World Guide to Greece* is exemplary, though one needs a jeweler's loupe to read some of the print. *The Road Map and Tourist Guide of Greece*, published by the Automobile and Touring Club of Greece, is indispensable: its detailed maps in a ringed binder trace every erratic road in Hellas (copies can be purchased at Zeno Booksellers, 6 Denmark Street, London W.C.2, the best Hellenic bookshop outside Athens).

Next is M. I. Finley, *The Ancient Greeks* (London: Penguin, 1963), a model of concision. Mimi Granaki, in *Greece* (New York: Vista, 1964), provides a companion volume about the country today. Canon Guy Pentreath, *Hellenic Traveler* (London: Faber, 1964), describes the principal sites in a dry, unhurried manner, while a slim volume in a new series of specialized guides provides more details: Robert and Kathleen Cook, *Southern Greece: An Archaeological Guide* (London: Faber, 1968).

Homeric archaeology is a world to itself, and I would suggest as a starter Denys Page's engaging and readable *History and the Homeric Iliad* (Berkeley: University of California Press, 1963). Page leads the reader through an involved labyrinth with a firm hand and disarming wit in arguing the historicity of the Trojan War (for a dissenting view, see Finley's essay in *Aspects of the Past, op. cit.*). For a lively introduction to the Mycenaean-Minoan controversy, see Joseph Alsop, *From the Silent Earth* (New York: Harper & Row, 1964).

Three books by Heinrich Schliemann form the cornerstone of a serious library on Greek archaeology: *Troy and Its Remains* (London: John Murray, 1872); *Mycenae* (London: John Murray, 1878); and *Ilios: City and Country of the Trojans* (London: John Murray, 1880). Expensive reprint editions are available, but they lack the attractiveness of the older volumes with their gilt-engraved covers. There is regrettably no adequate full-scale biography of Schliemann. For my own interpretation of the pioneer, I am indebted to E. M. Butler, *The Tyranny of Greece over Germany* (Boston: Beacon, 1958).

The travel literature about Greece is dauntingly vast. A standard early account is Christopher Wordsworth, D.D., *Greece* (London: Wm. S. Orr & Co., 1853), written by the nephew of the poet and notable for its steel engravings. More recent books that I particularly liked include: F. L. and Prudence Lucas, *From Olympus to the Styx* (London: Cassell, 1924); Osbert Lancaster, *Classical Landscape with Pictures* (London: John Murray, 1947); Kevin Andrews, *The Flight of Ikaros* (London: Weidenfeld and Nicolson, 1959); Henry Miller, *The Colossus of Marousi* (New York: New Directions paperback, 1958); Patrick Leigh Fermor, *Mani: Travels in the Southern Peloponnese* (New York: Harper, 1960); Robert Lidell, *The Morea* (London: Cape, 1958); Nikos Kazantzakis, *Travels in Greece* (Oxford: Cassirer, 1966); Helen Hill Miller, *Greek Horizons* (New York: Scribner, 1961); and Robert Payne, *The Splendor of Greece* (New York: Harper, 1960). Copies of J. P. Mahaffy's entertaining *Rambles and Studies in Greece* (London: Macmillan, 1878) are easy to come by in London's second-hand bookstores. Finally, special mention should be made of Patrick Anderson's *The Smile of Apollo* (London: Chatto and Windus, 1964), a literary companion to Greek travel, in which an original idea is admirably executed.

The novels of Mary Renault are sufficiently well known not to require listing, but even the diligent reader may have passed by Lawrence Durrell's *The Dark Labyrinth* (London: Faber, 1963), an archaeological fantasy set in Crete which, if not one of Durrell's great novels, is nevertheless diverting.

VI
Realm of Power: Italy

The story of Italian archaeology is admirably related in Paul MacKendrick, *The Mute Stones Speak* (New York: St. Martin, 1960), and the useful but ineptly translated *In Search of Ancient Italy* (New York: Hill and Wang, 1964) by Pierre Grimal.

Of the innumerable books about Rome, ancient and modern, the works of Rodolfo Lanciani are notable for their enthusiasm and fine illustrations, especially *The Ruins and Excavations of Ancient Rome* (London: Macmillan, 1897). The original editions are, unfortunately, hard to find, and the high-priced reprints not especially attractive. Margaret R. Scherer, *Marvels of Ancient Rome* (London and New York: Phaidon, 1955), is an excellent blend of text and pictures. The most urbane of modern commentaries is supplied by Eleanor Clark, *Rome and a Villa* (New York: Atheneum paperback, 1962).

On specific subjects I liked E. M. Winslow, *A Libation to the Gods* (London: Hodder and Stoughton, 1963), written by an American economist in celebration of the ancient aqueducts; Joseph Day Deiss, *Herculaneum: Italy's Buried Treasure* (New York: Crowell, 1966); Marcel Brion, *Pompeii and Herculaneum* (London: Elek, 1960); Victor W. Von Hagen, *The Roads That Led to Rome* (London: Weidenfeld and Nicolson, 1967); and H. V. Morton, *The Waters of Rome* (London: Michael Joseph, 1966), the latter being a richly illustrated study of Rome's pride of fountains.

A book in a special category is Gilbert Highet's *Poets in a Landscape* (New York: Knopf, 1957), which is a guided tour of the terrain described by Catullus, Vergil, Propertius, Horace, Tibullus, Ovid and Juvenal—a literary pilgrimage conducted by a civilized and unobtrusive cicerone.

The literature about the Etruscans is exceptionally rich, beginning with Mrs. Hamilton Gray's charming early account, *Journey to the Sepulchers of Etruria in 1838* (London: J. Hatchard & Son, 1840), and with the classic pioneering report of George Dennis, *Cities and Cemeteries of Etruria* (London: John Murray, 1880), in two fat, amply illustrated volumes. D. H. Lawrence, *Etruscan Places* (London: Heinemann, 1956) is a classic of a different kind. The great modern authority is M. Pallotino, whose *The Etruscans* (London: Penguin, 1956) is virtually the standard work. For a tour of the sites, see Henry Harvel-Courtés, *Etruscan Italy* (London: Oliver and Bond, 1964), and for a more detailed analysis consult H. H. Scullard, *The Etruscan Cities and Rome* (London: Thames and Hudson, 1967).

To all of this Luigi Barzini, *The Italians* (New York: Atheneum, 1964) is an essential supplement, a book about Italy that brings the past and present into judicious accord.

VII
Miss Havisham's House: England

The English devotion to the past finds a rewarding expression in the guides and maps published by Her Majesty's Stationery Office. For a comparatively few shillings one can acquire the excellent guides describing Stonehenge, Hadrian's Wall and the Roman Forts on the Saxon Shore. Three maps are outstanding: *Map of Ancient Britain* (in two sheets); *Map of Roman Britain;* and *Map of Hadrian's Wall*. These maps are keyed to the even more detailed Ordnance Survey maps, meaning that there is hardly a cairn or milepost that cannot be precisely pinpointed.

General works that I have consulted with profit include Gordon Childe, *The Dawn of European Civilization* (London: Routledge and Kegan Paul, 1961); Grahame Clark, *Prehistoric Britain* (London: Batsford, 1962); I. A. Richmond, *Roman Britain* (London: Penguin, 1967); and I. D. Margary, *Roman Roads in Britain* (London: John Baker, 1967). The indispensible Baedeker is Jacquetta Hawkes, *A Guide to Prehistoric and Roman Monuments in England and Wales* (London: Chatto and Windus, 1954), which has a comprehensive gazeteer. Roman ruins are described with gusto by Leonard Cottrell in *Seeing Roman Britain* (London: Evans, 1963), which is also available in a paperback. For anecdotal oddments about the search for the British past, see Ronald Jessup, *The Story of Archaeology in Britain* (London: Michael Joseph, 1964).

Concerning the Stonehenge controversy, some basic works are R. J. C. Atkinson, *Stonehenge* (London: Penguin, 1960); Gerald S. Hawkins, in collaboration with John B. White, *Stonehenge Decoded* (London: Souvenir Press, 1965); and A. Thom, *Megalithic Sites in Britain* (Oxford: University Press, 1967). More generally, see also Glyn Daniel, *The Megalithic Builders of Western Europe* (London: Penguin, 1963). Anent Hadrian's Wall, David Harrison, *Along Hadrian's Wall* (London: Cassell, 1962) is an engaging account of a personal exploration; David Divine, *The Northwest Frontier of Rome* (London: Macdonald, 1969) is a detailed military analysis; and the Rev. J. Collingwood Bruce, *A Handbook to the Roman Wall* (Newcastle, many editions) is the standard guide. Bruce was a vicar who a century ago popularized Wall-walking; his *Handbook* has been revised and pruned by I. A. Richmond, but the older editions, which can be found in second-hand bookstores, are pleasant artifacts; limp green covers, a profusion of steel engraving, a fold-out linen map, and period prose like this: "[The traveler] may, if he thinks proper, indulge in the use of wheels as far as Sewingshields, alighting at every point of interest." About Camelot, a fine introduction to the entire Arthurian controversy is Geoffrey Ashe, *The Quest for Arthur's Britain* (London: Pall Mall, 1968). Finally, among the many novels about ancient Britain, I was especially impressed by Alfred Duggan, *Conscience of the King* (London: Faber, 1962), which convincingly evokes the decay of Roman Britain, the ferocity of the encroaching Anglo-Saxons, and the offstage figure of Arthur as he must have seemed to his more barbarous adversaries.

VIII

The Moon's Dark Side: Mexico

Where does one begin? The question may be put in despair by the layman who approaches the vast literature about Mexico, the Conquest, and pre-Columbian archaeology in general. I would propose Prescott, whose *Conquest of Mexico* still stands alone, like a temple carved from living rock, its judgments amended but not superseded. Prescott's achievement surely ranks with that of Gibbon, all the more so when one recalls that the Bostonian was half blind and never visited the country whose subjection he describes.

Of the narratives left by the conquerors, Bernal Díaz del Castillo, *The Discovery and Conquest of Mexico* (New York: Farrar, Straus and Cudahy, 1956) is pre-eminent. A useful anthology, in Spanish, of the various accounts of Indian life is Luis Nicolau d'Olwer, ed., *Cronistas de las Culturas Precolumbinas* (Mexico: Fondo de Culture et Económica, 1963). An admirable new popular narrative of the Conquest of Mexico and Peru is Hamilton Innes, *The Conquistadors* (London: Collins, 1969).

The broader controversy over New World cultural origins can be appraised in Robert Wauchope, *Lost Tribes and Sunken Continents* (Chicago: University Press, 1962), an *omnium gatherum* of fantasies collected by a non-believer; Kenneth Macgowan and Joseph A. Hester, *Early Men in the New World* (New York: Doubleday Anchor Books, 1962), a generally sober diffusionist analysis; and Constance Irwin, *Fair Gods and Stone Faces* (London: W. H. Allen, 1964), typical of many enthusiastic tracts by non-scholars. See also Glyn Daniel, *The First Civilizations* (London: Thames and Hudson, 1968) for an analysis that puts the dispute in a global context. On the unsettling finds in Ecuador, see Betty J. Meggers, *Ecuador* (London: Thames and Hudson, 1966).

A book about the Aztecs that is still standard though superseded in some important details is George C. Vaillant, *The Aztecs of Mexico* (New York: Doubleday, 1962), preferably in this edition, as revised by his widow. Fray Diego Duran, *The Aztecs* (New York: Orion, 1964) is an invaluable source by an early friar. Two sympathetic accounts of Aztec civilization by Miguel León-Portilla cannot be ignored: *Aztec Thought and Culture* (Norman: University of Oklahoma Press, 1963), and *Broken Spears: Aztec Accounts of the Conquest of Mexico* (Boston: Beacon, 1962). Also see Ignacio Bernal's concise *Mexico Before Cortez* (New York: Doubleday, 1963).

My approach to modern Mexico has been influenced by three outstanding books: Octavio Paz, *The Labyrinth of Solitude* (London: Penguin, 1967); Lesley Bird Simpson, *Many Mexicos* (Berkeley: University of California Press, 1966); and Victor Alba, *The Mexicans* (London: Pall Mall, 1967). The best of modern guides is Kate Simon, *Mexico: Places and Pleasures* (Cleveland: World, 1963), though the old Terry *Guide to Mexico,* in its early red-covered editions, is still unique.

Of the multitude of travel books, I especially enjoyed Aldous Huxley, *Beyond the Mexique Bay* (London: Chatto and Windus, 1950); Graham Greene, *Lawless Roads* (London: Heinemann, 1960); and A. t'Serstevens, *Mexico: Three-Storeyed Land* (London: Hutchinson, 1959).

Two anthologies, which overlap to some extent, bring together the pioneering accounts of the first discoverers of pre-Columbian civilizations: Robert Wauchope, ed., *They Found the Buried Cities* (Chicago: University Press, 1965); and Leo Deuel, ed., *Conquistadors Without Swords* (New York: St. Martin, 1967). On pre-Columbian art, a classic analysis remains Miguel Covarrubias, *Indian Art of Mexico and Central America* (New York: Knopf, 1957).

Three excellent introductions to the Maya are Sylvanus Morley, *The Ancient Maya* (Stanford: University Press, 1958), as revised by George W. Brainerd; Michael D. Coe, *The Maya* (London: Thames and Hudson, 1966); and J. Eric Thompson, *The Rise and Fall of the Maya* (Norman: University of Oklahoma Press, 1956). A useful companion is Tatiana Proskouriakoff, *An Album of Maya Architecture* (Norman: University of Oklahoma Press, 1963), and a pleasant human document is J. Eric Thompson, *Maya Archaeologist* (Norman: University of Oklahoma Press, 1963).

Finally, the serious student will acquire, in either original or reprint form, the two matchless narratives by the first great American travel writer, John Lloyd Stephens, *Incidents of Travel in Central America, Chiapas and Yucatan* (1841), *and Incidents of Travels in Yucatan* (1843). With their illustrations by Catherwood, these books are the cornerstones of any serious library on the Maya.

IX
Utopia Lost? Peru

As in Mexico, Prescott's *Conquest of Peru* retains its unique interest. An account of Pizarro's feat that comes close to Bernal Díaz's Mexican narrative is Agustin de Zarate, *The Discovery and Conquest of Peru* (London: Penguin, 1968), as edited and translated by J. M. Cohen. The two best sources on Inca life are Pedro Cieza de León, *The Incas* (Norman: University of Oklahoma Press, 1959) in the admirable edition translated by Harriet de Onís; and *The Incas: The Royal Commentaries of the Inca Garcilaso de la Vega* (New York: Orion, 1961), as translated from the critical French edition by Alain Gheerbant. Nearly everything written about the Incas is indebted to these primary sources, the one written by an admiring Spaniard and the other by a proud descendant of the Inca royal house.

I have benefited from J. Alden Mason, *The Ancient Civilization of Peru* (London: Penguin, 1957); Philip Ainsworth Means, *Ancient Civilizations of the Andes* (New York: Scribner, 1936); Burr Cartwright Brundage, *The Empire of the Inca* (Norman: University of Oklahoma Press, 1963); and *Lords of Cuzco*

(Norman: University of Oklahoma Press, 1967); and Victor W. Von Hagen, *The Desert Kingdoms of Peru* (London: Weidenfeld and Nicolson, 1965). (A prolific popularizer, Von Hagen is sometimes patronizingly dismissed by professional archaeologists, but his zest is so contagious that one can forgive him much, and his *Ancient Sun Kingdoms of the Americas* [Cleveland: World, 1961], which collects in one volume his paperbacks on the Aztecs, Mayans and Incas, is worth acquiring.)

Louis Baudin, *A Socialist Empire: The Incas of Peru* (Princeton, N.J.: Van Nostrand, 1961); the wholly absorbing *Cuzco: A Window on Peru* (New York: Knopf, 1970) by Miriam Beltran; and Sally Falk Moore, *Power and Property in Inca Peru* (New York: Columbia University Press, 1958) give contrasting views on the dispute over the degree to which the Incas developed a planned, socialist state. Hiram Bingham, *The Lost City of the Incas* (New York: Duell, Sloan and Pearce, 1948) is an account of the discovery of Machu Picchu by the original explorer. Ephraim G. Squier, who was President Lincoln's envoy to Peru, is the Andean equivalent of John Lloyd Stephens; his *Peru: Incidents of Travel and Exploration in the Land of the Incas* (New York: Harper, 1877) is the most invaluable pioneering account of Inca sites (one of its illustrations, of the rope bridge on Apurimac River, inspired Thornton Wilder to write *The Bridge of San Luis Rey*). Of modern travel books, I can commend Sacheverell Sitwell, *Golden Mirror and Mirador* (London: Weidenfeld and Nicolson, 1962), and George Woodcock, *Incas and Other Men* (London: Faber, 1959). See also Selden Rodman, *The Peru Traveler* (New York: Meredith, 1967).

Index

Karl E. Meyer

Born in Madison, Wisconsin, Karl E. Meyer is a third-generation newspaperman. After attending the University of Wisconsin and receiving a Ph.D in politics from Princeton, he cubbed for *The Milwaukee Journal* and *The New York Times* before joining *The Washington Post* as a staff writer in 1956. Since then he has ranged widely over the world for his paper, covering the Cuban revolution, the Soviet occupation of Prague and the pop scene of London, where he was Bureau Chief for five years. His writings have appeared widely in magazines on both sides of the Atlantic, including *Harper's, Esquire* and *The Spectator*. Mr. Meyer is presently New York correspondent for the *Post* and traces his interest in archaeology to a fortuitous trip to Machu Picchu, the ancient Inca city in Peru.